FAMILY DRAMAS

Most of Shakespeare's tragedies have a family drama at their heart. *Family Dramas: Intimacy, Power and Systems in Shakespeare's Tragedies* brings these relationships to life, offering a radical new perspective on the tragic heroes and their dilemmas. It focusses on the interactions and dialogues between people on stage, linking conflicts in their intimate emotional worlds to wider social and political contexts.

Exploring the diverse relationships in Shakespeare's tragedies sheds a different light on the predicaments faced by each of the protagonists. It shows how moral and ideological struggles are worked out within family relationships. The book introduces a family systems approach to literary criticism, relating these ideas to other approaches within Shakespeare studies. Gender features strongly in the analysis since it is within gender relationships that intimacy and power most compellingly intersect and frequently collide.

For Shakespeare lovers and psychotherapists alike, this application of family therapy theory opens up new vistas on a familiar literary landscape.

Gwyn Daniel has practised as a family therapist, trainer and clinical supervisor within the National Health Service and she co-founded the Oxford Family Institute. She is a visiting lecturer at the Tavistock Clinic, London. She has authored or co-authored many professional books and articles. In the past ten years she has given presentations, both nationally and internationally, on her family systems approach to Shakespeare's tragedies.

"This book is a feast for family therapists and Shakespeare lovers alike. How pleasurable to see systemic ideas reflected in different light as Gwyn Daniel puts them to use in her lively reading of Shakespeare's plays. And how pleasurable to appreciate, yet again, across time and culture and contexts, the drama and complexity of human relating and the beauty of Shakespeare."

– **Carmel Flaskas**, Adjunct Associate Professor, School of Social Sciences, University of New South Wales, Australia

"Gwyn Daniel is a phenomenally astute and sensitive reader of people and relationships; she is also a phenomenally astute and sensitive reader of Shakespeare's plays. This book combines her skills in family therapy and in Shakespeare. The result is a fresh reading of major plays, with new insights in every chapter. It is a book that also displays acute theatrical sensitivity: what we see on stage is characters performing relationally. The Shakespeare lover, the therapist, and the theatre-goer will find much to treasure in this valuable book. Gwyn Daniel distils her immense knowledge and her close reading of Shakespeare into precise observations that consistently offer perceptive articulations of social systems and family relations."

– **Laurie Maguire**, Professor of Shakespeare, University of Oxford and Tutorial Fellow, Magdalen College

The Systemic Thinking and Practice Series

Series Editors: Charlotte Burck and Gwyn Daniel

This influential series was co-founded in 1989 by series editors David Campbell and Ros Draper to promote innovative applications of systemic theory to psychotherapy, teaching, supervision and organisational consultation. In 2011, Charlotte Burck and Gwyn Daniel became series editors and aim to present new theoretical developments and pioneering practice, make links with other theoretical approaches, and promote the relevance of systemic theory to contemporary social and psychological questions.

Recent titles in the series inlcude:

Family Dramas: Intimacy, Power and Systems in Shakespeare's Tragedies
Gwyn Daniel

The Heart of the Matter: Music and Art in Family Therapy
Hilary Palmer

Staying Attached: Fathers and Children in Troubled Times
Gill Gorell Barnes

Creativity in Times of Constraint: A Practitioner's Companion in Mental Health and Social Care
Jim Wilson

Surviving and Thriving in Care and Beyond: Personal and Professional Perspectives
Edited by Sara Barratt and Wendy Lobatto

Emotions and the Therapist: A Systemic-Dialogical Approach
Paolo Bertrando

Creative Positions in Adult Mental Health: Outside In-Inside Out
Edited by Sue McNab and Karen Partridge

FAMILY DRAMAS

Intimacy, Power and Systems in Shakespeare's Tragedies

Gwyn Daniel

Routledge
Taylor & Francis Group
LONDON AND NEW YORK

First published 2019
by Routledge
2 Park Square, Milton Park, Abingdon, Oxon OX14 4RN

and by Routledge
52 Vanderbilt Avenue, New York, NY 10017

Routledge is an imprint of the Taylor & Francis Group, an informa business

British Library Cataloguing-in-Publication Data
A catalogue record for this book is available from the British Library

Library of Congress Cataloging-in-Publication Data
A catalog record has been requested for this book

ISBN: 9781138335769 (hbk)
ISBN: 9781138335776 (pbk)
ISBN: 9780429443541 (ebk)

Typeset in Palatino
by Apex CoVantage , LLC

MIX
Paper from responsible sources
FSC® C013056

Printed and bound in Great Britain by
TJ International Ltd, Padstow, Cornwall

To my sister, Anne Harrison

CONTENTS

ACKNOWLEDGEMENTS

I owe the genesis of this book to my friend and colleague, Paula Boston from Leeds University, who had the creative idea of inviting psychotherapists to illustrate the differences between their theoretical approaches by analysing a Shakespeare play. A psychoanalyst, Richard Rusbridger, and I had some fascinating discussions of *Hamlet, King Lear* and *Othello*. Various conference presentations and lectures at the Tavistock Clinic, London and elsewhere followed and this book is the result.

A key principle of systemic thinking is that ideas evolve in collaboration through dialogue and that other minds act as resources in multiple ways. I have benefitted from the input of many such minds and from the support of colleagues, friends and family, who have either read drafts, offered feedback, asked challenging questions, or just exhorted me to get on with it. Two friends and colleagues have played a pivotal role. Charlotte Burck and I are joint editors of the *Systemic Thinking and Practice Series*. She edited the final draft of this volume with characteristic empathy and intellectual rigour. Gill Gorell Barnes, who combines knowledge of systemic therapy and English literature, has been a huge help in urging me to sharpen my arguments and keep my potential readers in mind. She also generously agreed to write the preface.

Marian Allsopp, Sara Barratt, Felicity Bryant, Dante Ceruolo, Mary Chamberlain, Alan Cooklin, Spencer Grey, Elsa Jones, Laurie Maguire, Gill

Marshall Andrews, Sue McNab, Bebe Speed, Patricia Williams and Bernadette Wren have all provided inspiration, offered comments, or made it seem a worthwhile thing to be doing. I am deeply grateful to them all.

Among my family, I extend especial thanks to my daughter, Tamar Shlaim, whose razor-sharp mind, knowledge of the publishing world and up-beat and positive attitude have been invaluable. My cousin, Margaret MacMillan, has been consistently supportive, commenting on drafts and encouraging me to trust my own voice. My brother, David Daniel, and sister-in-law, Mary Daniel, made helpful comments on chapter drafts. My niece, Amanda Barokh, constantly found just the right words to revive a writer's flagging morale.

My debt to Avi Shlaim, my supportive and loving husband, is immeasurable. Despite being a formidably disciplined and accomplished writer himself, he has somehow managed to tolerate my different writing habits, intellectual peregrinations, grammatical sloppiness and eccentric referencing, only occasionally moved to fury by my disrespect for the semi-colon. He has always encouraged me to keep faith with my project and knows what a massive debt I owe him.

My beloved sister, Anne Harrison, who died suddenly of a brain haemorrhage in March 2017, was passionate about the theatre and Shakespeare. She had a profound knowledge of the tragedies. She read earlier drafts of the book with a mixture of finely tuned critical faculties and sisterly solidarity. In my sorrow that she cannot be present at its long overdue publication, it is to her that this book is dedicated.

Gwyn Daniel
Oxford
March 2018

SERIES EDITOR'S FOREWORD

It has always been perplexing that systemic ideas have not become more widely known outside the psychotherapy and organisational fields. This has been the case despite the capacity of systemic theoretical frameworks to illuminate and elaborate the complex links between the personal and political and to highlight and examine the ways in which cultural and societal influences play out in our personal interactions and relationships. Systemic concepts are ever more relevant to the challenges of our current times.

It is therefore particularly exciting to be publishing my series co-editor Gwyn Daniel's book in our *Systemic Thinking and Practice Series*. It offers a fascinating way to introduce systemic ideas to a wider readership. Gwyn Daniel's exploration of Shakespeare's tragedies through a systemic theoretical lens provides us with a unique perspective on his plays – plays that will be familiar to many if not all readers and that have been analysed countless times from other theoretical viewpoints. Produced, viewed and analysed so frequently and with good reason, Shakespeare's work continues to offer us thought-provoking commentary on and questions about our human dilemmas.

What is so radical about Gwyn Daniel's systemic analyses of the tragedies is that she has managed not to become captivated and captured, as so many of us have, by the power of the individual tragic figures seen to be primary in these plays, but shifts the complexities of their relationships to centre stage. This opens up unexpected and novel perspectives. She invites us to entertain a multiplicity of views and ideas, challenging received wisdoms, particularly of many of the female characters. As a systemic thinker, she is continually helping us make links to Shakespeare's context and the contexts in which the plays' actions are set to highlight the different meanings these convey to the struggles of all those involved in the interactions. It is wonderfully stimulating to have new interpretations of such familiar plays.

Interwoven with the discussion of the plays, Gwyn Daniel offers us a succinct and clear exposition of a range of systemic ideas – ideas that she not only applies in original interpretations of the tragedies but through which she illustrates how they can inform an understanding of families and their relationships with their contexts. This invites us to consider anew our own interactions within our contemporary contexts.

Gwyn Daniel's book establishes a landmark. It is a very fine introduction to systemic ideas for those who are unfamiliar with them, demonstrating their richness, timbre, scope and potential. The book should also prove to be useful and provocative to systemic thinkers and therapists in demonstrating the creative application of these ideas in new contexts and inspire others to be bolder in their own applications of these powerful and helpful ideas to the many dilemmas and issues of our current times.

Charlotte Burck
Systemic Thinking and Practice Series Co-editor

PREFACE

Gill Gorell Barnes

The tragedies of Shakespeare are deeply embedded in the English language and in our culture. This unique book invites us to re-examine Shakespeare's tragic heroes and heroines using a systemic framework for linking these great individuals to their social contexts. In laying out before us the wider dimensions of the societies within which their original creator, Shakespeare, has framed their lives, Gwyn Daniel engages the reader not with the internal workings of the characters alone but with the ways in which the minds depicted are themselves contextualised and constrained by the larger beliefs of their societies. The words, discourses, arguments and inner conversations of those who live in them are shaped by and in turn shape these larger beliefs. Social mores, political workings, religious and supernatural beliefs – tropes about morality and duty affecting most areas of intimate life and the assumptions about gender, role and power that are formed by these beliefs over time are in turn revealed for us to consider. In considering them through the lenses of each heroic figure, their relationships, potential paths of action and choices of these paths, we will inevitably reflect upon our own.

Without specifying this intent, Gwyn Daniel invites us to reflect at many levels, not only upon the social constraints in the plays but in the society of Shakespeare himself, the author of the plays in the first Elizabethan era. Identifying these discourses also provokes us to think reflexively about our own world now, our society and the choices for living in intimate relationships, as these are lit up by the language and dialogues of Shakespeare. In the exploratory, interactional and interdependent discourses of the tragedies, dilemmas for living are reflected, independent of century. Linking her work as a family therapist to her focus on interactional experience in the plays, she also highlights systemic interdependence in her clinical work – the ways in which family members and others in the intimate social system, of which the 'referred person' or patient is a part, act to maintain the problem, even when that behaviour can be seen to set a participant on a negative rather than positive pathway. Looking always at 'the pattern that connects,' she examines the ways in which apparently rule-governed behaviour keeps the family equilibrium in balance as well as the dangers for each member when this balance is contested. She considers the ways in which people mutually influence each other – their participation in sequences of interaction in which one person's speech or behaviour is both influenced by and in turn influences others.

She uses a systemic framework in which she demonstrates how individual speech acts are additionally embedded within episodes of behaviour that in turn are guided by both allocated and chosen social definitions of relationship and role. The ways in which family stories, life scripts and allocated roles are held at a higher level of patterning in the accepted social hierarchy are experienced by protagonists as legacies from society, sometimes additionally blessed by higher forces, such as divinity or the supernatural. In tragedy, such patterns may be pre-scripted in heavily defined ways.

In his tragedies, Shakespeare used intimate relationships and the interactions and speech between people within these and wider kinship systems, as well as a range of participant observers, to explore universal themes about nature and instinct, and how these should be constrained through social patterning. Focussing on the meanings given to blood and kin, Gwyn Daniel explores how actions derived from interpreting the meanings in these words serve further as a microcosm for exploring wider social and moral concerns. She focusses not only on how these are condensed into the minutiae of everyday thought and exchange in the tragedies but the way that the players perceive and experience their options for living in the light of these concerns, as they evolve or are constrained by choices that are shaped by the historical and current conversations found within the worlds in which they have developed. Concepts like blood and kin, in which assumptions about family, humanity and what it is to be a human being – the boundaries between mind, emotions and body, body and spirit, human and divine, and the ways social constructions of both intellect and emotions are housed precariously within fragile relational structures – are deconstructed. These go side by side with contested explorations of lineage, legitimacy and social order within the societies portrayed in the dramas, the structure and fabric of these, and their secure maintenance, also being a reflection of constant preoccupations in the Elizabethan age.

Within the dramatic narratives, she shows us how Shakespeare crafts words for individuals in soliloquy as well as in conversation between participants to show not only what is but what is not, or what might have been, as well as the range of alternatives that have not been considered or have been too readily discarded. She offers us the idea of outer and inner talk – that even when we might believe a key player is talking to themselves, there is an invisible other present in their minds, an interlocutor who poses questions and to whom they feel responsible for their answers. These inner ways of positioning moral dilemmas can aid in expanding options or can narrow them down to inevitable and disastrous consequences. Self-monitoring, as shown in these inner discourses, can include the dictates and constraints constructed by limitations and blindness of power or gendered role: men must be men and reject anything that hints of femininity, uncertainty, kindness or compassion. The chaos that can ensue when meanings are narrowed to only one interpretation – counter narratives are closed and cannot be considered and multiple possibilities are shut down too early – form a key part in the tragedies and their unfolding.

Gwyn Daniel delights in demonstrating how the plurality of perspectives on the dilemmas of being human that Shakespeare so richly contributed to drama and to the English heritage is not only laid out through the grand narratives of the central characters, but is constantly positioned throughout the plays by other voices – characters with minor roles holding different social perspectives in the worlds of each play. These voices comment on the main action and suggest or invite thought about alternative possibilities for the main protagonists – intimate servants, servants positioned within an ordered court hierarchy, soldiers who are friends, soldiers who hold a different moral position. In the later tragedies, these voices are expanded into the more extreme and marginalised or unacknowledged voices in and out of society, including the voices of the very poor and dispossessed, hired murderers, the deliberately mad and the supernatural. Positions of moral protest, of saying the unsaid but 'right' thing as well as commentary on wrong doing or evil, are often held in these voices so that the debate for the audience about choices of action that have been made in relation to other possible ways of seeing and doing remains open until the end of the drama. Cultural interpretations through these minor voices – the giving of possible alternative meanings to what is going on that the main protagonists have elided from their thinking due to their allocated positions in society as they have interpreted them – are also powerful. These include comments on gender, patriarchy, race and otherness and on the performances of power, given or taken. As Gwyn Daniel notes in Chapter 11, "In Shakespeare's tragedies, we are presented with many instances of the 'almost said' – with brief glimpses of the alternative narratives that can emerge from significant dialogue."

One of the author's many gifts to us lies in her ability to link the level of close and intimate human interactions with their particular emotional dilemmas, patterning, language and dialogue, to higher levels of patterning from the wider world that shapes them. In her approach, as stated in Chapter 11, she resists a "focus on individuals [which] creates the temptation to . . . fix them in some kind of essence, which does not do justice to the complexity of their interactions. A focus on relationships creates a more dynamic means through which identity can be revealed as fluid, contested and expressed in diverse ways, depending on the contexts, which confer meaning."

The detailed way the recursive loops between social constraints and the possibilities for individual action are laid out, especially as these relate to gender and power, are always present in her thinking. The larger influences that permeate smaller discourses and shapes what takes place are returned to as the dramatic actions unfold, always revealing not only what is included in the decision-making processes but crucially what is left out.

The author offers us a continual exploration of how, in Shakespeare's tragedies, identity is fluid and changing, how identity based on status and power can fragment and how illusions of power are held onto by a refusal or inability to see its effects on others or to recognise a right to difference of perceptions. Gender and power intersect in complex ways, creating possibilities either for insight or obtuseness, for moments of clarity or agency or for terrifying experiences of helplessness or fragmentation.

In linking her work on Shakespeare's dramas about families and their entanglements with wider society to her own work with families, Gwyn Daniel comments on how therapists are often faced with families who act as if there is only one possible narrative:

> Part of the ethics of therapy is to support the expansion of choices. The most helpful ways of supporting this process are through identifying those very constraints that limit them, which may include gender stereotypes, beliefs

> about material success and achievement, or precepts about how parents and children should properly relate to each other. Identifying exceptions and counter-narratives is an intrinsic part of this process as it is in Shakespeare's texts.

The exploration of meaning-making is central to drama as well as to therapeutic conversations but the author does not mislead the reader into thinking that human processes allow for tidy categorisation in either context. As Gwyn Daniel notes in Chapter 4,

> If experiences of fragmentation and madness arise in the gap between the signifying systems of different worlds, this teaches us to be humble about those aspects of human experience that, however hard we try to understand them, are always beyond our grasp.

For me, reading this book has been an inspiration to study further the texts of a man who I first studied sixty years ago at school, and later as a student of English Literature at university. I come at the plays with a new outlook on many issues, which I had previously glimpsed but never before truly entered intellectually or emotionally. This makes the reading of each chapter in relation to the original text a feast.

Introduction

Family relationships, as we know, can be tragic at times and most of Shakespeare's tragedies have some kind of family drama at their heart. For families, whether 'real' or on stage, when relationships unravel, it is often because power struggles have developed with the capacity to undermine or destroy intimacy. The dimensions of power and intimacy thus provide a crucial framing of this exploration of Shakespeare's tragedies from the perspective of family and other relationships. Drama is, by its very nature, interactional, so a focus on what is going on *between* people on stage should be a completely obvious approach, yet it is surprisingly neglected. The lure of the tragic eponymous heroes of *King Lear, Hamlet, Othello, Macbeth* and *Coriolanus* is compelling and reinforced by pairing them with great individual Shakespearean actors/celebrities. We tend to talk about "Benedict Cumberbatch's Hamlet," "Glenda Jackson's Lear," "Patrick Stewart's Macbeth" or "Lenny Henry's Othello" and this inevitably focusses attention primarily on their interpretation of the individual protagonist.

Of course, the great celebrity sell-out performances are matched by countless other productions from small companies, each with a collective ethos and culture. Nevertheless, the cultural narrative of the 'compelling individual' can risk obscuring an alternative way of exploring Shakespeare's plays. This alternative is to pay close attention to how and why protagonists relate to each other in the ways they do. As well as the three tragedies that are actually named after a relationship, there are compelling relationships within all the plays that illuminate the dramatic themes and dilemmas of the main protagonists. Precisely because family relationships are made up of interactions over time, they can be seen as a microcosm for wider social concerns. Thus, the 'little theatre' of family life with all its idiosyncrasies is so often one in which larger tensions are played out. Families absorb and enact social ideologies, so relationship conflicts within the family often expose the conflicts and ambiguities that all ideologies contain. I use a family systems framework to bring these crucial dimensions into the limelight.

When I write of 'family' I am, of course, speaking to a later era, as the word does not actually appear in any of Shakespeare's tragedies. This reminds us of the diverse and complex meanings given to close blood ties at different historical junctures. Shakespeare himself used 'kin', a word that has a somewhat broader scope. In the tragedies, we see very few 'intact families' in the modern sense. Of the plays foregrounding parent/child relationships, in *Othello, King Lear* and *Troilus and Cressida,* mothers are absent or off stage. In *Coriolanus,* the father is missing; in *Hamlet,* he is a ghost. In *Troilus and Cressida* and *King Lear,* sibling relationships are key. In *Coriolanus,* we have, tantalisingly, two parents and their young child but there is little interaction between them. Only in *Romeo and Juliet,* in which the protagonists are very young, do we have a scene involving two living parents and their daughter.

As well as portraying family relationships, in many of the plays, the meaning of the kinship bond itself is subjected to remorseless scrutiny. Parents' disappointment at their children failing to perform filial duty is forcefully expressed by Lear, Gloucester, Volumnia and Capulet. No less vociferous are Desdemona, Cordelia, Cressida, Coriolanus, Hamlet and Juliet as they confront, in their different ways, the complex question of where family loyalty and duty might properly lie. The two plays that do not overtly foreground family relationships – *Macbeth* and *Anthony and Cleopatra* – are nevertheless deeply concerned with questions of procreation, dynasty and succession. In each of the eight plays selected, I argue that the actions of the tragic protagonists can take on completely new meanings if relationships rather than individuals are foregrounded. This means that other relationships within the plays are equally important: those between friends, soldiers, servants and their masters or mistresses and between political rivals. It is often within these relationships that intimacy can flourish in quite unexpected and illuminating ways and barriers to intimacy can just as suddenly loom into focus. The relationships between, for example, Desdemona and Emilia or Hamlet and Horatio – to name only two – illustrate powerful extra-familial bonds that transcend divisions of class or status. These relationships too are multi-levelled, complex and frequently highly ambivalent.

I use my perspective as a family therapist to explore these relationships but my scope extends beyond a narrowly psychological perspective and a focus only on family itself. Family therapists try to resist the temptation to interpret the 'inner motivations' of individuals and are equally reluctant to extend this essentialist type of analysis to family relationships by, for example, highlighting family dysfunction. Instead, we pay attention to interactional patterns and to the contexts that give meaning to people's actions and communications. Thus, rather than take the families in Shakespeare as some kind of case example, I draw upon this approach to explore the many levels at which relationships in Shakespeare's tragedies can be read. The family therapy approach has a great deal to contribute to our understanding of how people act within their intimate relationships but it also encompasses the wider systems within which these relationships are performed.

Our cultural and social contexts play a vital role in shaping both our identities and our expectations of each other. At one level, this is something we take for granted. However, one of the contributions of the family systems approach lies in its capacity to show in detail just how wider power structures and social discourses can be seen to reach into the heart of intimate relationships and into the diverse ways that people define themselves and each other. It provides valuable analytic tools to observe at close range how these processes are enacted within the dialogues and actions of individuals in relationships.

I have two parallel aims in the book. The first is to introduce a systemic framework and argue for its relevance and applicability within the field of Shakespeare studies as a whole. In this way, I wish to make a contribution to what might be called 'popular literary criticism.' The second involves applying this approach in depth to each of the selected tragedies to provide new understandings while keeping the theory implicit. All approaches to drama, even those that claim, disingenuously, to have no theoretical position, have to grapple with the extent to which they make their theory the servant of the texts or extract from the texts those features that fit our theory. I plead guilty to straying at times on the side of having a theoretical 'axe to grind' but I hope to keep my proselytising urges reasonably under control. Shakespeare's work, due to its very status as a cultural monument, can only thrive through constant challenge, renewal and reinterpretation, of which mine is only a tiny dot in a very long and continuously expanding line.

The systemic approach is the theoretical framework that underlies the practice of family therapy, so the terms 'systemic,' 'family systems' and 'family therapy' are used variably throughout the book. This varies according to whether theory or practice is being discussed and whether the focus is on family relationships or wider systems. In Chapter 1, I introduce a theoretical framework that may well be new to many lovers of Shakespeare, describing the systemic concepts that seem most relevant to drama. These range from observing and describing the detail of family or couple interactions to a wider focus on political and ideological contexts. Addressing these different levels means that, instead of using one 'template' for approaching the plays, I highlight different ideas in each play, following the systemic principle that there is a reciprocal relationship between theory and context. Different contexts call for different aspects of theory. Family therapy evolved out of the need to engage with multiple perspectives – it questions fixed or rigid viewpoints and gives positive value to uncertainty, ambiguity and paradox. This makes it well suited to explore these dynamic, mutable processes within Shakespeare's dramas.

In Chapter 2, I locate my approach alongside existing traditions of Shakespearean criticism, exploring a selection of scholarly standpoints. This diversity of perspectives also reflects the multiple levels to be found within the plays and the contradictions within them. Shakespeare's plays are always open to alternative readings because they are polyphonic: they contain multiple perspectives and thrive on contradiction, inconsistency and paradox. Among the approaches to Shakespeare I explore are those that analyse the social and ideological codes permeating the plays and that tend to 'decentre' the main protagonist/s in favour of illuminating the surrounding context. I am aware, however, that these approaches can often seem too remote from the intense emotions that the individuals on stage arouse in us.

The focus on what is happening in relationships provides a bridge between close attention to the dilemmas and struggles of the people on stage and the wider social worlds they inhabit. It would be absurd to ignore the prominence Shakespeare gave to a Hamlet or a Macbeth and treat them as just another protagonist; the challenge is not to discount the individual but reach beyond consideration of their inner world to explore the dilemmas and struggles in their relationships. In the tragedies, these dilemmas manifest themselves in confrontation with the big questions of love, sex, intimacy, loyalty, loss, power, ambition, violence and death – the same concerns that permeate therapeutic encounters.

Shakespeare's tragedies have thus held an honoured place in the minds of many psychotherapists, providing fertile ground for witnessing intense emotional dilemmas. Their very familiarity serves, in turn, to reinforce their status as exemplars of emotional conflicts. There is a natural affinity between drama and the practice of psychotherapy, and many approaches to therapy – including systemic – use drama as a creative vehicle for therapeutic change. Drama enables people to express powerful and previously unexpressed emotions, to step outside their habitual view of themselves and their relationships and to engage with the perspectives of others. Shakespeare's background as an actor seems to have provided him with an exceptional talent for engaging with multiple perspectives and for holding different positions in tension.

Each experience of drama is one in which a confrontation with ambiguity is inscribed, just as it is in therapy. In each, there is an inevitable tension between our rational and emotional selves. In theatre, suspension of disbelief, as Coleridge put it, means responding to protagonists in their 'real' flesh and blood form; at that moment, we put aside our knowledge that these are the creations of the playwright.[1] On the other hand, the rational, sceptical audience that Berthold Brecht encouraged through his concept of the 'alienation effect' was intended to block just this kind of identification with the characters on stage.[2] His aim was to make the audience aware of how powerfully theatre can manipulate our emotions. As audience, we are in both positions simultaneously in a similar way to our stance as therapists. Therapists move between close engagement with and acceptance of the emotional world before us, but we also step back to reflect, drawing upon the cognitive maps that our theory provides.

Although each play chapter draws upon systemic ideas that seem especially relevant to the work at hand, there will be some key recurring themes. As well as focus on relationships and how they can be understood in context, the dimension of gender features strongly in the analysis of all the plays, as it is within gender that intimacy and power most compellingly intersect and frequently collide. Feminist approaches, both to Shakespeare and to therapy, influence my approach, as attending to gender patterns requires a constant shifting of levels between macro and micro processes in human relations.

I have structured the book so the first two chapters introduce most of the theory, with Chapter 1 describing my family systems approach and

Chapter 2 exploring other approaches both from within the psychotherapy world and from those works on Shakespeare that have most enriched my understanding and underpinned my approach.

It is possible for readers to proceed directly to the subsequent eight chapters, each of which is devoted to a single play. I have organised the book so that each play chapter can be read as a 'stand-alone' to appeal to a range of different readers, including those who might just wish to gain a new perspective on a play they are about to see performed. Because it is impossible to write about Shakespeare plays without addressing the key question of their interpretation on stage, I illustrate my arguments at times with references to performances on stage or in film.

I have provided plot summaries in the appendix and have used throughout the *Oxford World's Classics* (OWC) versions of the plays. In *King Lear,* the OWC text has continuous scenes with no Act breaks and I have therefore used this format for Chapter 4.

Notes

1 Samuel Taylor Coleridge, *Biographia Literaria* (Oxford: Clarendon Press, 1817).

2 Berthold Brecht, 'Alienation Effects in Chinese Acting', *The Tulane Drama Review*, 6:1 (1961), 130–136.

CHAPTER 1

A family systems approach

The lights dim in the auditorium and the performance begins. It might be any one of Shakespeare's tragedies. The stage set, the costumes, the actors, their postures, expressions and accents, their locations on stage all give us clues about what sort of production this will be. But in this opening scene, we are highly unlikely to meet the individual or couple for whom the play is named. In virtually all of Shakespeare's tragedies, the scene is set by other characters well before the main protagonists appear on stage. The significance of this delay is that the wider canvas of the drama can be laid out before we engage with the leading individuals. It also means that our first encounters with them are in the eyes and through the voices of others. This immediately invites us, the audience, into a relational world. We learn what the Roman soldiers think about Anthony's relationship with Cleopatra before we meet the lovers themselves. Macbeth's soldierly prowess and brutality is reported to King Duncan before Macbeth himself appears on stage.

We also learn about the key themes and leitmotifs that will recur throughout each play. In *Hamlet,* the watchmen and Horatio first grapple with the question of whether to give credence to the supernatural; they implant the narrative of another son avenging his father and we are introduced to Claudius' skills as a political operator. In *Coriolanus,* the citizens and Menenius lay out the key debates about political power that will permeate the plot. In *Romeo and Juliet*, we witness the workings of the feud with its all-pervasive effects on family relationships. We meet the parents of Romeo and Juliet, each with their particular concerns about their offspring, before our first encounter with either of the teenage lovers.

These openings can certainly be said to heighten dramatic anticipation for the appearance of the 'hero/s.' At the same time, however, they have the effect of 'decentring' the hero by reminding us that we can never focus on just one person or one couple without taking into account the contexts that give meaning to their words and actions. The key actors in the tragedies are most likely to capture our attention and engage our emotions but the relationships that surround them are what bring their dilemmas and struggles into relief and give the production its texture.

Family therapists frequently meet families in which one individual – the equivalent of drama's hero or villain – is presented as the person upon whom we should all be focussed. Without discounting their individual troubles or suffering, understanding them in the context of their surrounding relationships is usually the most creative and helpful approach. John Donne's line "No man is an island" has acquired the status of cliché, but it is striking to what extent in Western cultural practice, especially in psychotherapy, but also in some Shakespearean criticism, individuals are still viewed in isolation from their context.

In family therapy, by contrast, we highlight the idea of interdependence – the ways in which others act to maintain the behaviour of the 'problem person' even when that behaviour is unwelcome. In drama, the more dominant or domineering the protagonist, the more important it is to explore the actions of others that might be maintaining or sustaining it. For example, Iago, the master manipulator, actually depends to a large extent on Rodrigo, his 'gull', for his success. Rodrigo's frequent and unexpected appearances, just when Iago appears most confident that everything is under control, highlights his disruptive potential and his capacity to undermine a conspiracy that depends on his participation.

The practice of family therapy involves understanding individuals and their communications through the relationships that surround them. In this process, I have come to rely on some key conceptual frameworks as I immerse myself in the complex and often conflictual world of the individuals, couples and families who seek help. Most of the ideas I find useful as a therapist also lend themselves to understanding the relationships we see on stage.

Lives and relationships are complex, diverse and multi-levelled. When we communicate with each other, our speech is likewise heard and responded to in a diversity of ways. In families and other intimate relationships, as with protagonists on stage, people will, whatever their inward emotions, perform their relationships in myriad ways. They may cling to rigid positions, contest the positions taken by others, or acquiesce in or reject the account of them provided by others; they will do all of these things overtly or covertly. However persuasively families may seek to convince us that there is one single truth about the problem or about the person brought to therapy, looking at their interactions in the present, exploring influences from past family relationships and from all the other contexts surrounding them creates a more fertile context within which to offer help. Many therapists of course do this but the family systems approach has especially useful conceptual tools for analysing relationships and the contexts in which they are embedded.

One analogy for what we do in systemic therapy is that of a photographer who uses both a zoom and wide-angled lens. We engage closely with people and their intimate relationships, immerse ourselves in their emotional worlds and respond to their language and narratives. However, we also widen the frame to keep the context of extended family, community and social environment within our field of vision. This wider lens is especially important when working with people whose worlds are different from that of the therapist but it is also important for all therapists to step back from their close engagement, to take a broader view and reflect on the assumptions we might be making about families or they will be making about us. This challenges us to entertain alternative viewpoints and think about other contexts that might render more intelligible the complex dynamics we see in front of us.

The concepts I use in exploring the tragedies encompass this key idea of close range and wider context. The former emerge from direct observation of families and their interactions and the latter are more concerned with how individuals and families construct their worlds within the social and cultural discourses that surround them. In the latter, there is more attention to the workings of power, the effects of ideologies and the way language operates in the construction of identities. In understanding Shakespeare, it is likewise important to move between a close 'reading' of the interactions we see on stage and a wider appreciation of all the contexts that surround them and give them meaning.

Shakespeare's tragedies are suffused with double meanings, contradictory perspectives and examples of how intimate relationships can be a site in which wider political or social questions are contested. A multilevel approach greatly adds to an appreciation of the processes involved in creating the 'reality' that we see on stage. Our emotions are engaged by the protagonists and their narratives; we respond to them at some level as if they are 'real,' but at the same time, we hold a parallel appreciation of the constructed nature of the play and its dramatis personae, of the production and the acting. In therapy, we are likewise moved by the story narrated to us, we believe in its emotional 'truth' but are simultaneously aware that this is only one of a range of possible stories and are mindful of the rhetorical devices employed to persuade us of a favoured story-line. A family who all agree that one particular member is 'the problem' will inevitably have a powerful narrative about that person and will produce evidence to support their view. Therapists obviously need to engage with this perspective but at the same time stand back from it and hold other narratives in mind.

The early family therapists drew upon systems theory to guide their work because interventions based on the study of internal states of mind had so often proved inadequate when working with long-term and intractable psychiatric problems. They were equally ineffective in working with families suffering the effects of poverty, marginalisation and other social disadvantages. One of the most enduring ideas in family therapy has been that of the 'pattern that connects.'[1] This is a way of determining that, within the complexity, confusion and often chaos of family life, patterned sequences and apparently rule-governed behaviour can be elicited. The process of observing and identifying patterns is a way of keeping relationships in focus because we are alert to how people influence each other. They participate in sequences of interaction in which each person's speech or action creates feedback for others and is in turn affected by this feedback. This level of analysis is particularly relevant to drama, opening up as it does a close view of the interactions on stage; it also avoids making simplistic assumptions about the internal states or motivations of any of the participants.

Theatre directors are inevitably alert to pattern and sequence because these are part of the spatial dimension within which Shakespeare's words are conveyed to the audience. This choreography is a key part of meaning-making. On first encountering a family, I will be aware of spatial relationships: who sits where, who is closer to whom, who looks at whom etc. This highlights patterns within relationships that family members may be unaware of or experiencing as a constraint. Inviting people to change their positions in the room can have a powerful effect on their ways of experiencing each other, just as a theatre director will experiment with actors' positions on the stage.

The opening scene of *Romeo and Juliet* is a beautifully choreographed sequence in which we immediately see patterns in operation. The audience, primed by the chorus, already know that they are witnessing a scenario that has been repeated in much the same way over a long period of time. The serving men from the Montague and Capulet households pick a fight in which each responds quite predictably to the provocations of the other. Their fracas brings in others, and then, as if on cue, the Capulet and Montague parents. Finally, Prince Escalus appears and brings the warring factions to heel. The pattern up to this point can be described as a 'symmetrical escalation' in which there is an exchange of similar types of behaviour.[2] In this particular case, it is a trading of threats and insults but the pattern can be maintained by any type of interchange. The content is less important than the process, which is mainly a competitive one. Identifying these symmetrical patterns is a useful way to highlight the quasi-ritualistic nature of the feud, which appears to have taken on a life of its own, affecting the behaviour of all the protagonists. It also serves to dramatise the moment when the feud reaches a tipping point with the deaths of Mercutio and Tybalt.

In this first scene, the prince does not participate in the fight but takes a position above the fray, on the basis of his authority. The symmetrical pattern is thus temporarily replaced by a complementary one in which different interactions can be observed. In this case, it is a ruler and his subjects who cannot directly challenge him, but are expected to obey. Complementary (unlike symmetrical) patterns are essentially exchanges of different behaviour, usually from different positions within a system. They can again be maintained by any type of interaction; teacher and student, doctor and patient or abuser and victim will all be complementary relationships.

This type of analysis can also illuminate interactions within couple relationships in which it can seem as if the pattern has the power to organise a couple, almost despite their volition. For Desdemona and Othello, their first interactions on stage are marked by symmetry, with each boldly and publicly claiming their right to love the other in the face of social disapproval. As the play progresses, however, the symmetry of their relationship is eroded and in its place emerges the complementarity of victim and abuser. This is not before each makes attempts to change the pattern – Desdemona engages in a competitive exchange over the handkerchief in which symmetry is temporarily restored and Othello makes an ambiguous and short-lived attempt to evoke Desdemona's compassion by citing the power she has over his life: "*But there, where I have garnered up my heart/ Where either I must live or bear no life.*" This evokes the complementary at the outset of their relationship when her love was equated by Othello with her pity for him.

For Antony and Cleopatra, shifts between symmetry and complementarity are embedded in the very fabric of the relationship and observable at virtually every exchange. Although the overall framework of their relationship is complementary, i.e. coloniser/colonised, their first meeting involves a symmetrical exchange – competing over who should host the other to dinner. Their exchanges are so choreographed that, if a symmetrical exchange escalates too far, one of them will take a complementary position to temporarily restore equilibrium. The changes in position that each of the lovers makes also serve to maintain some distance in the relationship, meaning that the romantic narrative they tell about themselves is not exposed as fiction.

Distance regulation is another idea from the early period of family therapy, which explores the way many couples, however volatile they appear to be, can also be seen as collaborating to keep a fixed distance in their relationship.[3] When one attempts to get closer, the other will find a means of distancing. When they get too distant, one will find a way of getting closer again. For example, Cleopatra reserves her most adulatory comments about Anthony for when they are apart; when they are together, she is more disparaging of him. This pattern, however frustrating, means that each member of a couple protects themselves from the feared consequences of too much intimacy and, at the same time, it keeps them from separating.

We can also identify patterns in the language people use, especially in the way that different modes of talk can be amplified within interactions. In *Hamlet*, for example, we notice the difference between Hamlet's speech when he performs his 'antic disposition' and that of the people at the receiving end of it. Hamlet does 'crazy talk' in a variety of ways, including flights of the imagination, verbal tricks, puns, non-sequiturs and plain nonsense. He is mostly responded to in language that is prosaic, rational, concrete and condescending. The more elusively and crazily he acts, the more stolid and impoverished is the language of his interlocutors, in turn acting as a spur to creativity in enacting madness:

Polonius "*How does my good lord Hamlet?*"

Hamlet "*Well, God-a-mercy*"

Polonius "*Do you know me my lord?*"

Hamlet "*Excellent, excellent well. You're a fishmonger*"

Polonius "*Not I, my lord.*" (2.ii.172)

It carries on from here in the manner of an inventive patient undergoing a rather substandard psychiatric assessment, although Polonius is not entirely fooled by the display – *"Though this be madness, yet there is method in't."* The point is that, were Hamlet to be seen in isolation, with critical energy only going into debating his inner state or whether his madness is real or feigned, less attention would be paid to the effect of the relational context on how he actually speaks.

This is a particularly important principle for therapists because they need to be mindful of how the positions they take and the language they use influence the responses they receive. If a person comes across as defensive, this is just as likely to be the result of an interaction in which there is a judgemental tone that emphasises deficits as it is to be an attribute of the person. When Othello accuses Desdemona of having lost the handkerchief, she replies shiftily and mendaciously: *"It is not lost; but what an if it were?"* Rather than being an 'attribute' of Desdemona, this can be understood in the context of Othello speaking to her *"so startingly and rash."* He likewise becomes even more agitated and enraged as she seeks to deflect him from the matter of the handkerchief and onto the question of Cassio's commission.

When communication happens that makes little sense, even to those participating in it, let alone to an observer, it is often because a crucial context is missing. When family therapists encounter communication that we cannot understand, we do not consider that this signifies an inability or unwillingness on the part of the person to articulate their innermost feelings; we assume there are other levels to which we need to pay attention. This is often the moment to widen the lens to include other contexts that can help us make better sense of ambiguities or misunderstandings that may be arising. A model called the Coordinated Management of Meaning (CMM) helps clarify how various levels of context influence communication.[4] These levels are defined as:

Culture/Society
Family Story Life Script
Definition of Relationships
Episode
Speech Act

Each communication can be understood within a 'higher order' context; for example, a speech act such as a 'disrespectful' comment might mean one thing within a relationship defined as a friendship but quite another within a particular family or set of cultural rules. The influence can also be seen in reverse with 'lower order' contexts able to create new meanings for 'higher.' For example, a couple relationship that demonstrates equality might lead to changes in attitudes within family or cultural contexts. In therapy, it is a useful way of exploring whether there is a good enough 'fit' between therapist and client. A therapeutic conversation intended to be helpful but which meets with resistance might contradict a 'higher order' rule from family or culture that you should only trust your own kin. The reverse order might mean that a trusting and affirming therapeutic relationship creates the confidence to change relationships at other levels such as friendships or family.

What this model facilitates, both in therapy and in drama appreciation, is a flexible way of thinking in which we can constantly shift levels. Shakespeare's tragedies are never just about one key emotional or political dilemma – they contain multiple levels and are always exploring contradictory responses to political, moral and ideological concerns.

An example of CMM follows from *King Lear* when the old man explodes into rage at a seemingly innocent reply.

Speech act

Lear "*O you sir, sir, you sir, come you hither. Who am I, sir?*"

Oswald "*My lady's father.*"

Lear "*My lady's father? My lord's knave, you whoreson dog, you slave, you cur.*"

Oswald "*I am none of these, my lord, I beseech you pardon me.*"

Lear "*Do you bandy looks with me, you rascal?*" *(Lear strikes him)*

Oswald "*I'll not be struck, my lord.*"

Kent *(Tripping him)* "*Nor tripped neither, you base football player.*"

Lear (to Kent) "*I thank thee, fellow. Thou serv'st me, and I'll love thee.*"

(iv.73–84)

Episode

Lear is staying with Gonoril, who is increasingly fed up with his behaviour and that of his one hundred knights. She has instructed Oswald, her steward, to be cool towards Lear. Lear is incensed by being disrespectfully treated and attempts to get Oswald to acknowledge his status as king.

Definition of relationship

Because Lear has handed over his kingdom to his two older daughters and their husbands, he is now dependent on them for shelter and for his standard of living. Gonoril wants to indicate that she is now in control. Oswald's accurate definition of Lear as Gonoril's father exposes the reality of the change in relationships, evoking a violent reaction. The disguised Kent also cannot bear the loss of status and position. Oswald moves from superficial servility to stating his right not to be hit, which in turn challenges the ex-king's omnipotence. Lear defines love for Kent in terms of Kent's willingness to serve him.

Life script

Lear, facing old age and death, has given up his kingdom, which means losing the power, status and identity that have accompanied him all his life. He has little idea of his own agency other than through the exercise of unilateral power and control. He is not high on the emotional intelligence quotient and, according to Regan: *"hath ever but slenderly known himself."*

Family story

The family is composed of a father and three daughters – the mother presumably died some time ago. Relationships are characterised by the exercise of hierarchical patriarchal power. There is an overlap between affectional bonds and the political domain. There is one favoured daughter, Cordelia, upon whom Lear had hoped to rely for nurture in his old age but whom he has now banished.

Culture/society

A transition is in progress between a mediaeval social system and a more capitalist and individualistic age. In the feudal system, identity is bestowed on the basis of position within a rigidly hierarchical society. Giving up a position is tantamount to being an outcast. In a rigidly patriarchal society, there are complexities involved in transferring inheritance to daughters.

These are some of the contextual forces that might influence a particular episode of interaction. In this way, we can think of Lear, Kent and Oswald as acting 'in context,' i.e. being influenced by higher-level rules about relationships. The process can also be seen as bi-directional; the model can be used to identify 'sites of resistance' with people acting 'into context,' i.e. acting in ways that challenge and perturb these rules. In therapy, we often see change at one level having profound reverberations throughout the system. We can, however, only speculate on the implications for the Lear family story if the old king had responded differently to Oswald by saying: "Yes and how lovely to have the opportunity to be a real father to my eldest daughter at last!"

In Shakespeare's tragedies, ambiguity and contradiction feature so strongly that there are many examples of communication that seem to get caught up in paradoxes and double binds. Hamlet is one protagonist who is often portrayed as being at the receiving end of confusing messages, which place him in a bind. Gregory Bateson, who developed the concept of the double bind, identified four components in a double-binding process.[5] A message is given at one level and contradicted at another, often by non-verbal means but also through language; for example, "you must do as I say, but you must do it of your own volition." The other two components of the double bind are that the recipient is unable to meta-communicate, i.e. to comment on the communication, and cannot leave the field. These processes are typically enacted in repeated ways over time, meaning that they are most commonly observed in parent/child relationships. According to this model, the result is a state of confusion in the recipient to which their response may be to become mute, mindless or crazy.

I identify these processes at work in several of the plays, especially *Hamlet* and *Coriolanus*. The question of course arises of why any parent would choose to subject their child to these madness-inducing processes. This is where thinking at different levels of context is so useful. What Bateson failed to do was supply the missing contexts – whether familial, social or cultural – that might make sense of a parent enacting this type of process. Having developed his theory through observing the interactions of mainly mothers subjecting their children to double binds, Bateson did not include the mother's context in his analysis. So, for example, when I describe this process at work in the relationship between Volumnia and her son Coriolanus, the context might include the constraints on an intelligent and ambitious Roman mother who can only exercise power and influence vicariously through her increasingly uncooperative son.

Hamlet, I argue, is placed in a bind by the ghostly father. He must avenge his father's death but not harm his mother. One wider context at work here is the way mothers are frequently depicted. They are singled out for particular condemnation – in this case, for sexual transgression – but at the same time, they are treated as inferior moral beings who need to be protected from the consequences of this 'transgression.' The bind Ophelia's father, Polonius, places her in reveals an even more disqualifying level of psychic life. She has to possess desire to be 'bait' for Hamlet but desire, that most ungovernable of feelings, has to be switched on and off to suit her father's strategising. As a result, Ophelia opts first for mindlessness and then for craziness. In the interests of gender equity, we should also think of the context for Polonius: his absolute determination to maintain his family's position at court under the new Claudius regime.

I do not describe these processes as double binding to uncover 'family pathology.' It is a way of exploring the interactions that can occur when there are contradictions between different rules in a relationship system. Close emotional bonds may be irreconcilable with other social imperatives; for example, Coriolanus has to 'obey' his mother to fulfil her political ambitions for him but if he does this, he is 'disobeying' her by not being the autonomous self-reliant male she has brought him up to be. Again, these ways of understanding family interactions can capture some of the nuances and ambiguities in Shakespeare's multi-levelled portrayals of relationships.

Language and dialogue

Nuance and ambiguity is above all revealed through language use and in dialogue. Attention to the specificities of language is, of course, a key feature of both psychotherapy and drama criticism. Family therapists are particularly concerned with the material effects of language, i.e. with the actions and responses that follow from the use of some words rather than others. In therapy, we are alert to those situations in which language is employed in a way that constrains people into demeaning or restricted identities. For example, whether Othello is addressed by his own name or as 'the Moor' indicates the extent to which he is being treated as an insider or an outsider. In *King Lear*, the language employed by Gonoril and Regan about Lear changes from the intimate (if ironic) "*dearest father*" to the generic "*old man*" to the even more distancing *"lunatic king."* Each shift, as well as reflect changing constructions of relationships also serves to constitute those relationships. They open up possibilities for certain actions and close down others as the conflict between Lear and his two eldest daughters moves out of the familial and into the political domain.

In families, words used about certain family members have profound consequences, however descriptive they might appear to be. If a child is always referred to as 'trouble' or a father as 'emotionally cut off,' their opportunities for demonstrating alternative aspects of self are likely to be diminished or closed down and a single restrictive narrative about them will prevail.

When language is used in derogatory ways to marginalise or demean, it will provoke different responses on the part of the recipients who may or may not challenge it. Edmund in *King Lear* does a thorough job of interrogating the word 'bastard' – *"Why 'bastard', wherefore 'base' . . . Why brand they us with 'base, base bastardy'?"* – and indeed reclaiming the word – *"Now gods stand up for bastards!"* On the other hand, the word 'whore,' which features particularly strongly in *Othello* and *Troilus and Cressida,* is mainly taken up in terms of whether women are thought to have earned the epithet. Its instrumental use as a means of demeaning, silencing and exclusion receives less attention, although, when Iago uses it of his wife Emilia at the end of *Othello,* his menacing intent is pretty clear. The impact of the word shifts according to context and whether it is employed within private or public domains. Cressida is named 'whore' by Ulysses and Thersites, but not to her face. Desdemona, directly called whore by her husband, can hardly bear to let the word pass her lips:

> Desdemona "*Am I that name, Iago?*"
>
> Iago "*What name, fair lady?*"
>
> Desdemona "*Such as she says my lord did say I was.*"
>
> Emilia "*He call'd her 'whore:'.*" (4.ii.117–120)

Emilia demonstrates, as does Bianca later in the play, that she knows the word's lethal charge and immediately and forcefully rebuts it. Desdemona, having no such hinterland, barely attempts to defend herself.

That language carries profound implications beyond the merely descriptive is highlighted by Juliet, who, detaching the signifier from the signified, interrogates the meaning of the name Montague, a name that has exercised such a baleful influence on her family. She questions its materiality by comparing it to parts of the body and opens up the liberating prospect that Romeo might simply discard it:

> "*Tis but thy name that is my enemy*
>
> *Thou art thyself, though not a Montague*
>
> *What's Montague? It is nor hand nor foot*
>
> *Nor arm nor face nor any other part*
>
> *Belonging to a man. O be some other name!*" (2.ii.81–85)

As well as interrogating the use of particular words, family therapists pay particular attention to dialogue because it is within dialogue that language use and relationships intersect. Dialogue is, of course, the stuff of drama. Even monologues are inevitably public utterances that are preceded and succeeded by dialogue of some kind. Family therapists have drawn upon the work of the Russian linguist Mikhail Bakhtin to open up ways of bringing the idea of multiplicity into the process of therapeutic discourse.[6] Bakhtin argued that language has to be seen as inherently dialogic: it can be grasped only in terms of its inevitable orientation towards another. Language is heterogeneous because it is composed of many conflicting influences. Bakhtin's work is also helpful in clarifying the relationship between what we can call 'outer talk' and 'inner talk.'[7] These two levels intersect in dialogue, although one is of course more visible than the other.

When members of a family or any other system engage in a debate or argument, their dialogue constitutes of 'outer talk' – what people actually say to each other. This, as we have seen in the example of Hamlet, develops its own patterning. If we witness a dialogue between family members, we will notice who talks most, who interrupts, who lapses into silence or who invites others to speak on their behalf. We will also notice differences in language use – careful factual language or imaginative flights of fancy, for example, or critical tirades being met with defensiveness. With an eye for interactions, we will also notice how when strong positions are taken, they invite responses from others that either reinforce or soften them and we explore how these positions may become rigidified over time.

In a family in which parents are struggling with a dilemma over, for example, how much autonomy a young person should be allowed, it is quite likely that each person's position is actually more nuanced than might superficially be evident from observing their debate. If someone moves out of a predictable position, this can free others up to express a different view. If a point of view is expressed strongly, despite being held more ambivalently, even hearing the same thoughts emerge from the lips of another person can be enough to perturb it.

Juliet delivers a diatribe against Romeo when he has killed her kinsman, Tybalt, but the nurse's agreement is enough to make her change her stance:

> Nurse "*Shame come to Romeo!*"
>
> Juliet "*Blistered be thy tongue for such a wish!*
>
> ... *O, what a beast was I to chide at him!*" (3.ii.89–95)

When we explore what takes place in dialogue, the idea of 'positioning' is especially helpful because it creates links between the individual's own expression of beliefs and opinions and the social world within which they are received and responded to. In this view, each person is a subjectively coherent participant but within a jointly produced story-line. They are thus part of a discursive process, i.e. they are drawing upon a similar set of what Rom Harré calls 'semantic polarities.'[8] For example, the polarities of independence/dependence, freedom/constraint or trust/mistrust are likely to shape a family argument around what a sixteen-year-old is allowed to do. They take up different positions but around the same semantic frame. Because positioning theory translates so well into exploring dialogue, I find it useful to explore how the position taken up by one person creates a 'vacancy' or opening for a different position that is then taken up by another person.

I use this idea extensively to analyse the relationship between Macbeth and Lady Macbeth, whom, I argue, employ their different positions to collaborate in constructing a joint story-line, narrowing the options so as to lead inexorably to the murder of Duncan. The two family debates in *Troilus and Cressida* show relational positioning at work, strongly influenced by the competitive dynamic between the brothers. In the first debate, the semantic polarities of natural law and family loyalty and honour are initially set in opposition to each other, but converge with Hector's change of position. In the second, in which semantic polarities are taken up around fighting or preserving family unity, the belligerent position taken by Troilus edges Hector away from the compromise he might otherwise have reached with his wife, sister and father.

The second level of dialogue is what we call 'inner talk.' These are the thoughts and feelings that we each have but to which we may not give voice. Bakhtin argues that even here, when we might be most inclined to believe we are talking only with ourselves, what he calls the 'invisible interlocutor' is always present.[9] By this, he means that there is always an imagined audience, either an influential voice from the past or a set of precepts or cultural norms that are framing our inner conversation.

In family debates or discussions, 'inner talk' takes place for each participant. This might be entirely conscious, such as "My Mum might be cross if I say that," but it may also take the form of influences on us that have become so patterned they are beyond our awareness. These may emerge from previous family experiences; for example, a person whose voice has been disqualified or silenced in childhood may take a particularly rigid or dogmatic position in dialogue because they are determined not to be talked out of their viewpoint. There may be social or cultural influences at work, such as a 'rule' that men must not give way to women in an argument or they will lose their authority. In therapy, we are attentive to what we think of as the inner voices of everyone in the room, including, of course, that of the therapist.

In Shakespeare's tragedies, we have the privilege of listening to soliloquies, which give us access to the inner voice of participants in dialogue. Cressida, for example, having roundly dismissed all of Pandarus' attempts to get her interested in Troilus, tells the audience that, despite her love for Troilus, she fears she will be devalued if she admits it because "*Men prize the thing ungained more than it is.*" In Hamlet's famous soliloquies, he can be seen to be responding to a whole series of 'invisible interlocutors,' including other sons who have not shirked from avenging their fathers and, of course, the voice of his own dead father.

In family therapy, we pay particular attention to exploring how relational and cultural influences are revealed in our words and how they act as blueprints for how we think we should live our lives. These might include canons of parenthood that mothers and fathers draw upon in bringing up their children, societal messages about work and achievement or more subtle cultural messages about independence or family duty. Often, enquiring about these inner voices helps bring forth tensions that people may be experiencing between what is actually happening within their relationships and what they think 'should be' happening. A parent struggling to cope because of mental illness and reliant on a child to help out may be influenced by a dominant discourse about parenting, which is that parents should look after children and not vice versa.

The relationship between discourse and power was developed by the French philosopher Michel Foucault, who explored the way that language operates to specify certain ways of living. We tend to 'read' ourselves against social discourses and absorb their normative power.[10] Whether we comply or not, we become 'docile bodies,' according to Foucault, in the ways that we speak of ourselves, revealing how these discourses act upon us as subjects. This idea can seem elusive and abstract, making it essential to locate these processes in the words people actually use to describe themselves and their intimate others. A systemic therapist will be alert to the social discourses behind such descriptions as "I'm a hopeless mother" or "he's a weak man." Being 'captured by discourse' does not mean acquiescence, but rather that people frame their moral dilemmas within its terms.

Juliet's speech to Romeo in the 'balcony scene' is a good example of this; she articulates a conflict between her sexual desire and the social norms she has to transgress if she, as a woman, takes the initiative in courtship. As a 'docile body' in Foucault's sense, she responds to the discourse, which she rhetorically locates in Romeo; she indicates how she could 'play by the rules' but as a self-confident young woman, she decides upon transgression.

> "*Or if thou thinkest I am too quickly won*
>
> *I'll frown and be perverse and say thee nay,*
>
> *So thou wilt woo; but else, not for the world.*
>
> *In truth, fair Montague, I am too fond*" (2.ii.138–141)

In this example, Juliet speaks directly to Romeo but, while inter-personal exchanges show the influence of social discourses, especially those of gender (which many families are particularly eager to monitor), struggles between competing discourses are often evident within 'inner talk.' In the tragedies, this appears in soliloquies but can also be seen in speeches within dialogues when the speaker seems suddenly to deviate from the immediate context of the conversation. Old Capulet in *Romeo and Juliet* erupts into a rage that takes everyone in the room by surprise when he is confronted with the implications that his daughter's defiance has for his role as father. Coriolanus, in the Act 3 scene with Volumnia, appears to be responding to two voices simultaneously – his mother's external voice and that of his own internalised beliefs about masculinity, autonomy and pride. The idea of the inner dialogue is particularly useful in showing how a polyphony of voices can be present in a single speech. Lear's speech outside Cornwall and Regan's house (vii. 253–279) is a beautiful example of this. Here, his discourse shifts between, on the one hand, his current state of powerlessness, which requires patience and self-restraint, and, on the other, his prior state of absolute entitlement, according to which the need for any such restraint is unthinkable. In drama, from our position as the 'real' audience witnessing the emotional struggles unfold, we can think of an imagined but invisible 'audience' in which ideology, duty and social canon assert their unseen presence and against which characters respond, even to their own speech and actions.

In the therapeutic context, dialogue can be emancipatory if people are able to move beyond their habitual positions and gain new perspectives on self and other. Unsurprisingly, there are fewer examples of such emancipatory dialogues in the tragedies. After all, the closing down of alternatives is what drives the tragic denouement. What is powerful, however, as *Hamlet* and *Othello* in particular demonstrate, are the glimpses of dialogic potential that Shakespeare provides in the last scene between Desdemona and Emilia at the end of *Othello* and between Hamlet and Horatio in Act 5, scene 2. In each of these scenes, there is a moment, just before it is all too late, when alternative ways of talking or of seeing the world are opened up. The dialogue between Macduff and Malcolm in *Macbeth* illustrates a crucial distinction between dialogue that involves an 'other' who takes a different stance leading to new understanding, and the instrumental and uni-directional exchanges of the Macbeths.

'Performing' gender

One of the most powerful ways in which social discourses can be seen to operate is through specifying the ways that we 'perform' our gender.[11] In family therapy, we pay attention to the ways in which men and women, girls and boys talk about gender and sexual identities. I find it helpful to think about gender as performative because gender identity is so much more fluid than the binary terms of male and female allow. Gender as performance is absolutely the stuff of Shakespeare's plays, with female parts originally played by boys and with cross-dressing and gender deceptions at the heart of so many of the comedies. In the tragedies, gender playfulness of this kind is less in evidence but gender anxieties, particularly for men, are much more to the fore. I have employed three ways of analysing gender in the tragedies.

First, I explore the social discourses that invite men and women into performing gender identities in ways that frequently restrict them. All the plays can be explored in this way but in *Coriolanus, Hamlet, King Lear* and *Troilus and Cressida,* it seems especially compelling. How what we might call 'gender self-monitoring' takes place is more obvious for male than female characters. Men in Shakespeare's tragedies are enjoined to be men and to renounce anything that hints at femininity, including vulnerability, indecision, kindness or compassion but, typically, Shakespeare also provides counter-narratives to these dominant injunctions. The requirement on women to 'be women' is rarer and more subtle, usually evoked in the event of gross 'deviation' from an apparent norm, as Albany castigates his wife Gonoril: "*Proper deformity shows not in the fiend/ so horrid as in a woman.*"

The second level involves interactions between men and women that lead to ways of 'collaborating' to support troubled gendered identities. *Macbeth* and *Anthony and Cleopatra* are good examples of plays in which this process can be identified. It may take the form of the gender provocations that Lady Macbeth excels at delivering to her husband or the more overt sexual invitations at which Cleopatra is expert. In each case, the temporary effect is to shore up a troubled sense of maleness.

The third level is the way that practices of power can be seen to intersect with gender tropes so that 'gender performance' can also be linked to the effects of power. Experiences either of power or powerlessness open up different spaces within which women and men might define or redefine their gendered selves. We might thus question within a particular interaction whether power or gender is acting as the higher context in meaning-making.

Two examples of this can be seen in relation to the constructs of 'reason' and 'emotion,' themselves so often ascribed gendered meanings. They are amplified in interaction, so that the more one person evokes 'reason,' the more another appeals to 'emotion.' In scenes from *King Lear* and *Coriolanus,* each of the men, in the midst of a troubled relationship to power, challenges the idea of 'reason' – something they might previously have simply taken to reflect their own position. In scene 7, faced with Gonoril and Regan's 'impeccable logic' that he should reduce the size of his retinue, Lear emits the impassioned cry: "*O, reason not the need!*" With so many levels at work in this speech, it is easy to overlook his emotional response to his daughters' appeal to reason and logic. This discursive shift could be seen to create a terror in Lear that, if his daughters have occupied 'reason,' he is left only with 'emotion,' which must at all costs be resisted:

"*You think I'll weep*

No I'll not weep

I have full cause of weeping, but this heart

Shall break into a hundred thousand flaws

Or ere I'll weep – Oh fool I shall go mad." (vii.440–444)

Excess of emotion, unless it is justified, reasonably, as "*noble anger,*" can only lead to madness.

The second example is in Act 5, scene 3, when Coriolanus is confronted by his mother, Volumnia, petitioning him not to attack Rome. Although she couches her pleas in emotional language, he can easily resist her because he has already anticipated and set his mind against such entreaties – *out affections!* – but her formidable use of logic and reason is what unsettles him. It invites him to position himself as emotional and thus less in control: "*Desire not/T'allay my rages and revenges with/Your colder reasons.*" In these two examples, the novel experiences either of being unable to exert authority or of being on the losing side of an argument lead to interactions in which gender stereotypes about men being 'reasonable' and women 'emotional' are challenged. For both protagonists, the change in discourse comes about through a reconfiguration of power. Similar processes often occur in families in which social changes create challenges to previous assumptions about 'proper' gendered behaviour.

Power and resistance

In therapy, we are alert to the ways that power operates both within families, between families and therapists and in families' interaction with social institutions. Power does not only operate through coercive mechanisms but also through the discourses and ideologies that construct the ways that individuals and families think about themselves and their relationships. However, rather than addressing power only in terms of its uni-directional effects, we also incorporate the idea of points of resistance. In family therapy, these are identified and highlighted to support and sustain alternative courses of action that will enhance wellbeing or create more rewarding relationships. Because we can hardly do this on behalf of any of Shakespeare's protagonists, we are always left with intriguing questions of what might have been. However, a disposition towards interrogating power practices and identifying resistance is just as important in literary criticism as it is therapy. Attention to the detail of counter-currents to totalising discourses is what is crucial and Shakespeare excels at this.

In Shakespearean criticism, as well as in therapy, it requires an attentive eye and ear to notice small variations within rigid or oppressive systems when protagonists can be seen to act 'against the grain' or to identify exceptions to otherwise homogenous narratives. For two men constrained by Roman ideology, Coriolanus' cry of "*there is a world elsewhere*" or Antony's seemingly derisory request to Caesar to let him *"breathe between the heavens and earth/A private man in Athens"* are examples of counter-narratives that contain the potential for liberation, even if they are over within seconds. Often, counter-narratives can be seen in the utterances of minor characters such as Cornwall's serving man in *King Lear* or Cassandra in *Troilus and Cressida*. These characters, although marginal, also speak truth to power.

Being open to families' views about the therapeutic process underscores the way that the powerful and privileged world of therapy and its institutions might be perceived when oppression, discrimination or stigma is part of life's experience. The voices of the least powerful are often the most trenchant in family life and in family therapy; for example, the very young or those with psychiatric diagnoses. I have found the process of 'learning from the margins' – i.e. from those whose views might easily be ignored – invaluable in therapy but it has been useful in drama criticism, as peripheral characters and their voices are so easily expunged from Shakespearean productions.

Because Shakespeare's drama is so multi-facetted, there are always voices in the tragedies that open up alternative narratives. They may occupy ambiguous positions – they are either already on, or about to be on the margins, too lowly to have their views taken seriously, easily discountable because they are fools, mad or (of course) women. Indeed, speaking truth to power can in itself be constructed as a form of madness. The tribunes dismiss Volumnia's rage when her son is banished with the lofty words: *"they say she's mad."* Women speaking up for themselves are also likely to be constructed as whores, as Iago does to Emilia. When minor characters speak truth to power or when they deconstruct power, their status is usually ambiguous. Cassandra's 'madness' in *Troilus and Cressida* also carries another and more persuasive attribute – that of foresight – *"Cassandra doth foresee"* – as well as the dismissive epithet: *"our mad sister."* When her words suit Hector's argument for returning Helen, he emphasises Cassandra's foresight:

> "*Now youthful Troilus, do not these high strains*
>
> *Of divination in our sister work*
>
> *Some touches of remorse*" (2.ii.112–114)

His brother, Troilus, arguing for the other side, uses her 'madness' both to dismiss her and to undermine his brother's case.

> "*Nor once deject the courage of our minds*
>
> *Because Cassandra's mad. Her brainsick raptures*

> *Cannot distaste the goodness of a quarrel*
>
> *Which hath our several honours all engaged*" (2.ii.120–124)

The fool in *King Lear* is in an 'all licensed' position to speak truth to power; his truth-telling is brutal:

> Lear "*Dost thou call me fool, boy?*"
>
> Fool "*All thy other titles thou hast given away.That thou wast born with.*" (iv.141–143)

Whether he would have spoken in quite this way when Lear was still king is another matter; as he says: "*there's not a nose among a hundred but can smell him that's stinking*." For Lear himself, it is loss of power that opens up space for an extraordinary deconstruction of its workings. Those in positions of power or privilege (including, of course, therapists) are often the least likely to interrogate their own assumptions or to be aware of how their opinions come across to others.

In *Coriolanus*, the perspectives offered by minor characters provide not only a commentary on events, but highlight the poverty of debate between those at the centre. The citizens in Rome provide a lacerating analysis of the way power operates, which is more sophisticated than that of the senators. The serving men of Aufidius' court, debating the various advantages of war or peace, expose the inadequacies of the individualised heroic narrative about warfare that has suffused the play so far.

In this chapter, I have argued that the ideas informing family therapy can create innovative readings of the tragedies in several ways: first, through describing patterns of interaction and showing how communication is influenced by the relational and social contexts in which it is embedded; second, through understanding the different ways that discursive practices are manifested and contested within dialogue; and, third, through the expectation that, although power acts upon and is enacted in relationships, there are always counter-currents and perspectives – often unexpected ones – that emerge from the margins and unsettle dominant narratives. Because family therapy from its very inception has grappled with and mostly delighted in the need to engage with multiple realities, Shakespeare's plays, which "are framed and qualified as only one version of things,"[12] seem to me to be a natural intellectual playground for a systemic family therapist. In the following chapter, I describe some of the ways that other psychotherapists have written about Shakespeare as well as some approaches from Shakespeare studies that have guided my own journey in this rich territory.

Notes

1 Gregory Bateson, *Mind and Nature* (London: Fontana, 1979).
2 Gregory Bateson, *Naven* (Stanford: Stanford University Press, 1958).
3 John Byng Hall and David Campbell, 'Resolving Conflicts in Distance Regulation: An Integrative Approach', *Journal of Marital and Family Therapy*, 7:3 (July 1981), 321–330.
4 Vernon E. Cronen and W. Barnett Pearce, 'Toward an Explanation of How the Milan Method Works: An Invitation to a Systemic Epistemology and the Evolution of Family Systems', in David Campbell and Rosalind Draper, eds., *Applications of Systemic Family Therapy* (London: Grune and Stratton, 1985).
5 Gregory Bateson, *Steps to an Ecology of Mind* (St Albans: Paladin, 1973).
6 Mikhail Bakhtin, *Problems of Dostoevsky's Poetics* (Minneapolis: University of Minneapolis Press, 1984).
7 Peter Rober, 'The Therapist's Inner Conversation in Family Therapy Practice: Some Ideas about the Self of the Therapist, Therapeutic Impasse and the Process of Reflection', *Family Process*, 38:2 (June 1999): 209–228.
8 Rom Harré and Luk Van Langenhove, *Positioning Theory: Moral Contexts of Intentional Action* (Oxford: Wiley-Blackwell, 1999).
9 Mikhail Bakhtin, *Speech Genres and Other Late Essays* (Austin: University of Texas Press, 1986).
10 Michel Foucault, *The Archaeology of Knowledge and the Discourse of Language* (New York: Pantheon, 1972).
11 Judith Butler, *Gender Trouble* (New York: Routledge, 1990).
12 Kiernan Ryan, *Shakespeare* (Basingstoke: Palgrave Macmillan, 2002).

CHAPTER 2

Interpretations of the tragedies

Berthold Brecht's idiosyncratic phrase conjures up an image of audiences and critics alike dismembering and devouring the individual tragic hero and disregarding his social connections:

> Shakespeare drives the great individual, Lear, Othello, Macbeth, out of all his human connections with family and state . . . into total isolation, where he must show himself great in his ruin. . . . The object of the exercise is the great individual experience. Later times will call this drama a drama for cannibals.[1]

As we are well into Brecht's 'later times,' we can report back to him that individual character analysis of the kind he derided is assuredly out of fashion in Shakespeare studies and that much scholarship has emerged, some of which, influenced by his own theories of drama, views individual consciousness as inextricably linked to socio-political context. But he would not expect any kind of consensus about the individual, nor would he find one. Within contemporary culture, there is a continuing fascination with the individual characteristics of our heroes or villains at the expense of the contexts that sustain them. As well as in responses to drama, this pervades many domains of public life from the arts to politics.

Within Shakespeare studies, we continue to see fault-lines between approaches that tend to take the texts to represent individual turmoil and tragedy outside of their social contexts and those that foreground these contexts and their influence on the construction of the drama. The contrast is most evident between many of the approaches informed by psychoanalysis and those employing a materialist perspective of the kind Brecht favoured. Intersecting with these polarities is a practical distinction between what can loosely be called text-based studies and those broadly concerned with an historical approach; that is, between studies that focus mainly on the content and structure of the plays and those concerned with the playwright and his milieu – those that take the plays as 'givens' and those that regard them as cultural productions.

Text-based studies themselves vary enormously and include Shakespeare's use of language,[2] imagery,[3] sex and love,[4] semiotic analyses,[5] and deconstruction,[6] to name only a few. Among these, some apply an explicitly theoretical lens and others consider themselves to eschew theoretical impositions on the text. All of these nuances and differences are relevant to this chapter because they relate to how systemic thinking finds itself an entry point into the world of Shakespeare studies. Psychotherapeutic approaches to Shakespeare's plays inevitably focus primarily on the text, and a systemic approach, exploring the detail of interactions within the plays, is no exception.

However, because systemic therapists take as axiomatic that any depiction of persons is necessarily context-bound, this means that it is those Shakespeare scholars who take an historical/contextual approach to questions of selfhood and relationship in the plays who have most influenced my own understanding of Shakespeare.

Tensions between text and history/context-based approaches within the field of Shakespeare studies often result in complaints that text-based approaches tend towards conservatism or are – even worse – guilty of the crime of 'essentialism.' Context-based studies, on the other hand, are accused of superficial reading or the ideological hijacking of texts. These are not so very different from the kinds of criticisms that psychoanalytic and systemic therapists level at each other, although perhaps not as rudely as literary critic Harold Bloom when he decried the scholarship of the "gender-and-power freaks."[7]

The different levels at which I explore the relationships portrayed in drama are described in Chapter 1. 'Close range' engagement involves observing interactional patterns, the positions taken up by individual protagonists, both verbally and non-verbally, exploring language use and its material effects. It also includes understanding how human emotions, desires and attachments shape and are shaped by relationships. Wider perspectives involve placing all of these actions and emotional transactions within the social and ideological contexts that frame them.

I broadly follow this framework in exploring the literature selected from the vast corpus of Shakespeare studies. The distinction between, on the one hand, a 'close-up' engagement with observable interactions and, on the other, a wider perspective on social and ideological influences can be mapped broadly – if somewhat crudely – onto the distinction between text-based and historically based approaches. Although the vast body of Shakespearean scholarship will, just as his own works do, slip effortlessly outside the confines of any category we try to impose on it, in practice, most Shakespeare scholars will tend to privilege one type of approach over the other.

In this chapter, I take these two levels as a framework for my survey of some of the literature. A systemic framework is well equipped to explore the reciprocal relationship between the levels of text and context. A creative interplay between close textual readings and wider socio-historical perspectives – 'double description,' to borrow Bateson's term – means that, even if the text itself is the main focus, other contexts are always in the frame. As well as the relationship between these two levels, what is significant for systemic thinkers is the stance taken by the observer/interlocutor, whether they are therapist, drama critic or Shakespearean scholar.

In this chapter, I first explore psychotherapeutic interpretations of Shakespeare's drama – in particular those informed by psychoanalysis – and then describe other contributions from Shakespeare studies. It is within the 'close range' analysis of the plays that the absence of the interactional perspective described in Chapter 1 is perhaps most evident. Among those Shakespeare studies that explore wider contexts, a relational analysis is also lacking but those approaches that look closely at the workings of power, ideology and gender are most relevant because they posit the 'conditions' for selfhood and thus for enacting relationships.

Psychotherapeutic interpretations of Shakespeare's tragedies

Psychotherapists can make valuable contributions to an appreciation of drama because of their close acquaintance with a wide range of human dilemmas, their powers of observation, their attention to the nuances in verbal and non-verbal communication and their understanding of the wellsprings of extreme emotions. This very advantage can also be a drawback in drama criticism if we remain too wedded to our own assumptions about human relations. Psychotherapists are often tempted to use Shakespeare's dramatic characters as a means of elucidating the finer points of clinical theory. In this case, protagonists are treated as if they are 'real' people and the main purpose is to communicate with other therapists rather than contribute to Shakespeare criticism. In this kind of writing, references are more likely to be drawn from other psychotherapists than from academics, leading to a somewhat circular process as if we are taking part in a rarefied case discussion with shared premises about human behaviour and emotions.

The idea that Shakespeare's appeal lies in his ability to represent fundamental truths about human emotional life is widespread but becomes problematic if it leads to thinking about human nature itself as timeless and unchanging. The idea of drama holding – to use Hamlet's phrase, a "*mirror up to nature*" – captures this tendency. It echoes the Aristotelean conception of drama as a means of revealing universal truths: "Characters do what they do because they must – that is to say, because their nature impels it."[8] Drama and psychotherapy, Michael and Margaret Rustin go on to argue, demonstrate in their different ways a "passion for truth" – they seek to understand what "unrecognized beliefs, desires or compulsions make people do what they do even sometimes seemingly against their will or against their better nature."[9]

A systemic approach, although not of course discounting individual subjectivity, locates this sense of what we 'must do' more in the way we have come to understand and position ourselves within our relational worlds. Identity is performed differently within different contexts. From this perspective, Shakespeare's enduring quality lies less in an inherent 'truth status' about human nature and more in his capacity to see many truths, embrace contradictions and inconsistencies and represent multiple perspectives. This means not only that different social contexts and time periods bring forth new ways of viewing the individuals and relationships he portrays but also that diverse perspectives and paradoxical positions arise within the plays themselves, often within the course of a single speech.

Psychoanalysis and Shakespeare

Psychoanalysis has made a massive contribution to our understanding of literature and to Shakespeare studies in particular. It has firmly established itself within the canon of literary theory. Freud himself was fascinated by Shakespeare and fond of quoting his work. As well as being the founder of such a ground-breaking, compelling and complex theory of human development, Freud made significant contributions to our understanding of *Hamlet, Lear* and *Macbeth* in particular. His famous dictum, "The poets and philosophers before me discovered the unconscious,"[10] speaks to the respect Freud held for other fields of knowledge and to his radical and creative imagination. Occasionally, however, his imagination ran ahead of him as he advanced various far-fetched theories about who was the 'real' author of the plays.[11] The fact that Freud was speculating about Shakespeare's drama at the same time as developing his own innovative theories provides a vivid sense of 'work in progress,' of the interconnection and feedback between drama and psychology, theory and practice, and art and scientific endeavour.

Margaret and Michael Rustin raise the question, "How it is that the themes of so much classical drama and those of psychoanalytical investigation overlap to such an extent?"[12] Posing the question in this way emphasises the circular nature of the process. Freud selected this particular genre as a launch pad for some of his most creative ideas. This became, reciprocally, a means of finding further evidence of it, 'discovering' in Sophocles' *Oedipus Rex* and *Oedipus the King* the inspiration for understanding "the repression of human desires and the potential catastrophe inherent in attempting to bring them to the surface."[13]

An insight derived from drama is then applied to drama. Freud argued that Hamlet's inability to kill Claudius was based on an unconscious identification with his uncle because of his Oedipal longing to kill his father himself.[14] At the time, this answer to the question, "Why did Hamlet delay?" was decidedly more sophisticated than most of the other explanations on offer.

Freud also developed other psychoanalytic concepts such as the death wish alongside his reading of *King Lear*. He connected the succession scene to mythology, drawing from this the inference that, as the third and silent participant, Cordelia represents death.[15] This was reinforced by Lear's appearance in the final scene carrying her body, after which he too dies. Freud also drew attention to Lear's repressed incestuous desires for his daughters, which Gonoril and Regan could resist but Cordelia could not. In his writing about *Macbeth*, Freud advanced several theories including an elaboration of the idea that because expressions of guilt, remorse and anguish shift from him to her as the play develops, Macbeth and Lady Macbeth could be seen as psychically the same person.[16]

Freud approached Shakespeare as he did human development in general, with a pioneering spirit, surprising lack of dogmatism and breadth of vision that has at times eluded some of his acolytes. The tendency towards a construction of Shakespeare's plays as exemplifying only internal psychic states is illustrated by Michael Jacobs:

> Shakespeare draws upon imagination and a depth of insight that prefigures and even overshadows later attempts to reflect upon the nature of personality and of human relationships. What psychologists have added to this are names and labels and theories that attempt to explain the wellsprings of emotions, actions and relationships.[17]

There is a frozen quality to this argument that never strays out of its own terms of reference; the 'eternal truth' of Shakespeare's insights into 'human nature' is one that broadly reflects psychoanalytic understandings.

When psychoanalysts interpret Shakespeare plays, they often end up approaching the individual protagonist and even the playwright himself from the position of therapist to patient. Attempts to psychoanalyse Shakespeare himself have usually proved to be comically disastrous and, although Michael Jacobs does not attempt this, his book is nevertheless entitled, revealingly, *Shakespeare on the Couch*.

Approaches to Shakespeare that attempt to diagnose and categorise have the unfortunate effect of replicating processes whereby we have an 'expert' psychotherapist seeking out 'the truth' about patients whose 'inner nature' they know more about than the patients themselves. This tendency reaches its apogee in an approach to literary criticism more akin to detective work. An extreme example of this is Martin Wangh's triumphant pronouncement on *Othello:*

> Iago's various projections may be summarised: the Moor has lain with Emilia; therefore Cassio has lain with Emilia; Emilia equals Desdemona; therefore Cassio has lain with Desdemona. All of these serve the function of warding off anxiety and enable Iago to deny by projection his homosexual drive to lie with the Moor.[18]

Quite apart from its homophobia, this approach illustrates the peril of focusing a critique entirely on the inner world of one protagonist with the other dramatis personae taken up as mere projections. This tendency is repeated in many psychoanalytic studies, even those that aim to take a more relational view.

The temptation to assume insight into the inner motivations and drives of an invented character is especially strong when certain drives and fantasies are taken as axiomatic, such as the Oedipus complex. This accounts for the narrow and somewhat orthodox flavour of some psychoanalytic Shakespearean criticism. It takes up a metaphor as unquestioned truth, using a theoretical construct to ride roughshod over specificities, moulding them to fit the conceptual imperative. It is often as if the oedipal drama is the only drama in town. Peter Hildebrand pushes this to the limits: deciding there must be an oedipal conflict to be uncovered in *Macbeth*, he creates a Lady Macbeth who is older than her husband and royally born so she can stand for the desired but forbidden mother. Duncan, the symbolic father, is therefore killed so that Macbeth can possess her.[19] In another example, Michael Jacobs argues that *Hamlet* "is so powerful because the audience can witness his repressed version of Oedipus, as they themselves similarly struggle with these universal desires."[20]

Although some of these approaches can be drearily orthodox, it is not surprising that some of the most compelling and creative psychoanalytic writing about Shakespeare has emerged in the process of renewing the field, often from the margins, by challenging its tendency towards universalising human experience and opening up a space for thinking about modes of representation. Once we question the ways in which characters are portrayed and the language employed in so doing, we inevitably raise the issues of who is doing the representation, from what perspective and in which context.

Feminist psychoanalytic writing

Feminist writers have critiqued psychoanalytic theory for erasing women as subjects, for representing women via developmental theories designed to describe the male psyche and for over-loading onto women the burden of men's 'emotional vulnerability.' Janet Adelman, a psychoanalytically informed professor of English Literature, has used the twin perspectives of literary criticism and feminist psychology to dig deeply into the imaginative structures of the works. Her book *Suffocating Mothers: Fantasies of Maternal Origins in Shakespeare's Plays* is a brilliantly argued work in which she explores the twin themes of male fear of engulfment by the female and male terror both of female sexuality and maternal abandonment.[21] In her analysis of the tragedies, she traces male fantasies of merger with the maternal body and the accompanying fear this generates. More importantly, she highlights the implications that these processes of male projection have for the women "who must pay the price for the fantasies of maternal power invested in them."[22] Despite the compelling nature of her analysis and fine attention to the nuances of language, Adelman still at times seems implicitly to load onto mothers the burden of being the cause of male suffering.

Jacqueline Rose, in a study of *Hamlet* and *Measure for Measure*, challenges portrayals of women that always problematise them as subjects.[23] She takes up the idea of Gertrude in *Hamlet* being portrayed in a way that leaves her 'carrying' a weight of emotion far in excess of the play's ability to support it. Both Gertrude in *Hamlet* and Isabella in *Measure for Measure* stand accused, respectively, of either excessive or deficient sexuality. In *Hamlet*, Rose argues that Freudian readings based on the idea of an oedipal struggle end up taking for granted that Gertrude is a sexually charged object arousing erotic feelings in her son. A Lacanian informed feminist analysis focusses instead on language and representation, so "failure of integration within language and subjectivity itself" takes the place of 'failure' within the female characters.[24] Exploring processes of representation rather than psychological drives makes it possible to lift the onus off the women and their positioning as 'guilty' for possessing either 'too much' sexuality as in the case of Gertrude or 'too little' as in the case of Isabella.

Psychoanalytically informed readings of Shakespeare of course vary hugely in terms of the theoretical connections they make with the plays and the extent to which they either impose universalising psychological theories on them or take up the ambiguities and contradictions within the text and interrogate language and modes of representation. One compelling strength of psychoanalysis lies in its deep and radical understanding of human desire, including, most importantly, an appreciation of its unruliness and excesses. One major disadvantage is that it does not – perhaps cannot, given its orientation – theorise the way in which selfhood and intimate relationships themselves are socially determined, instead "projecting the family of developed capitalist society onto all periods of history."[25] Stephen Greenblatt writes ironically of "the bafflement of psychoanalytic interpretation by Renaissance culture." Freudian understandings of the self, he argues, would be of supreme irrelevance to anyone in the sixteenth century; an irrelevance, he adds, that "need not itself discourage us – the universalist claims of psychoanalysis are unruffled by the indifference of the past to its categories."[26]

A systemic approach, having developed intellectually rigorous ways of engaging with diversity and difference, is well placed to engage with radically different ways of 'doing' family and 'doing' subjectivity at different historical junctures. Systemic therapists are trained to reflect on the taken-for-granted within our own thinking. This is particularly important because, by definition, we can only ever think about the past from the standpoint of the present. The best we can hope for perhaps is to keep being explicit about our own perspective and the inevitable lacunae in our knowledge. Systemic psychotherapy having made very few forays into Shakespeare studies has no track record in this area but, being so new to the field, can at least avoid the accusation of succumbing to orthodoxy.

Systemic family therapy contributions

Although the last thirty years have marked a shift in the systemic field into a focus on language and discourse and the development of narrative approaches to therapy, this has not to date been accompanied by many excursions into Shakespearean criticism. There has been one essay on the fool in *King Lear* in which the author mischievously portrays the fool as an amateur family therapist trying to help his master by naming the brutal truth of his situation and, as a result of such provocations, sending him further into madness.[27]

A chapter on "Family Games" in *Hamlet* bases its analysis on a systemic family therapy text of the same name.[28] The author locates Hamlet's narrative within the communicational patterns of his family, most of which, he argues, emerge from positions of ambiguity and are thus designed to confuse and obfuscate. He pays particular attention to what different family members are striving to achieve and what strategies and alliances they employ in doing so. He also makes imaginative hypotheses about intergenerational patterns, especially about the relationship between King Hamlet and his brother Claudius. His piece does have a tendency, however, to take a somewhat clinical approach, replacing individual pathology with family pathology.[29]

One of the most theoretically rigorous pieces of drama criticism, although not of Shakespeare, comes from the early period of family therapy. In an analysis of Edward Albee's play *Who's Afraid of Virginia Woolf?*, Paul Watzlawick and his colleagues demonstrate how, amid their high levels of conflict and extreme emotional volatility, the protagonists George and Martha collaborate in maintaining the equilibrium of their relationship through adhering to certain communicational rules.[30] They do this by drawing upon both complementary and symmetrical patterns of communication, so when conflict threatens to escalate into a 'runaway,' which could lead either to a complete breakdown of the relationship or to a resolution, each employs a manoeuvre to maintain homeostasis. These mechanisms keep the relationship in the frozen state of eroticised conflict that we see on stage. An escalating exchange of symmetrical communication (competitive trading of insults) will lead one of the couple to take a complementary position (a 'one down' move such as a plea for pity or call for another drink) until the symmetry reasserts itself. The other manoeuvre they employ to manage the relationship is the co-option of a third party as a means of detouring conflict (the other couple or George and Martha's own mythical child). The elegance of Watzlawick's analysis is that it is theoretically consistent and makes no claims to interpret what either of the two protagonists might 'really' be thinking or feeling but provides instead a compelling account of the observable pragmatic workings of the relationship itself.

We can never find out what characters 'really' think or feel, addictive as this quest is for those of us in the psychotherapy profession. All we can know is what people 'perform' in relation to each other, which may or not be consistent with more hidden thoughts and feelings. Although actors inevitably use their imagination and emotional resources to convey the intensity of a character's inner world, what we view on the stage is what they perform relationally. Even soliloquies are inevitably public utterances, directed at the audience with particular rhetorical intent. A systemic approach would assume, for example, that when Lady Macbeth or Volumnia in *Coriolanus* speak about being prepared to sacrifice their own child for the sake of political ambition, it is impossible to make any assumption about what this 'really' means for them. We would instead explore the way that these women – created by a man with, inevitably, his own assumptions about women and mothers – employ rhetoric aimed at bringing about particular outcomes in the context of different social worlds – Republican Rome and eleventh-century Scotland – imagined by Shakespeare from the standpoint of Jacobean England and responded to by audiences from different historical, geographical and social locations.

These wider perspectives are a long way from the views of A.C. Bradley who, writing over a hundred years ago about character in Shakespeare's tragedies, proclaimed that "in the circumstances where we see the hero placed, his tragic trait which is also his greatness, is fatal to him."[31] Although this essentialist view has long been contested and discredited within the academic field, there are many ways in which his approach continues to resonate with the way audiences actually respond to the tragedies. The concept of individual character, greatness brought low, inherent flaws, a moral order in which good prevails over evil and where those who overstep acceptable boundaries are punished, continue to be powerful tropes within Western cultural experience. They are likely to suffuse the experience of watching the tragedies in which visceral reactions overlay more detached critical faculties.

Because Shakespeare created such rich and complex psychological dramas, the lure of the inner world of protagonists is irresistible to those who are passionate about understanding human behaviour and human interactions. A reflexive stance on drama involves taking both positions simultaneously. We are fascinated by the protagonists on stage, wonder how and why they have come to be 'like that' and, at the same time, wonder how and why they are constructed in this way. The second question is illuminated by the textual and contextual understandings of Shakespeare scholars.

In my voyages around the vast universe of Shakespeare studies, I have been most drawn to writers who link the social and ideological ambience of the period to the construction of identities in the plays, who take ambiguity, multiplicity and contradiction as axiomatic, who interrogate language and representation and who deconstruct gender categories. These writers can be found across the spectrum from close textual readings to broader historical scholarship and my selection is inevitably partial and somewhat idiosyncratic.

Tragedy, history and ideology

Literary scholars who write about the Renaissance in such a way as to stimulate us to reflect on connections to our own times also invite critical thinking about subjectivity and relationships. Thus, although they locate their work in Shakespeare's time, their contribution is not only to look at the past but enable us to take a reflexive view of our present.

Historical approaches that address this dimension broadly locate tragedy within those power practices and ideologies that shape the identities and conflicts we view on stage. There are inevitably many different levels at work in these studies. Some tend to take social process and ideology as a uni-directional flow, whereas others are more concerned with countercurrents and resistance.

For systemic thinkers, to conceive of historical readings in conversational terms – "speaking with the dead" in Stephen Greenblatt's words[32] – involves a dynamic process in which we look for "fresh understanding of the rootedness of our present uncertainties, derived by some kind of engaging dialogue with the textual residue of history."[33] This requires recognising that we are responding at particular moments in history and that Shakespeare's plays inevitably have changing resonances for different audiences over time.

An eloquent example of this is Lisa Jardine's discussion of *Henry V* in which she describes seeing the play, which she knew well, at a time of vicious ethnic conflict and the collapse of multi-culturalism in the former Yugoslavia. Her response was to engage with the "complexity of representation within the play of nationalism and ethnic identity." She adds, "I find it hard to believe, personally, that I failed for so long to see the fractures in the play's nationalistic rhetoric."[34] These elements are of course supremely relevant to today's UK. Additionally, in the aftermath of the 2003 invasion of Iraq, it would be hard for audiences not to be alert to the contemporary resonances of the long and spurious series of claims produced by the Archbishop of Canterbury to legitimise Henry's desire to invade France.[35]

Jonathan Dollimore, whose cultural materialist approach employs a broadly Marxist perspective on tragedy, takes up the idea of 'decentring' the tragic hero. He argues that sixteenth-century theatre's sceptical representations of religion meant that individuals came to be seen as socially rather than divinely constructed. "The self is decentred," he argues, "not through misanthropy but in order to make visible social process and its forms of ideological misrecognition."[36] Ideas about such ideological constraints were already available to Jacobean playwrights through the writings of Machiavelli, Hobbes and Montaigne, in particular. Montaigne wrote of the way that social norms – 'custom' in his words – "does so entangle us that it shall hardly lie in us, to free ourselves . . . to discourse and reason of her ordinances . . . Custom doth so bleare us that we cannot distinguish the true visage of things."[37] We can take from Montaigne's writing that entanglement in 'custom' links to his description elsewhere of identities as fluid and fractured: "We are all framed of flaps and patches and of so shapeless and diverse a contexture, that every piece and every moment playeth his part. And there is as much difference found between us and ourselves as there is between ourselves and others."[38]

In *Troilus and Cressida*, it is the outsider, Cressida, who, speaking to her lover Troilus, explicitly identifies this kind of self-division; in her case, it is between her own desires and the 'custom' of power relations between men and women that she well knows will shape and manipulate these very desires: "*I have a kind of self resides with you/But an unkind self that itself will leave/To be another's fool.*"

From a systemic perspective, this example of the 'split subject' creates the need not to delve deeper into the psyche but to explore the tensions between individuals, their relationships and their social orders: "In theatre we see these things operating at all levels simultaneously – the psychic, the private, the familial, the public."[39] Because late Elizabethan and Jacobean dramatists had grasped the problematic and shifting nature of identity, they were concerned with exploring identity as a struggle rather than with portraying consistent characters or a strictly realistic plot. The credibility of these plays thus lies in their grasp of the dilemmas of power and positioning and the possibilities they open up for subverting fixed or oppressive positions: "One effect of the notorious discontinuity of 'character' in Jacobean tragedy is to make it virtually impossible to telescope the implications of all of this back into the individual . . . seeing it as ultimately a question of his or her moral culpability."[40]

Shakespeare and other Elizabethan dramatists were capturing, among other things, those diverse experiences that emerged within societies caught between a world of declining feudalism and one of nascent capitalism, with its increasing emphasis on the individual and his/her desires and ambitions rather than on social hierarchies and social bonds. This forms the background to, for example, *Romeo and Juliet*. The idea of the individual struggling to find a way to exist within a set of oppressive structures and conventions might also be seen in a Coriolanus crying out in extremis, "*there is a world elsewhere,*" or more reflectively by a Hamlet, struggling with the question of an emergent 'core self' asserting itself against both social and familial constraints: "*that within which passeth show.*" At the same time, because Shakespeare always presents contradictory perspectives, this treatment of selfhood is offset against a portrayal of the negative consequences of rampant and unbounded individualism, a standpoint that suffuses, for example, *Macbeth*.

Scholars whose approach is called new historicist and whose leading exponent is Stephen Greenblatt are especially concerned with both the effects of and responses to power. They use narratives from individuals or families in Shakespeare's time to illustrate the contemporary dilemmas that suffuse his plays. They are influenced by Michel Foucault as much as by Marx; as well as being alert to the effects of discourse, they explore counter-currents in social and cultural life and engage with contradictory positions. A discernible change in "the intellectual . . . social, psychological and aesthetic structures that govern the generation of identities . . . is difficult to characterise in our usual ways because it is not only complex but resolutely dialectical."[41] This dialectical framework is especially useful in analysing relationships because, rather than look only at how ideologies shape identities, we can also explore how these tensions may be worked out through the different positions taken up by individuals within their relationships. This can be seen, for example, in the struggle Romeo and Juliet have in trying to free themselves from the ideology of the feud.

A portrayal of individuals and their relationships at a cusp of socio-political change has an inevitably ambiguous flavour. Within Shakespeare's tragedies, it can evoke nostalgia for the social bonds and loyalties forged within a feudal system. In *King Lear,* this conflict is represented by the relationship between the rampant cruelty of the Duke of Cornwall and Edmund on the one hand and the steadfast loyalty of the Earl of Kent and Cordelia on the other. However, modern audiences are also likely to respond to the play's challenges to authoritarianism and to pick up its many appeals for a more egalitarian social system. Plays that seem to capture moments of profound social or political upheaval express diverse and contradictory responses to these changes and these are often played out within relationships.

The concept of ideology is crucial to cultural materialist scholars. Ideology offers the subject "an imaginary, compelling sense of reality in which crucial contradictions of self and social order appear to be erased."[42] If ideology is successful, people no longer question the way we have come to view our worlds – we take it as a given. In this sense, ideology is less a set of explicit political ideas than what Althusser calls a "lived . . . relationship with the real . . . in which men and women see and experience, before they think about, their place within a given social order, with its specific structure of class and gender relations."[43] Taking ideology as a framework sharpens our appreciation of its workings in the tragedies when we see how protagonists such as Macbeth end up acting as if a course of action 'has to be' so that alternative possibilities simply fade away.

Ideology is often made visible at times of crisis. Two writers have described the workings of ideology in *Othello* at such a moment. Ania Loomba writes: "Othello moves from existing on the terms of white Venetian society and trying to internalise its ideology, towards being marginalised, outcast and alienated from it in every way, until he occupies his 'true' position as its other."[44] Alan Sinfield adds:

> In the last lines of the play when he wants to reassert himself, (Othello) recognises himself for what Venetian society has really believed him to be: an ignorant, barbaric outsider – like he says the base Indian who threw away a pearl. Virtually this is what Althusser means by 'interpellation'; Venice hails Othello as a barbarian and he acknowledges that it is he they mean.[45]

Linking the somewhat abstract concept of ideology to the world of human relationships and emotions calls for a detailed and intimate level of analysis, as it is not just a set of ideas, but is woven into the fabric of 'ordinary' life. Finding ways to link these frameworks to the drama and emotion of everyday living to connect the levels of 'macro' and 'micro' can be an elusive task. Exploring gender patterns, as I discussed in Chapter 1, is a particularly powerful way of making such connections.

Gender and power

Feminist critiques of Shakespeare's tragedies confront many different levels, including rampant misogyny in many of the plays, theatrical practices in which women are played by boy actors, the gender composition of Elizabethan audiences and the sexist biases of critics. Feminist approaches have varied from celebrating heroines who are taken to represent certain feminine virtues[46] to the way that transvestism and disguise, mostly in the comedies, contribute to dissolving rigid categories of gender, sex and sexuality.[47]

Feminist scholars have tackled in a variety of ways the task of interrogating the hegemonic discourses drawn upon in depicting men, women and sexuality and developing alternative understandings. For some scholars, it can involve drawing upon alternative sources for understanding the lives of the women depicted by Shakespeare. Jyotsna Singh, in exploring the representation of prostitutes in Shakespeare's plays, argues for the development of 'anti-histories' or 'histories from below.' Her study of the lives of prostitutes in Shakespeare's time provides a radically different knowledge base that allows for a different and more nuanced understanding of the many depictions of prostitutes in his plays.[48] In this way, by drawing upon other contemporary narratives, a sense of subjectivity or agency can be restored to those Shakespearean heroines who are portrayed in ways that are diminished or stereotyped.

In many of the tragedies, ideologies of manhood and masculinity have been analysed by cultural materialist writers. In *Anthony and Cleopatra* and

Coriolanus, Jonathan Dollimore explores the Roman concept of male *virtus*, describing how this 'quality' is both intensified and undermined at times of political danger or crisis. The sense of *virtus* is that it is "close to valour but with the additional and crucial connotations of self-sufficiency and autonomous power."[49] Dollimore argues that these tropes of manhood, far from being essential qualities of the individual, are dependent on power and position. They rely on the acquiescence of others in constructing the hero as hero. This analysis has strongly influenced my reading of *Coriolanus*. In the case of Mark Antony, his weakening sense of manhood is buttressed by the exercise of sexual passion, although this too is ambiguous: "the heroic virtus which he wants to reaffirm in and through Cleopatra is in fact almost entirely a function of the power structure which he, again ambivalently, is prepared to sacrifice for her."[50] It is important to highlight, as Dollimore does not, that an appreciation of the effects of power is no less central in the construction of Cleopatra, whose support for Antony's heroic *virtus* is a matter of her own survival and that of her dynasty.

Language

Teasing out the workings of ideology in everyday life and dramatic representation involves an exploration of language, signification and discourse. It is through a focus on the specificity of language that our ways of processing our social worlds come to be highlighted. Shakespeare scholars take up language use at a semantic level, i.e. a focus on what words are taken to *mean*, or at a semiotic level, i.e. assuming that words have no intrinsic meaning but are a system of signs and signifiers on which wider social meanings are inscribed.

An exploration of language use at a semantic level is to be found in James Shapiro's book *1606*.[51] He looks at how the changing use of the word 'equivocation' worked its way into Shakespearean drama. In the midst of the anti-Catholic purges that followed the discovery of the 'gunpowder plot,' the meaning of the word 'equivocation' shifted from being synonymous with ambiguity to that of "concealing the truth by saying one thing while deceptively thinking another."[52] In this new definition, 'equivocation' was tantamount to a thought crime, as the mere suspicion of harbouring Catholic sympathies was enough to condemn someone. Shapiro describes how Shakespeare's use of the word in *Hamlet* as meaning to use words imprecisely – "*we must speak by the card, or equivocation will undo us*" – was radically different by the time he wrote *Macbeth*, at the height of the interrogation and persecution of Catholics. When Macbeth says, near the end of the play, "*to doubt the equivocation of the fiend/That lies like truth,*" he reflects this new usage. Its more sinister meaning had already emerged from the lips of the porter in Macbeth's castle, who could have been describing Macbeth himself: "*here's an equivocator that could swear in both the scales against either scale, who committed treason enough for God's sake yet could not equivocate to heaven.*" The climate of the times in which 'equivocating' over secret Catholic sympathies was punishable by death thus found its way into drama, creating another level of meaning for processes otherwise commonplace in theatre, such as subterfuge, concealing intentions, or saying one thing and meaning another. It infuses the dialogues between Macbeth and Banquo in Act 2, scene 1, and Malcolm and Macduff in Act 4, scene 3, adding an additional layer of fearfulness and suspicion to these relationships.

Post-structuralist Shakespearean criticism involves the deconstruction of language itself and is based on the idea that the linguistic sign has no inherent meaning but is unstable and context dependent. These theories have had a major impact on Shakespearean scholars, as they have on all literary criticism. Jonathan Goldberg advanced the idea – unsurprisingly about *King Lear* – of the text as a void in which "the very language which would seem (to us) solidly to locate the world slides into an abyss, an uncreating, annihilative nothing-ness."[53] As I discuss in Chapter 4, the unreliability of language – detaching the signifier from what is being signified – underscores the emotional experience of the unreliability of relationships.

This gap between symbol and symbolised was explored by Slavoj Zizek, using the example of *Richard II*. Richard questions how he, as king, can give up the crown when in the very act of giving it up, he is nothing – he is 'not-king.' The crown is at that moment an empty signifier. Richard's questioning of where his own 'kingness' could be said to reside at that moment leads to his response to Bolingbroke's demand that he resign the crown: "*Ay, no; no, ay: for I must nothing be.*"[54] Language, as we see in *King Lear*, breaks down at moments of transition, when 'reliable' symbols no longer confer identity.

The earlier work of Mikhail Bakhtin, discussed in Chapter 1, was less concerned with language as an abstract theory of signs and more with the concrete utterances of individuals in particular social contexts. Although Bakhtin's most famous work was on novels rather than plays, his exploration of dialogue is highly relevant to drama. The 'linguistic community,' Bakhtin contended, was "a heterogeneous society composed of many conflicting interests . . . language, in short was a field of ideological contention."[55] It is especially relevant to a systemic approach because of Shakespeare's own capacity to call up multiple voices, in the way that he used so many different speech genres, cutting across divisions of class and gender and assimilating a diversity of theatrical voices, thus expressing the "restless dynamic of dramatic polyphony whose aim is to situate and qualify everything it touches."[56]

Frank Kermode argued that, in the focus on ideology, an appreciation of the aesthetics of the verse that is at the heart of the plays can be lost.[57] It is a timely reminder that excessive theorising can drain the life out of the subject and that imposing frameworks of thought might have the effect of rendering the plays themselves dramatically inert. One can disagree fundamentally with Kermode's lofty dismissal of Marxist, feminist or other political approaches to Shakespeare and yet see his point.

This strengthens the argument for a creative interplay between close textual readings and wider socio-historical perspectives. There are many examples of this in the literature even though the analytic approaches can seem to be fundamentally different. One example comes from two works that look at the character of Iago from different theoretical perspectives. Laurie Maguire's work on language in *Othello* involves close textual reading to analyse the many dimensions of language use.[58] One section illuminates the linguistic means whereby Iago both exerts influence over the other dramatis personae and shapes audience responses. Exploring the use of aphorisms and proverbs in the play, Maguire comments on the fact that, although other characters use these as a rhetorical device, they "can usually be found in one of the great collections of proverbs." For Iago, on the other hand "his language is only made to sound proverbial. He invents proverbs, giving his language the status of truth, preventing questioning."[59] This illustrates the craft with which Shakespeare constructed a Iago capable of seducing the other characters and semi-persuading the audience into believing that his ideas, outlandish as they are, were commonplace or, in his words, "*probal to thinking*."

This level of fine textual detail fits beautifully with a work of new historicism. In *Renaissance Self Fashioning,* Stephen Greenblatt explores the structuring of selfhood and identity in sixteenth-century life. Exploring the reciprocal effects of ideas of selfhood and their representation in drama, he argues that in this period, there was "an increased self-consciousness about the fashioning of human identity as a manipulable, artful process."[60] Improvisation Greenblatt argues, is "the ability to capitalize on the unforeseen and to transform given materials into one's own scenario. The spur-of-the-moment quality of improvisation is not as important here as the opportunistic grasp of what seems fixed and established."[61] He describes Iago as a 'Renaissance skeptic,' inserting himself into the "symbolic structure of the centuries-old Christian doctrine of sexuality, policed socially and psychically, as we have already seen by confession . . . the orthodox doctrine that governs Othello's sexual attitudes – his simultaneous idealisation and mistrust of women – seems to Iago sufficiently close to be recognisable, sufficiently distant to be malleable."[62] To this somewhat abstract view, Laurie Maguire's fine textual analysis brings us to the specificity of *how* these processes might unfold within the interactions we witness on stage.

In *Hamlet in Purgatory,* Stephen Greenblatt situates the play and its hero within the religious doctrines and conflicts of the time, taking the ambiguous nature of the ghost as a sign of wider religious unease.[63] This framework becomes another prism though which the profound ambiguities in the play can be highlighted as Hamlet struggles with questions of life and death, corporeality, bodily excess and decay. Pinpointing opposing positions that "challenge each other, clashing and sending shock waves through the play"[64] opens up a space for these positions to be explored in relationships and through dialogue. Placing the pragmatic Wittenberg student Horatio, who *"will not let belief take hold of him,"* alongside Hamlet opens up a potential relational space in which these conflictual questions can be struggled with.

The impossibility of resolution, such a compelling leitmotif of *Hamlet,* is, as Kieran Ryan argues, a core feature of all the tragedies. Effects of wider oppressive ideologies are offset against the progressive and liberating potential within the texts themselves. Their value to the present stems from

> their refusal to resolve the intolerable contradiction between justified human desires and their unjustifiable suppression: the heart-breaking contradiction between what men and women want to be and what the particular social scenarios into which they have been scripted by history cruelly condemns them to be.[65]

Asserting that an alternative potentiality is always present leads to reading the plays both *within* and *against* ideologies. This accords well with a systemic approach, which, as well as holding alternative perspectives in tension, focusses on the detail of *how* these alternative positions come to be worked out within relationships.

So far, I have focussed on Shakespearean scholars who mainly address the links between cultural and political contexts and the shaping of the individual subject. One of the few writers who approaches Shakespeare's plays from a relational perspective is René Girard. In his book *A Theatre of Envy,* he employs the concept of 'mimesis,' by which he means a fundamental orientation towards others and what they possess. Thus, he argues that desire is always experienced in relation to another person, to their attributes or possessions.[66] Mimetic desire is, Girard claims, to be found in all Shakespeare's plays, as Shakespeare had understood both the competitive emotions it unleashes and the inevitable violence that ensues from such a competitive dynamic. Girard's approach seems tailor-made for a play such as *Troilus and Cressida,* in which the relationship between Greeks and Trojans involves much uneasy gazing on each other's attributes and possessions. His analysis of *Hamlet* is iconoclastic, castigating those critics who take for granted that the problem for Hamlet is his failure to act, 'problematising' his so-called indecision rather than challenging the ethics of revenge.

Girard challenges these kinds of a-contextual approaches and his method of analysis involves ascribing agency to the different protagonists, eschewing a top-down approach in which people are seen as victims of ideological pressures and bringing a dynamic interactional understanding to the plays. However, although Girard has an immense intellectual range, and his interpretations of the plays are invariably engaging and creative, the concept of mimetic desire itself is a limited framework for the exploration of relationships in all their diversity and complexity. I have therefore found it a more useful framework in some plays than others. It illustrates the risk of trying to fit all of Shakespeare's tragedies into a single explanatory framework and of imposing theories too enthusiastically onto the multi-layered worlds they encompass.

This selection of Shakespeare scholarship is inevitably impressionistic; its aim has been to locate my own approach broadly within the existing canon. What follows is a textual analysis of eight different plays, taking the relationships depicted in them as the key framework. Those authors who have enriched my understanding of wider social and political contexts and their manifestation through language and dialogue form a crucial background to the analysis. Through their authorial traces, the contexts of politics, power and ideology are visible in the interplay between individuals, their intimate relationships and their struggles within their familial and social worlds. It is in the detail of relationships – in language, dialogue and gender patterning – that the fractures and fissures generated by ideological and political tensions and undercurrents can be most starkly discerned. But, above all, in none of the eight plays do these weightier concerns settle too narrowly on any one protagonist or relationship. Instead, family dramas are enacted in all their particularity and diversity – with passion, humour, playfulness, cruelty and duplicity and, above all, ambiguity.

Notes

1 Margot Heinemann, 'How Brecht Read Shakespeare', in Jonathan Dollimore and Alan Sinfield, eds., *Political Shakespeare* (Manchester: Manchester University Press, 1994), 229.
2 Frank Kermode, *Shakespeare's Language* (London: Penguin, 2000).
3 Caroline Spurgeon, *Shakespeare's Imagery, and What It Tells Us* (New York: Palgrave Macmillan, 1935).
4 Stanley Wells, *Shakespeare, Love and Sex* (Oxford: Oxford University Press, 2010).
5 Alessandro Serpieri, 'The Breakdown of Medieval Hierarchy in *King Lear*', in John Drakakis, ed., *Shakespearean Tragedy* (London: Longman, 1992).
6 Jonathan Goldberg, 'Perspectives: Dover Cliff and the Conditions of Representation', in Kieran Ryan, ed., *King Lear* (Basingstoke: Palgrave Macmillan, 1993).
7 Harold Bloom, *The Best of the Best American Poetry, 1988–1997* (New York: Simon and Shuster, 1998).
8 Margaret Rustin and Michael Rustin, *Mirror to Nature* (London: Karnac, 2002), 3.
9 Ibid., 3.
10 Sigmund Freud, *The Interpretation of Dreams* (Harmondsworth: Penguin, 1899).
11 Sigmund Freud, *Autobiographical Study* (New York: W.W. Norton, 1927), 130.
12 Margaret Rustin and Michael Rustin, *Mirror to Nature* (London: Karnac, 2002), 14.
13 Ibid., 2.
14 Sigmund Freud, *The Interpretation of Dreams* (Harmondsworth: Penguin, 1899), 367.
15 Sigmund Freud, *Theme of the Three Caskets,* Collected Works, vol. XII (London: Hogarth, 1913).
16 Sigmund Freud, *Some Character Types Met with in Psychoanalytic Work,* Collected Works, vol. XIV (London: Hogarth, 1916).
17 Michael Jacobs, *Shakespeare on the Couch* (London: Karnac, 2008), 7.
18 Martin Wangh, 'Iago: The Tragedy of Othello', *Psychoanalytic Quarterly,* 19:2 (1950): 208.

19 Peter Hildebrand, 'The Caledonian Tragedy', in Inge Wise and Maggie Mills, eds., *Psychoanalytic Ideas and Shakespeare* (London: Karnac, 2006).
20 Michael Jacobs, *Shakespeare on the Couch* (London: Karnac, 2008), 5.
21 Janet Adelman, *Suffocating Mothers: Fantasies of Maternal Origin in Shakespeare's Plays, 'Hamlet' to 'The Tempest'* (New York: Routledge, 1992).
22 Ibid.
23 Jacqueline Rose, 'Sexuality in the Reading of Shakespeare: *Hamlet* and *Measure for Measure*', in John Drakakis, ed., *Alternative Shakespeares* (London: Routledge, 1996).
24 Ibid., 118.
25 Dymphna Callaghan, 'The Ideology of Romantic Love', in Dymphna Callaghan, Lorraine Helms and Jyotsna Singh, eds., *The Weyward Sisters* (Oxford: Wiley-Blackwell, 1994), 64.
26 Stephen Greenblatt, *Learning to Curse* (New York: Routledge, 1990), 183.
27 Robert Wilkins, 'The King and His Fool,' *Journal of Family Therapy*, 11:2 (May 1989), 181–195.
28 Mara Selvini Palazzoli, *Family Games* (London: Karnac, 1989).
29 John V. Knapp, 'Family Games and Imbroglio in *Hamlet*', in John V. Knapp and Kenneth Womack, eds., *Reading the Family Dance* (Newark: University of Delaware Press, 2003).
30 Paul Watzlawick, Janet Beavin and Don Jackson, *Pragmatics of Human Communication* (New York: W.W. Norton, 1967).
31 A. C. Bradley, *Shakespearean Tragedy* (Basingstoke: Palgrave Macmillan, 1904), 15.
32 Stephen Greenblatt, *Shakespearean Negotiations* (New York: Oxford University Press, 1988).
33 Lisa Jardine, *Reading Shakespeare Historically* (London: Routledge, 1998), 1.
34 Ibid., 14.
35 William Shakespeare, *Henry V*, Act 1, scene 2.
36 Jonathan Dollimore, *Radical Tragedy* (Basingstoke: Palgrave Macmillan, Third Edition, 2004), 191.
37 Ibid., 17.
38 Stephen Greenblatt and Peter G. Platt, eds., *Shakespeare's Montaigne* (New York: New York Review Books Classics, 2014), 98.
39 Jonathan Dollimore, *Radical Tragedy* (Basingstoke: Palgrave Macmillan, Third Edition, 2004), lvii.
40 Ibid., 47.
41 Stephen Greenblatt, *Renaissance Self – Fashioning* (Chicago: University of Chicago Press, 1980), 1.
42 James Kavanagh, 'Shakespeare in Ideology', in John Drakakis, ed., *Alternative Shakespeares* (London: Routledge, 1996), 145.

43 Ibid.,145.
44 Ania Loomba, *Gender, Race, Renaissance Drama* (Manchester: Manchester University Press, 1989), 48.
45 Alan Sinfield, 'Cultural Materialism, Othello and the Politics of Plausibility', in Lena Cowen Orlin, ed., *Othello* (Basingstoke: Palgrave Macmillan, 2004), 51.
46 Marilyn French, 'The Late Tragedies', in John Drakakis, ed., *Shakespearean Tragedy* (London: Longman, 1992).
47 Catherine Belsey, 'Disrupting Sexual Difference: Meaning and Gender in the Comedies', in John Drakakis, ed., *Alternative Shakespeares* (London: Routledge, 1996).
48 Jyotsna Singh, 'The Interventions of History', in Dymphna Callaghan, Lorraine Helms and Jyotsna Singh, eds., *The Weyward Sisters* (Oxford: Wiley-Blackwell, 1994).
49 Jonathan Dollimore, *Radical Tragedy* (Basingstoke: Palgrave Macmillan, Third Edition, 2004), 208–209.
50 Ibid., 217.
51 James Shapiro, *1606: William Shakespeare and the Year of Lear* (London: Faber and Faber, 2015).
52 Ibid., 179.
53 Jonathan Goldberg, 'Perspectives: Dover Cliff and the Conditions of Representation', in Kieran Ryan, ed., *King Lear* (Basingstoke: Palgrave Macmillan, 1993), 153.
54 Slavoj Zizek, 'Troubles with the Real', *Lacan.com*, 6 April 2009.
55 Terry Eagleton, *Literary Theory* (Oxford: Wiley-Blackwell, Second Edition, 1996), 101–102.
56 Kiernan Ryan, *Shakespeare* (Basingstoke: Palgrave Macmillan, Third Edition, 2002), 113.
57 Frank Kermode, *Shakespeare's Language* (London: Penguin, 2000).
58 Laurie Maguire, *Othello: Language and Writing* (London: Bloomsbury, 2014).
59 Ibid., 43–44.
60 Stephen Greenblatt, *Renaissance Self-Fashioning* (Chicago: University of Chicago Press, 1980), 2.
61 Ibid., 227.
62 Ibid., 246.
63 Stephen Greenblatt, *Hamlet in Purgatory* (Princeton: Princeton University Press, 2001).
64 Ibid., 240.
65 Kiernan Ryan, *Shakespeare* (Basingstoke: Palgrave Macmillan, Third Edition, 2002), 75.
66 René Girard, *A Theatre of Envy* (New York: Oxford University Press, 1991).

CHAPTER 3

"O cursèd spite, that ever I was born to set it right!"

Legacies and alternative identities in *Hamlet*

Hamlet is generally seen as being all about Hamlet. Productions are judged by his performance, he is barely off stage, has many more lines than the other characters and a feast of soliloquies that invite the audience into his interior space. In reading the contexts that frame Hamlet's moral, relational and emotional dilemmas, we have few examples of interactions that really bring these to life. None of the other characters, especially the women, are set up to be remotely Hamlet's equal as a protagonist. These are mostly 'thin' depictions, revealing little of their inner worlds. Reclaiming Gertrude and Ophelia as active subjects in the drama is hard work even for determined feminist critics.[1]

Interactions are one-sided in other respects. The word games, jokes, puns and verbal acrobatics that Hamlet performs to communicate his 'antic disposition' are responded to by a series of humourless 'straight men,' including Claudius, Polonius, Rosencrantz and Guildenstern and Osric, offering little of dialogic interest. Even in the significant dialogues that do take place, the temptation can be to underplay them. A review of Benedict Cumberbatch's performance in Lyndsey Turner's 2015 production sums up this tendency: "In the big dialogue scenes, you're conscious of Mr Cumberbatch riding Shakespeare's rushing words like a surfboard, as if saving his interior energy for the monologues."[2]

Hamlet's centrality and the intense focus on his inner world could thus pose a challenge to a systemic approach. However, it also provides an opportunity to focus on the place of dialogue itself. In this chapter, I explore the relationship between inner talk and outer talk – between monologue and dialogue. I focus on the ways that moral and political imperatives reach into monologue and how dialogues can be restricted and compromised by the machinations of power. Those portrayals of Hamlet as driven to extremis by his crazy family[3] or by the sick and paranoid politics of the Danish court have an obvious relevance to a systemic approach. However, taking up a 'linear' narrative of cause and effect runs the risk of collapsing the struggles, complexities, paradoxes and subterfuges of the play into a single explanatory framework that does not do justice to its multiple levels and linguistic ambiguities.

The first clown digs into these ambiguities beautifully when he says: "*An act hath three branches – it is to act, to do and to perform.*" And *Hamlet* certainly deals with 'acting' and 'doing' as well as with 'not acting' and 'not doing.' However, it is above all concerned with performances, quite literally at times, of different positions and different identities. Hamlet's apparent search for authenticity, his concern with the gulf between '*seems*' and '*is*,' between "*actions that a man might play*" and "*that within that passeth show*," is enacted, paradoxically, by means of subterfuge, and through performing contradictory aspects of self. Rory Kinnear said of his Hamlet, "He's a different person every time he comes on, and that's brilliant!"[4] He might also have added that it depends on whom he comes on with.

The idea of authenticity is a chimaera that Shakespeare himself treats with irony. "*This above all – to thine own self be true*" is a line given, of all people, to Polonius. The play is, instead, full of questions, signalled by the very first line: "*Who's there?*" It "reverberates with questions, anguished, meditative, alarmed,"[5] most of which are uttered by Hamlet. This constant questioning underscores the play's resistance to closure through any fixed interpretation and reinforces the importance of moving beyond dualities. This is a key principle for systemic therapists and so, if I dare to rephrase Hamlet's most famous question, we might read the play as being concerned with 'how to be' as much as the binary oppositions implied in "*To be, or not to be.*"

Kiernan Ryan alerts us to the future orientation of *Hamlet*, emphasising its "untimeliness, its obstinate refusal to be fully intelligible in terms of its age because the unvoiced assumptions that govern it are indeed far ahead of its time."[6] This sense of the elusiveness of time – "*the time is out of joint*" – creates a powerful experience for the audience of being poised on the edge of something that is always just beyond our reach.

Alongside the dynamics of family and court are questions, again heralded at the very beginning of the play, about the place of rational knowledge in a context of dark subliminal forces and the supernatural, pointing to the 'not-yet-known' – in short, to all those things in heaven and earth that are not *"dreamt of in our philosophy."* This disjuncture of worlds reverberates throughout the play and is reinforced by linguistic devices through which contrasting modes of expression texture the dialogues, from the elusiveness, imaginative leaps and ambiguity of Hamlet's speech to the concreteness and superficial rationality of Gertrude, Claudius, Polonius and Rosencrantz and Guildenstern.

Hamlet's struggle with the question of 'how to be' in this uncertain world can be explored in many different contexts and through different relationships, including ways of 'doing family' and of enacting parent/child and especially father/son relationships. These relationships are in turn embedded in the various meanings attached to revenge, reason, death and the afterlife and they are enacted by individuals who, in responding to conflicting and contradictory imperatives about how to live one's life, find themselves, as a result, in various states of confusion, terror or craziness.

Family relationships

As well as Hamlet, his mother, dead father and uncle/stepfather, two other families feature in the play and provide alternative templates for relationships: Polonius, his son and daughter and, to a lesser extent, young Fortinbras, his dead father and uncle. Another son is referred to in the play-within-a-play: Pyrrhus, son of Achilles, avenges his father by slaying Priam in front of Hecuba, his wife. These three sons stand, in their different ways, as exemplars, intruding into Hamlet's reflections and forming a backdrop to his existential and strategic dilemmas. Additionally, they deepen and expand our understanding of these dilemmas by creating observer positions on the prince and his own family. Before Hamlet has uttered a word on stage, we encounter Laertes and Polonius. Fortinbras is introduced even earlier as the avenger of his dead father, killed by old Hamlet on the birthday of his own son. Horatio, assuming that old Hamlet's ghost is warning of military peril to Denmark, explains:

"our valiant Hamlet –

For so this side of our known world esteemed him –

Did slay this Fortinbras, who by a sealed compact,

Well ratified by law and heraldry,

Did forfeit, with his life, all those his lands

Which he stood seized on to the conquerer; ...

Now young Fortinbras

Of unimprovèd mettle, hot and full ...

But to recover of us by strong hand

And terms compulsative those forsaid lands

So by his father lost." (I.i.95–104)

This narrative is one of settling disputes through fighting, of old Hamlet's valour and of sons assuming a military identity to right the wrongs done to their fathers. The play thus opens with the 'simple' story of an external threat – a threat that only materialises at the very end, creating the first of many potential but rarely completed actions.

Our first introduction to Claudius is as an already-established king responding to the threat posed by young Fortinbras, while the 'internal threat' in the form of Hamlet remains a silent presence. Having sent ambassadors to Fortinbras' uncle in the expectation that he will exert authority over his hot-blooded nephew, Claudius' next act is to grant Laertes' request for permission to return to France. This again reinforces his authority as well as intensifies our sense of the anomaly of Hamlet's own position. The exchange sets Laertes up as an independent young man "*whose thoughts and wishes bend again towards France*" and who is confident of extracting his father's grudging consent, "*my slow leave.*" Hamlet, by contrast, having similarly returned to Denmark from abroad and equally keen to return to Wittenberg, faces a very different injunction:

"*It is most retrograde to our desire*

And we beseech you bend you to remain

Here in the cheer and comfort of our eye." (I.ii.114–116)

The two young men, Laertes and Fortinbras, who provide such a contrast to Hamlet, enact conventional forms of masculinity. Action is privileged over thought as they take up the stances of military adventurer or violent avenger. "Hamlet," argues Catherine Belsey, "is surrounded both textually and dramatically, by figures who behave like the heroes of tradition."[7] These make their way, elliptically, into Hamlet's soliloquies:

"*no more like my father/Than I to Hercules.*" (1.ii.152–153)

"*What's Hecuba to him or he to Hecuba*

That he should weep for her? What would he do

Had he the motive and the cue for passion

That I have?" (2.ii.145–146)

"*Witness this army, of such mass and charge,*

Led by a delicate and tender prince ...

Rightly to be great

Is not to stir without great argument,

But greatly to find quarrel in a straw

When honour's at the stake. How stand I, then?

That have a father killed, a mother stained." (4.iv.39–49, Q2)

As well as setting up alternative models for male behaviour, the two main families demonstrate parallel modes of enacting constraint, secrecy and evasion. In the family of Polonius, Laertes and Ophelia, overt mistrust and manipulation are the norm. The message is one of social conformity, the need to observe social rank and of profound fears of transgression. As Laertes conveys these precepts to his sister, he also highlights the constrained life that Hamlet leads:

"*Perhaps he loves you now,*

And now no soil nor cautel doth besmirch

The virtue of his will; but you must fear,

His greatness weighed, his will is not his own,

For he himself is subject to his birth.

He may not, as unvalued persons do,

Carve for himself, for on his choice depends
The sanity and health of the whole state;
And therefore must his choice be circumscribed
Unto the voice and yielding of that body
Whereof he is the head." (1.iii.14–24)

Laertes' speech highlights two ironies. First, the special power ascribed to Hamlet was in fact drastically reduced when Claudius usurped the crown. Other than a couple of offhand remarks, Hamlet himself does not cite deprivation of the succession as a major cause of resentment. However, the experience of being simultaneously deprived of his birthright and still circumscribed in his relational possibilities continues to echo elliptically throughout Hamlet's narrative: "*I could be bounded in a nutshell and count myself a king of infinite space.*"

Second, in a play that modern audiences are most likely to view in terms of individual psychology, that very discourse of autonomy and choice – *carve for himself* – has to be set within a context of constraint, of the responsibilities to state and society surrounding a Renaissance prince: "*therefore must his choice be circumscribed.*"

Constraints are enacted differently in the two families. Although trying in every way to circumscribe and control him, Hamlet's mother and stepfather are too fearful of him to do so directly. In Polonius' family, by contrast, the tight hand of parental control is everywhere visible. He showers the departing Laertes with advice, sends spies to check on him and micro-manages Ophelia's relationship with Hamlet.

Polonius' obsessive control over his children can be understood as his need to straddle the domain of intimate familial bonds and the harsh realities of power politics in which he has needed to transfer his allegiance from one king to another. Despite all the manipulations, the rules in the family of Polonius, Laertes and Ophelia could at least be said to be clear: parental authority rules and everything is subsumed to the need to maintain their position in court. This contrasts with the more confusing, generalised and dishonest injunctions enjoined upon Hamlet. He sums up the complexity of family relationships: "*You are the Queen, your husband's brother's wife, But – would you were not so – you are my mother.*"

As well as references to incest and adultery, these descriptions of family relationships contain embedded and contradictory codes about how to enact such relationships. Claudius' preference is for Hamlet to display *"gentle and unforced accord,"* a perfect paradox in the light of the firm injunction placed on him not to leave the court. Inevitably, power reconfigures the person of Claudius: *"For my uncle is King of Denmark. And those that would make mows at him while my father lived give twenty, forty, fifty, a hundred ducats apiece for his picture in little"* (2.ii.259–362).

Claudius' arrogation of the crown and marriage to Gertrude means that, however much he obsesses about revenge, Hamlet still has to find a mode of relating to Claudius inside this new and unwelcome family. One method he employs to avoid outright defiance of the king is to obey him obliquely through his mother, thus following protocol and showing contempt simultaneously: *"I shall in all my best obey you madam."* As he departs for England, Hamlet says farewell to Gertrude. Claudius rebukes him: *"Thy loving father, Hamlet."* Hamlet replies, *"My mother. Father and mother is man and wife; man and wife is one flesh; and so my mother."* The relationship between Hamlet and Claudius is often depicted as a battle of wills in which each alternately gains the upper hand. This 'battle,' however, is never played directly but at one remove. Claudius can never be quite sure of what Hamlet knows but his fear of him and of being overthrown increases as the play progresses.

Claudius makes it clear that this fear is not just based on Hamlet's rage, 'madness' and volatility, but from the political threat the young prince poses: *"He's loved of the distracted multitude."* However, although Claudius alludes to this wider public context, Hamlet's attention remains entirely fixated on the private context of family relationships, less appalled apparently by Claudius' usurpation of the throne than by his marriage to Gertrude.

The self that Hamlet performs in this new family configuration, an 'antic disposition,' is at one level a strategy – *"I am but mad north-north west; when the wind is southerly, I know a hawk from a handsaw"* – but it can also reflect melancholy, confusion, doubt and self-loathing. For many young people confronted with an intolerable family or social situation, this inner turmoil and outer performance co-exist as well as sit in tension with each other, although actors playing Hamlet sometimes seem to feel they have to choose one or the other.

The verbal tricks Hamlet engages in not only serve the function of concealing whatever his 'real' thoughts and feelings might be but also create a context from which he can observe and assess others. Additionally, they function to confuse the onlooker. Hamlet's 'crazy talk' increases with the amount of surveillance he is under. In the first two acts, there is a stark contrast between his erratic behaviour and the performance by Claudius and Gertrude of concerned parents 'reasonably' attempting to understand their ailing and unhappy son:

Claudius "*He (Polonius) tells me, sweet Queen, that he hath found*

The head and source of all your son's distemper."

Gertrude "*I doubt it is no other but the main*

– His father's death and our o'erhasty marriage." (2.ii.55–57)

When Rosencrantz and Guildenstern enter the play, they act as another pair of seemingly concerned and disingenuous onlookers.

Male friendships

Shakespeare frequently shows male friendships as providing opportunities for sharing unhappiness, love secrets or for creative problem solving. Because virtually all of Hamlet's relationships are circumscribed by power and hierarchy, suspicion and betrayal, the introduction of his old friends Rosencrantz and Guildenstern intensifies a sense that all relationships are corrupted. Although Hamlet initially engages in the intimate banter common to Shakespeare's young men, he is well aware that these former friends can no longer be trusted because they now serve Claudius: "*Were you not sent for? . . . You were sent for.*" The dialogue thus moves in and out of apparent confidences – "*I have of late – but wherefore I know not – lost all my mirth . . . man delights not me*" – and evasive game playing, especially in the later scenes:

Rosencrantz "*I understand you not, my lord.*"

Hamlet "*I am glad of it. A knavish speech sleeps in a foolish ear.*"

Power and status continue to suffuse the relationship, creating contradictions as when Hamlet curtly dismisses the pair – "*Have you any further trade with us?*" – only to receive the hurt response from Rosencrantz: "*My lord you once did love me.*" Although Rosencrantz and Guildenstern were apparently ignorant of the contents of Claudius' letter condemning Hamlet to death, he has no compunction about having sent them to their own deaths – "*They are not near my conscience*" – because, having "*made love to this employment,*" they deserved their fate. A modern audience hearing Rosencrantz's encomium to Claudius in Act 3, scene 3, on the subject of regal absolutism might well share this view.

Although these particular male friendships are contaminated by the manipulations of Claudius, Rosencrantz and Guildenstern are bound to

disown the fact and maintain a level of 'reasonable discourse' by acting as if they have Hamlet's rather than Claudius' interests at heart. By trying to control Hamlet, they both invite his 'crazy talk' and censure him for it: *"Good my lord, put your discourse into some frame, and start not so wildly from my affair . . . If it shall please you to make me a wholesome answer, I will do your mother's commandment."*
After denouncing their manipulation and pretence at friendship, Hamlet makes Rosencrantz and Guildenstern's status as lackeys of Claudius explicit:

> Rosencrantz "*Take you me for a sponge, my lord*"
>
> Hamlet "*Ay, sir, that soaks up the King's countenance, his rewards, his authorities.*"

Their presence in the play highlights not only Claudius' avoidance of confronting Hamlet directly, but also the way that these peer relationships recreate the same pattern of dialogue as with the older generation – phoney expressions of concern are countered by mystifying and elusive banter.

In the relationship with Horatio, by contrast, although Hamlet refers to his 'antic disposition,' he never actually performs it. The bond appears to be one of trust and affection – *"Horatio, thou art e'en as just a man/ As e'er my conversation coped withal"* – and one in which dialogue might be possible. With Horatio, Hamlet can reflect on the enormity of the ghost's revelations and his possible responses. The dialogues with Horatio (one-sided as most of them are) present a different range of discursive practices, privileging honesty, logic and rationality. This is presumably the result of a friendship developed in an intellectual milieu that encouraged critical thought. From the perspective of this 'Wittenberg identity,' Hamlet can show his contempt for the dishonesty, circumlocutory speech, surveillance and plotting of the Danish court.

Horatio's status at the court is never quite clarified; a student friend from Wittenberg, his visit to the court to attend old Hamlet's funeral seems to be a surprise to his friend – *"what in faith make you from Wittenberg?"* – yet he is well-known to the soldiers on the watch and well versed in the history of old Hamlet's battles. He remains central to the court after Hamlet has departed for England and seems to be trusted by Gertrude and Claudius. His insider/outsider status means he is less prone to indulge in the intrigue and sycophancy of courtiers. Indeed, Hamlet sets him up as something of a stoic ideal – *"not passion's slave"* – as well as someone whom Hamlet, a courtier himself, has no need to flatter: *"why should the poor be flattered?"*

More importantly, as much of the play is concerned with what credence to give to the supernatural, Horatio is already referred to by the other members of the watch as a sceptic: "*Horatio says 'tis but our fantasy/ And will not let belief take hold of him.*" The relationship therefore provides Hamlet with an opportunity to perform a different aspect of his identity – to be reflective and reasonable; most significantly, it is where he can meta-communicate by signalling a shift of contexts: "*They are coming to the play. I must be idle.*"

Much of Horatio's speech is terse and telescopic. His longer speeches are mostly descriptive rather than stating his own point of view, creating uncertainty as to how free he is to express his thoughts or whether he actually believes Hamlet. He rarely contradicts the prince unless to protect or restrain him. He conveys fear about Hamlet's vulnerability as he warns that the ghost might "*deprive your sovereignty of reason/ And draw you into madness.*"

Horatio's role in the relationship seems to be to hold onto rationality, to calm his friend down and block imaginative excess: "*These are but wild and whirling words, my Lord.*" But the relationship is also constrained by hierarchy, meaning that Horatio's participation is mostly confined to witnessing and affirming Hamlet's monologues.

One example of Horatio performing this role is in Act 5, scene 1, when he and Hamlet arrive at the grave being dug for Ophelia. There is a sequence of banter with the gravedigger/clown, culminating in the famous interchange with Yorick's skull. Here, a complex polyphonic sequence ensues in which monologue (addressed to Horatio) merges with dialogue with the skull, intensified by Hamlet taking on Yorick's own voice. This exchange is in many ways the antithesis of that with the father's ghost, with its harsh rage and calls for revenge, and it evokes a more loving and playful relationship with another male figure. It also evokes reflection on the inevitability of death – "*to this favour she must come*" – an inversion of the insistent calls for violent action. The recreation of a treasured childhood relationship and its corporeal remnant in the form of the skull provokes reflections on the nature of decomposition and transformation. Horatio acts both as a containing and supportive witness to Hamlet's troubled musings and as a pragmatic 'other' voice, attempting to confine his imagination: '*Twere to consider too curiously to consider so.*'

In Act 5, scene 1, following shared banter at the expense of Osric, who has delivered Laertes' challenge, Horatio ventures a more direct opinion: "*You will lose this wager my lord.*" The dialogue that follows hovers around a moment of intimacy when Horatio senses Hamlet's vulnerability only to have talk closed down:

Hamlet "*I shall win at the odds. But thou wouldst not think how ill all's here about my heart/ But it is no matter.*"

Horatio "*Nay, good my lord –* "

Hamlet "*It is but foolery. But it is such a kind of gain-giving as would perhaps trouble a woman.*"

Horatio "*If your mind dislike anything, obey it. I will forestall their repair hither, and say you are not fit.*"

Hamlet: "*Not a whit. We defy augury. There's a special providence in the fall of a sparrow.*" (5.ii.156)

A focus on Hamlet's inner world might lead this speech to be understood solely in terms of his final 'acceptance' of fate and death. A dialogic reading, however, highlights the interplay between a too-eager naming by Horatio of his friend's vulnerability and Hamlet's need to recoil from this, positioning himself within a stoical and fatalistic discourse.

Although Hamlet avoids too much intimate confidence, the trust he shows in Horatio allows his friend to provide a safe context for strange or painful narratives to be related. Hamlet first alludes in Act 2 to "*the circumstance/ Which I have told thee of my father's death,*" an account the audience has not been privy to. In Act 5, by contrast, the story of how Hamlet thwarted Claudius' scheme to put him to death is narrated to Horatio in front of the audience. The story of the events on the boat to England is told calmly and factually, with a certain amount of pride, but still ends with questions:

" *– is't not perfect conscience*

To quit him with this arm? And is't not to be damned

To let this canker of our nature come

In further evil?" (5.ii.68–70)

These questions may be rhetorical, but in the context of the relationship with Horatio, they still reflect a pattern of testing evidence before reaching conclusions or committing to action. Horatio's reply is indirect, pragmatic and cautious. Revenge narratives by contrast are designed to justify actions that are already decided upon. They tend to be one-dimensional, certain, self-exonerating and blaming of others.

Revenge narratives

Hamlet's speeches demonstrate the compelling cultural and social influence of revenge. If we think of revenge as an ideology, then this is an excellent example of how ideology becomes woven into the fabric of everyday life and speech, even when it is simultaneously resisted. Revenge narratives infiltrate most of Hamlet's soliloquies but Shakespeare has his hero rebound from them into other discursive positions, creating polyphonic speech in which every utterance is qualified almost as soon as it is voiced. Initially, however, before he even knows the identity of the killer, Hamlet has unhesitatingly acquiesced in his ghostly father's demand that he avenge his murder:

> Ghost "*Murder most foul, as in the best it is,*
>
> *But this most foul, strange and unnatural.*"
>
> Hamlet "*Haste, haste me to know it, that I with wings as swift*
>
> *As meditation or the thoughts of love May sweep to my revenge.*" (I.iv.27–31)

The self-injunction that actions must override reflection becomes a critical prism through which Hamlet judges himself as he becomes stranded in a revenge plot for which he has no real appetite. Caught up in this discursive frame, Hamlet castigates himself for inaction and cowardice – "*For it cannot be/ But I am pigeon livered and lack gall,*" goads himself towards action by evoking gory images – "*I should have fatted all the region kites/ With this slave's offal,*" and then recoils from this invective into a rational mindset that requires evidence – "*I'll have grounds/ More relative than this. The play's the thing/ Wherein I'll catch the conscience of the King.*"

Hamlet's dilemma is that the only way to live within his social milieu is to obey its rules, including, we assume, that of revenge. This means living a truncated, one-dimensional, impoverished existence, emotionally, intellectually and spiritually. René Girard calls this the "tedium of revenge."[8] Hamlet is also "caught between two worlds; unhappy with the dark revenge duty and yet unable to find another way to act. The Protestant university of Wittenberg has taught him to rely on reason and conscience – in the bloody business of feudal revenge, reason merely impedes him."[9]

Although the play, as we have seen, contains other avengers who take a more action-oriented approach, none do so without some ambiguity. Fortinbras allows himself to be deflected from the revenge he planned to carry out on the state of Denmark and Laertes expresses momentary qualms before he goes on to inflict Hamlet's death wound: "*and yet 'tis almost 'gainst my conscience."* As Catherine Belsey reflects, "When all these conventional revengers hang back, if only for a time, would we have more sympathy with a Hamlet who did not?"[10] Even Claudius, who orders Hamlet to be put to death on his arrival in England, has to make excuses to Laertes for failing to punish Hamlet earlier for killing Polonius:

> Laertes "*But tell me*
>
> *Why you proceeded not against these feats*
>
> *So crimeful and capital in nature*"
>
> Claudius "*O for two special reasons ...*
>
> *The Queen his mother*
>
> *Lives almost by his looks ...*
>
> *The other motive ... Is the great love the general gender bear him.*" (4.vii.5–18)

In fact, the only spontaneous act of violence in the play is Hamlet's murder of Polonius, mistaking him for Claudius. Thus, the binary oppositions – thought and action, activity and passivity, heroism and cowardice – so powerfully summoned up in Hamlet's soliloquies and so tempting for critics and audiences alike to see as located within his person are in fact undermined by the intricacies of the plot and the positions taken up by the other protagonists. These continually serve to challenge the idea that Hamlet's 'problem' is melancholy or indecisiveness or that the logic of the play unfolds towards the point when he has finally "put down the book and picked up the skull," accepting the 'reality of death' and thus able to take the action he has so far avoided.[11] Reading the play 'against revenge' involves accompanying Hamlet in questioning the ethics of revenge, even though this questioning is invariably indirect.

The performance of *The Murder of Gonzago*, a play based on Italian revenge dramas, as well as being an opportunity to entrap Claudius, also provides a context in which Hamlet can observe a re-enactment of his father's death, an important means of grounding himself in the 'reality' of what had only been narrated by a ghost. But it also dramatises the absurdity of revenge. This is conveyed by the deliberately old-fashioned, stilted and artificial performance of the play, with its dumb show, monotonous rhyming couplets and conventional emotional expression. When Hamlet cues in the players with *"the croaking raven doth bellow for revenge,"* he utters one of its most clichéd lines, underscoring an ironic stance towards revenge. He is both within and an observer to the play, employing it to bait and provoke Claudius:

> Claudius "*Have you heard the argument? Is there no offence in't?*"
>
> Hamlet "*No, no, they do but jest, poison in jest. No offence i'th' world ... 'Tis a knavish piece of work. But what o' that? Your majesty and we that have free souls, it touches us not.*" (3.ii.219–226)

Among the many levels of meaning to emerge from the play-within-a-play is a transformation of the idea that Hamlet can only punish Claudius by exacting physical revenge. Merely killing him is now "*hire and salary, not revenge.*" Claudius has to suffer, emotionally and spiritually, for his crime: "*And that his soul may be as damned and black/ As hell, whereto it goes. My mother stays./ This physic but prolongs thy sickly days.*"

A revenge narrative in order to summon up the hatred required to kill, needs to be simplistic and one-dimensional. To achieve this, Hamlet would have, in Bateson's words, to "chop up the ecology," that is, to think of his and Claudius' actions as outside the context of what has gone before and what will be to come.[12] "*To be, or not to be*" is the speech in which this dimension of time is most powerfully confronted as Hamlet contemplates the unknown consequences of taking "*arms against a sea of troubles*" by killing a man who, even if he is a usurper, even if he reveals his guilt, is still the king. The perils are not just that he in turn will most likely be killed but: "*that the dread of something after death,/ The undiscovered country, from whose bourn/ No traveller returns.*"

There are echoes in this speech of the ghostly father's injunction, "*taint not thy mind,*" which places Hamlet in a particularly tricky bind.

Double binds

Double binds emerge when opposing and incompatible but equally compelling injunctions occur within intimate relationships, meaning that to obey one involves disobeying the other with serious consequences for these very relationships.[13] The revenge imperative, as we have seen, creates its own set of impossible binds about how to live authentically and ethically within its exigencies and whether one single action can be separated from a series of acts, stretching into the future. However, the specific circumstances Shakespeare creates for Hamlet's family involve more profound binds. The ghostly father exhorts Hamlet:

"If thou hast nature in thee, bear it not

Let not the royal bed of Denmark be

A couch for luxury and damnèd incest.

But howsoever thou pursuest this act,

Taint not thy mind, nor let thy soul contrive

Against thy mother aught-leave her to heaven

And to those thorns that in her bosom lodge

To prick and sting her." (I.v.81–88)

In this passage, the ghost makes it clear that he is more preoccupied with incest and sexual infidelity than regicide. The first bind for Hamlet is how he can conceivably carry out an act that he has no natural disposition for without *"tainting his mind."* His attempts to resolve this question involve weighing up the consequences of different courses of action and, when contradictory imperatives clash, confronting them through a series of creative 'performances' or taking a rational position by questioning the nature of ghost itself: *"The spirit that I have seen/ May be the devil, and the devil hath power/ T'assume a pleasing shape."* Involving Horatio in the 'trial' of Claudius through observing his reactions to the play means collaboration in a 'scientific experiment' conducted by two people:

Hamlet *"Observe my uncle. If his occulted guilt*

Do not itself unkennel in one speech

It is a damnèd ghost that we have seen,

And my imaginations are as foul

As Vulcan's stithy. Give him heedful note;

For I mine eyes will rivet to his face;

And, after, we will both our judgements join

To censure of his seeming"

Horatio *"Well my lord.*

If he steal aught the whilst this play is playing

And scape detecting, I will pay the theft." (3.ii.75–84)

This interchange and their subsequent exchange of notes constitute a 'meta-position' from which realities can be checked out and feelings of confusion and craziness contained:

Hamlet "*Didst perceive?*"

Horatio "*Very well my lord.*"

Hamlet "*Upon the talk of the poisoning?*"

Horatio "*I did very well note him.*" (3.ii.271–274)

The second bind for Hamlet is that his mother is, by definition, a participant in the incest; how can he punish this offence without "*contriving*" against her? She has somehow to be compelled to feel for herself the pangs of conscience, the "*pricks and stings*" of its thorns. This latter dilemma is a more private one that Hamlet shares with no-one except, obliquely, with Ophelia. Thinking of Hamlet being caught up in this bind helps make sense of the particularly intense and desperate emotional climate of his encounter with Gertrude in her chamber. Just before he enters, he outlines the difficult 'edge' between violent emotions and violent actions, exhorting himself to employ self-restraint and escape the revenge clichés of his own first four lines:

"*'Tis now the very witching time of night,*

When churchyards yawn, and hell itself breathes out

Contagion to this world. Now could I drink hot blood,

And do such bitter business as the day

Would quake to look on. Soft, now to my mother.

O heart, lose not thy nature. Let not ever

The soul of Nero enter this firm bosom.

Let me be cruel, not unnatural

I will speak daggers to her, but use none." (3.ii.371–379)

The 'gothic horror' of witchcraft, sacrifice and matricide is countered in this speech by a display of self-restraining talk, underlying the paradoxical nature of Hamlet's mission.

In the bed-chamber scene, Hamlet frantically tries to induce in Gertrude those *"pricks and stings"* of conscience that she has to be forced to feel for herself because he cannot directly punish her. Gertrude, subjected to an abusive tirade, the purpose of which is to tell her what she ought to be feeling, is also in a bind. Her position as Hamlet's mother, which might lead her to tell her raging son to mind his own business and show her more respect – *"What have I done that thou dar'st wag thy tongue/ In noise so rude against me?"* – conflicts with her position as a subordinate to men, especially kings and princes. She therefore implicitly grants Hamlet the right to act as her moral judge: *"Oh Hamlet speak no more,/ Thou turn'st mine eyes into my very soul."* When she says this, Hamlet barely hears, rushing on to further invective and it is when she says for a third time *"No more"* that we have another appearance of the father's ghost, with an ambivalent effect, either of rescuing her or encouraging him *"to whet thy almost blunted purpose."* The result is that Hamlet is drawn back into a state of confusion about what exactly it is that he is meant to be doing.

> Ghost "*But look, amazement on thy mother sits.*
>
> *O step between her and her fighting soul!*
>
> *Conceit in weakest bodies strongest works.*
>
> *Speak to her, Hamlet*"
>
> Hamlet "*How is it with you, lady?*" (3.iv.104–108)

It is at this moment that, enmeshed as he is in the bind, Hamlet's 'madness' again intervenes in the dialogue. Once Gertrude, seeing nothing of what her son sees, is convinced of his craziness, she regains some composure: *"This is the very coinage of your brain/ This bodiless creation ecstasy/ Is very cunning in."* Hamlet has already spotted the danger:

> "*It is not madness*
>
> *That I have uttered. Bring me to the test*
>
> *And I the matter will re-word, which madness*
>
> *Would gambol from.*" (3.iv.137–140)

After the ghostly father's unsettling intrusion, Hamlet resumes his attempts to 'save his mother's soul,' begging her to keep out of his uncle's bed. The images of disgust at his mother's sexuality – *"reechy kisses"* – are usually read by psychoanalysts as a projection of Hamlet's oedipal longings, but they can also be read relationally as a frantic attempt to evoke feelings of revulsion in Gertrude so she would herself choose to reject Claudius and Hamlet would not need to *"contrive aught"* against her. The scene, one of a very few with sustained dialogue in the play, ends in a way that contrasts strongly with the intensity of emotion between mother and son throughout it. Hamlet reminds Gertrude of his imminent departure for England (thus leaving the field) and Gertrude's response verges on indifference.

> Hamlet "*I must to England. You know that?*"
>
> Gertrude "*Alack! I had forgot. 'Tis so concluded on*"

Gertrude's passive and evasive voice at the end of this scene opens the way for her only soliloquy. Just before the meeting with Ophelia, which she tries to avoid, she reflects on how easily she can betray herself:

> "*To my sick soul, as sin's true nature is,*
>
> *Each toy seems prologue to some great amiss.*
>
> *So full of artless jealousy is guilt,*
>
> *It spills itself in fearing to be spilt.*" (4.v.17–20)

The nature of the 'sin' is never specified – whether it is marrying Claudius, incest, adultery, knowledge that her husband murdered his brother, witnessing Hamlet murder Polonius or colluding in the plan to remove her son from Denmark. What we can, however, draw from this is that when Hamlet is no longer present, the boundary between controlled, rational talk and crazy discourse starts to break down and the paranoid fears of Gertrude and Claudius, always visible beneath the surface, emerge more powerfully. Crazy talk is then relocated in Ophelia.

Ophelia is the other protagonist subjected to double-binding processes. R.D. Laing, following Bateson, issued a powerful challenge for psychiatry to view schizophrenia in a relational context.[14] However, he does not extend this privilege to Ophelia: "In her madness there is no-one there. She is not a person. There is no integral selfhood expressed through her actions or utterances. Incomprehensible statements are said by nothing. She has already died. There is now only a vacuum where there was once a person."[15]

Well before her 'madness,' Ophelia's 'absence' is illustrated by this interchange between the king and his counsellor:

> Claudius "*But how hath she received his love?*"
>
> Polonius "*What do you think of me?*"

An enquiry about Ophelia's own desire is responded to in terms of the reputation of her father; she is erased as a subject and denied recognition of any feelings that might potentially displease her father. Even old Capulet's brutal invective against Juliet at least acknowledged his daughter's opposition.[16] Ophelia's attempts to convince her father of Hamlet's honest intentions are ruthlessly dismissed and her conclusion seems to be that it is easier not to have a mind:

> Ophelia "*He hath, my lord, of late made many tenders*
>
> *Of his affection to me.*"
>
> Polonius "*Affection, pooh! You speak like a green girl*
>
> *Unsifted in such perilous circumstance, Do you believe his tenders as you call them?*"
>
> Ophelia "*I do not know my lord, what I should think.*" (I.iii.99–105)

While Ophelia obeys her father and rejects Hamlet's advances, she is careful not to display any clue as to her own desires and volition; in her description of the 'mad' and frightening behaviour of the prince, she denies her own agency altogether. Her father's disingenuous question "*What have you given him any hard words of late?*" elicits the response "*No my good lord, but as you did command I did repel his letters, and denied his access to me.*" If the actor emphasises phrases such as "*I do not know my Lord what I should think*" and "*as you did command,*" Ophelia can be shown as registering a protest by naming the power practices at work.

Polonius, who has quickly worked out how 'evidence' of Hamlet's "*very ecstasy of love*" can be turned to his advantage, now moves into explicitly using his daughter as 'bait' to entrap Hamlet and assist Claudius in discovering exactly what Hamlet knows. Although Polonius' manipulation of Ophelia is plain to see, we need not succumb to the temptation of viewing her simply as a victim. Her treatment of Hamlet leaves him in as much a state of confusion about her feelings and intentions as the other way around, although on the basis of gender and position in the social hierarchy, she cannot use power or employ hurtful language as he can. Vicious and misogynist as it is, Hamlet's accusation "*God has given you one face, and you make yourselves another. You jig, you amble and you lisp, and nickname God's creatures, and make your wantonness your ignorance*" does speak to the ambiguity of Ophelia's communication. In this scene, even were she inclined to do so, she cannot name the deception practised on Hamlet because her father is listening. Instead, she receives the full force of his tirade against women, sex and generativity. Not understanding the context for his rage and not acknowledging her own complicity, her conclusion, like Gertrude's, is "*O, what a noble mind is here o'erthrown.*"

The relationship between Hamlet and Ophelia is hard to bring to life, constructed as it is to highlight the emotional manipulations of others. There are a few moments, however, when it is possible to imagine it differently. Hamlet, having set up the *Murder of Gonzago* as a trap for the guilty king, is so engrossed in the story, or more moved than he expected to be by witnessing the re-enactment of his father's death, that he completely fails to observe Claudius and needs reminding by a more alert Ophelia:

> Hamlet "*You shall see anon how the murderer gets the love of Gonzago's wife.*"
>
> Ophelia "*The King rises.*"

However, if Ophelia is to develop a capacity to speak any kind of truth to power, she is only given the opportunity to do so while simultaneously disqualifying herself through madness.

Confusion and madness

The forms of madness Shakespeare accorded Hamlet and Ophelia are deeply embedded in representations of masculinity and femininity. Hamlet has been portrayed as the prototype of the melancholy hero; the "epidemic of melancholy associated with intellectual and imaginative genius curiously bypassed women. Women's melancholy was seen instead as biological, and emotional in origin."[17] Throughout the play, Hamlet's 'madness' is the subject of avid debate by others and he draws upon a variety of discourses about madness according to the context he happens to be in. Ophelia, on the other hand, is generally shown as descending in lineal fashion deeper and deeper into a psychotic state with few possibilities for alternative understandings. She witnesses and reflects on Hamlet's excesses; he is absent for hers and Gertrude and Claudius are more concerned with monitoring her – "*give her good watch*" – than attempting to understand her. Even Ophelia's suicide is sanitised and left ambiguous, with Gertrude describing an accidental fall into the water – "*an envious sliver broke*" – and the priest pronouncing, "*Her death was doubtful.*" She is deprived of agency even in her mode of death.

Ophelia and Hamlet each name dangerous matters through mad talk. Polonius is aware that crazy talk has different levels of meaning – "*Though this be madness yet there is method in't . . . how pregnant sometimes his replies are. A happiness that often madness hits on, which reason and sanity could not so prosperously be delivered of*" (2.ii.204–210).

Even though Laertes expresses a similar idea – *"This nothing's more than matter"* – Ophelia's madness is rarely seen as feigned or strategic; merely as tragic.

Despite this, it would be hard to hear Ophelia in her sane state described as *'importunate'* and her allusions in madness to truths too dangerous to be spoken offer the chance for them to be rendered coherent, as Horatio describes:

> "*Her speech is nothing;*
>
> *Yet the unshapèd use of it doth move*
>
> *The hearers to collection. They aim at it,*
>
> *And botch the words up fit to their own thoughts,*
>
> *Which, as her winks and nods and gestures yield them,*
>
> *Indeed would make one think there might be thought,*
>
> *Though nothing sure, yet much unhappily.*" (4.v.7–13)

Ophelia's words in the scene that follows are a mélange of the crazily elusive, sexually charged, emotionally direct and pragmatic: *"We must be patient. But I cannot choose but weep to think they should lay him i'th'cold ground. My brother shall know of it."* She speaks enough nonsense to be dismissed as 'distracted' but enough logic for Gertrude and Claudius to fear the effect she could have on others: *"'Twere good she were spoken with, for she may strew Dangerous/conjectures in ill-breeding minds."* With the death of the father who so forcibly manipulated and constrained her sexual desire, Ophelia is both grief-stricken and liberated. The interwoven themes of sex and death are key elements in the many levels of relational subterfuge at work in the play and they emerge into the light in Ophelia's speech.

Although all these different verbal levels can be read into the text, representations of Ophelia have, as Elaine Showalter points out, historically relied on the visual, reinforcing the notion of her as surface: "The romantic critics seem to have felt that the less said about Ophelia the better; the point is to *look* at her."[18] Hamlets 'madness' by contrast creates acute anxiety in others and thus the need to investigate its causes and 'unpack' words and meanings that are fluid and elusive.

Hamlet is a play in which self-division and self-estrangement are rife and seem to be contagious. Hamlet is *"from himself . . . ta'en away"* and Ophelia is *"divided from herself."* This sense of alienation appears to reside in the difficulty each has in finding any context within which to experience agency or test out their potential for emotional attachments. The only dialogue between Hamlet and Ophelia of any emotional substance is orchestrated and witnessed by Claudius and Polonius. Hamlet returns from England with some experience of having acted effectively. Ophelia's world, by contrast, atrophies. Unlike Desdemona, she has no Emilia with whom to test out her sense of reality.

The sexual union between Hamlet and Ophelia is another of the many 'happenings' in *Hamlet* that never happens. Each of them remains stranded outside the possibility for generativity and growth. Ophelia's inability to determine whether or not she is able to express her own desire and Hamlet's shock and rage at his mother's sexuality combine to derail their relationship.

Hamlet and Ophelia have each been described in terms of their psychic absence. For Terry Eagleton, Hamlet has "no essence of being whatsoever, no inner sanctum to be safeguarded; he is pure deferral and diffusion, a hollow void which offers nothing determinate to be known. His 'self' exists simply within the range of gestures with which he resists available definitions."[19] Paradoxically, this 'lack of essence' is manifested by the hero with whom Shakespeare has provided the most words.

That these words appear, above all, in soliloquies or monologues means that Hamlet is caught up in a circular process of reflection in which no new ideas come in from outside to challenge his constructions. There is surely a relationship between this mad-making process and the lack of dialogue in the play; even though Horatio provides some opportunity for dialogue, his position in the social hierarchy constrains his ability to be an interlocutor. In dialogue,

> The speaker himself is orientated precisely toward such an actively responsive understanding. He does not expect passive understanding that, so to speak, only duplicates his own idea in someone else's mind. Rather he expects response, agreement, sympathy, objection, execution and so forth.[20]

The only person who even attempts to offer Hamlet such a dialogue is Ophelia and she is invalidated by her father's machinations.

Feelings of confusion and uncertainty emerge in part from ambiguities around death, the emptiness of ritual and doubts about the afterlife and the provenance of the ghost.

Death, ritual and the afterlife

When Claudius instructs the grieving Hamlet to cease his "*obstinate condolement*," his advice is likely to come across to modern audiences, sympathetic to the effects of grief, as cruel and self-serving. However, Claudius was not out of tune with contemporary views on the subject because "the last half of the sixteenth century witnessed an intense Protestant campaign against both the expression of grief or condolence toward those in mourning."[21] Some treatises regarded grief as a sign of "irrationality, weakness, inadequate self-control or impiety,"[22] not greatly at variance with Claudius' accusations of *"impious stubbornness," "unmanly," "a fault to heaven"* and *"to reason most absurd."* The theme of excessively prolonged grief is common in Shakespeare and the stances of either indulging in or trying to curtail it are employed strategically by many characters. Claudius describes it as unnatural when it is also inconvenient, as do Juliet's parents when her presumed mourning for Tybalt interferes with their plans to marry her to Paris. Excessive grief for one person is often a cover for other emotional attachments, as it is for Juliet, or a guise to avoid other relationships.

Neither of these applies to Hamlet. What the second scene in *Hamlet* shows most powerfully is the young prince's isolation in his grief. The word condolence means literally a 'being with in grief.' In a family in which most members want to move quickly away from painful or inconvenient expressions of grief, one person may feel it is their sacred duty to hold onto the memory of the dead person; they will therefore experience loneliness as well as grief. This is compounded if the message to 'move on' appears blatantly opportunistic. Gertrude's exhortation to *"cast thy nightly colour off"* is immediately followed by *"And let thine eye look like a friend on Denmark."* Her message to her son not to grieve is thus contaminated by her desire to please Claudius. Divergent experiences of grief are distorted by perceptions of time as the eloquent and poignant phrase *"a little month"* illustrates.

The reference to mixed rituals following Gertrude's rapid remarriage – *"The funeral baked meats/ Did coldly furnish forth the marriage tables"* – is echoed throughout the play in the theme of inverted weddings and funerals. Ophelia's funeral is the occasion Gertrude chooses to mention for the first time her wish that she might marry Hamlet:

> Gertrude "*I hoped thou shouldst have been my Hamlet's wife.*
>
> *I thought thy bride-bed to have decked, sweet maid,*
>
> *And not t'have strewn thy grave.*" (5.i.234–236)

As well as Ophelia's burial, for in which she is denied full rites, leading to her brother's agonised cries, *"What ceremony else?,"* Polonius also had a problematic burial ritual. Claudius admits that *"we have done but greenly/*

In hugger-mugger to inter him" and Laertes further laments his father's *"obscure burial _ / No trophy, sword, nor hatchment o'er his bones,/ No noble rite nor formal ostentation."*

Rituals have the effect of linking emotions to actions; performing ritual creates the possibility of connecting participants, creating a shared sense of agency and linking past, present and future. The curtailment of ritual thus creates another level at which all the main protagonists in *Hamlet* can be seen as stranded, lonely and fearful. After the death of Polonius, Gertrude initially rejects the grieving Ophelia: *"I will not speak with her – what would she have*?" As with Hamlet's father, this death is murder and carries all the imputations of guilt and complicity. In Claudius' ambiguous phrase, *"this is the poison of deep grief,"* a state of mind that calls for surveillance – *"give her good watch"* – rather than condolence. However, in her 'mad' state, Ophelia deals head on with the stark fact of death in a way that no other protagonist does:

> "*He is dead and gone, lady,*
>
> *He is dead and gone*
>
> *At his head a grass-green turf*
>
> *At his heels a stone*" (4.v.29–32)

Gertrude's attempt to divert her – *"Nay, but, Ophelia"* – is swept aside: *"Pray you, mark."* (She sings) *"White his shroud as the mountain snow."*

Claudius' endeavour to control this unregulated and potentially dangerous state of extreme distress has the opposite effect. On her second entrance, she seems 'madder' but is more insistent: *"And will he not come again?/ No, no he is dead."* Rather than call for retribution as Laertes thinks she would if she were sane: *"Hadst thou thy wits, and didst persuade revenge/ It could not move thus."* Ophelia unabashedly mourns.

By contrast Hamlet's grief is full of confusion and ambivalence. He only mourns Ophelia when competitively provoked by Laertes' excess: *"I'll rant as well as thou . . . the bravery of his grief did put me / Into a towering passion."* Quite apart from his mother's remarriage, and his uncle's usurpation of the throne, mourning his father is beset by uncertainty about the nature of the ghost: *"The spirit that I have seen/ May be the devil."* The 'existence' of the ghost inevitably intensifies speculation about the afterlife: *"For in that sleep of death what dreams may come/ When we have shuffled off this mortal coil."* Fear of the damnation that might follow a decision to *"take arms"* rather than suicidal intent is what concerns Hamlet in this speech, argues Catherine

Belsey.[23] However, Hamlet is not alone in fearing damnation in the afterlife, albeit in Laertes' case defiantly – *"I dare damnation."* Claudius is aware that he cannot escape divine retribution – *"O my offence is rank, it smells to heaven"* – even though he claims, implausibly in the light of his brother's murder, to have its protection on earth: *"There's such divinity doth hedge a king . . . ."*

Because of the play's revenge narrative, 'failure to act' becomes a critical prism through which thinking rather than acting becomes problematised. In most revenge dramas, enacting revenge results in the avenger's death so that 'accepting death' is infused with the implication that the ideology of revenge has also to be accepted.

This idea of Hamlet advancing towards a state of resignation in which he finally comes to terms with the inevitability of death and moves into decisive action is at variance with the whole tenure of the play. It is instead infused with contradictions, ambiguities and an avoidance of the finite, either of life, death or indeed of meaning. Death itself is one of the plays most interrogated areas with, Stephen Greenblatt argues, many ambiguous references as to whether the ghost, which comes in *"such a questionable shape,"* is speaking from hell or from purgatory, raising the question of how "a young man from Wittenberg with a distinctly Protestant temperament, is haunted by a distinctly Catholic ghost."[24]

If Hamlet has resolved anything at all by the final scene, what might he have resolved? Many actors playing the prince try to convey a sense of him as irrevocably changed on his return to Denmark, although not necessarily, as Nicholas Hytner puts it, that "there is a mystical, even spiritual element to him."[25]

It is tempting to see in Hamlet only an inner state in which he comes to accept death: *"The readiness is all. Since no man knows aught of what he leaves, what is't to leave betimes? Let be."* This, however, risks mistaking relational positions taken up in particular contexts, as in the conversation with Horatio, for evidence of internal 'resolution' with all the sense of closure this implies. In Hamlet's account of the events on the sea voyage to England, as throughout the play, we have competing discourses. There are many hints from Hamlet's account of foiling Claudius' plot that suggest he is drawing upon an idea of randomness sometimes at variance with and sometimes a sign of divine intervention. Hamlet has avoided death through his own *"rashness"*:

> "*Our indiscretion sometimes serves us well*
>
> *When our dear plots do pall; and that should teach us*
>
> *There's a divinity that shapes our ends,*
>
> *Rough-hew them how we will.*" (5.ii.8–11)

While congratulating himself on his performance in adversity however: "*Being thus benetted round with villains/Ere I could make a prologue to my brains/They had begun the play*," the notion of divine intervention is again in evidence: "*even in that was heaven ordinant*." Thus, if Hamlet is reflecting on anything, it is perhaps the utter unpredictability of life, death, his own agency or indeed of divine intervention. As the plot moves into its final stages, rather than provide 'closure' Shakespeare continues to extract ambiguities and contradictions from it. Hamlet accepts a duel with Laertes, whom he considers himself to have wronged, rather than a confrontation with Claudius who has clearly wronged him. Hamlet's death is certainly not presented as the result of a heroic duel but as one of a series of fortuitous actions, including Gertrude drinking the poison intended for her son, Laertes switching the rapiers and not one of his courtiers stirring to protect Claudius when he cries out "*O, yet defend me, friends, I am but hurt*." This last returns us once again to that very disjuncture between words and actions that so permeates the play.

Conclusion

The questioning quality of *Hamlet* which is both embedded in the texture of the play and verbalised by its hero emerges from the inconsistencies to be found at every level and which create such fertile ground for critics. The possibilities for radically incompatible accounts of almost everything in *Hamlet* seem endless. Although some questions relate to Hamlet himself, such as whether his madness is real or feigned or whether he really loves Ophelia, other key protagonists are equally inscrutable. We do not know whether Gertrude is innocent or complicit in the murder of her husband and we are left uncertain as to how much Ophelia loves Hamlet or whether Horatio believes anything that Hamlet tells him. These uncertainties create an imperative for audience and reader to reach beyond them, not to find alternative truths but, as so often in Shakespeare, to engage with inconclusiveness. Opposing positions about the key issues in the play are virtually all embedded in the soliloquies, rather than explored through dialogue. Hamlet emerges onto the stage as a silent witness to the conduct of the court, only reluctantly drawn into speech, and at the end of the play he disappears again into silence – "*O, I could tell you – But let it be . . . – the rest is silence*." His continuance in the world of the living will be through the remembrance of others but how this remembrance will be enshrined in narrative remains, unsurprisingly, uncertain. All the indications are that it will be appropriated by Fortinbras, who appears at the end of the play and, after surveying the array of corpses – "*this quarry*" – announces a military burial for Hamlet: "*and for his passage/The soldiers' music and the rites of war/ Speak loudly for him.*"

Horatio vainly attempts to tell a different tale:

"*Of accidental judgements, casual slaughters,*

Of deaths put on by cunning and forced cause;

And, in this upshot, purposes mistook

Fallen on the inventors' heads" (5.ii.335–338)

This distinctly unheroic account, while echoing Hamlet's own narratives, hardly fits the context of a heroic military intervention by an outside power. In the end Hamlet's complex identity is reduced to the unlikely, impoverished and simplistic one of the soldier prince, a narrative which, however unsuited to him, best suits the exigency of the hour: "*Bear Hamlet like a soldier to the stage.*"

This 'narrative failure' echoes the sense of Hamlet being stranded within his soliloquys while his interactions with others draw him into increasingly contradictory subject positions. Thus, the 'inner talk' that is so compelling for the audience further alienates him from his co-protagonists since their responses seem so inadequate, so compromised or so dishonest. The self-referential and somewhat omnipotent tone of the soliloquies in *Hamlet*, coupled with the impoverishment of dialogue, calls to mind Bakhtin's reflections on responses in dialogue: "And the speaker himself is oriented precisely toward such an active responsive understanding . . . Moreover any speaker is himself a respondent to a greater or lesser degree. He is not, after all, the first speaker, the one who disturbs the eternal silence of the universe."[26]

The issue is not that the questions raised in *Hamlet* remain unanswered – it is their very indeterminacy that provokes most thought – but that questioning fails to evoke active responses from others. In this way the creative potential of dialogue itself with its ability to imbue questions with a richer texture through the interchange of ideas remains elusive and out of reach.

Notes

1 Elaine Showalter, 'Representing Ophelia: Women, Madness and the Responsibilities of Feminist Criticism', in Martin Coyle, ed., *Hamlet* (Basingstoke: Palgrave Macmillan, 1992).
2 Ben Brantley quoted in the *Guardian* newspaper, 27 August 2015.
3 John V. Knapp, 'Family Games and Imbroglio in Hamlet', in John V. Knapp and Ken Womack, eds., *Reading the Family Dance* (London: Associated University Presses, 2003).
4 Rory Kinnear, *Interview with Ben Power* (Programme Notes for National Theatre Production of Hamlet, 2010).
5 Maynard Mack, 'The World of Hamlet', *The Yale Review*, 41 (1952), 504.
6 Kiernan Ryan, *Shakespeare* (Basingstoke: Palgrave Macmillan, 2002), 168.
7 Catherine Belsey, *Why Shakespeare?* (Basingstoke: Palgrave Macmillan, 2007), 109.
8 René Girard, *Theatre of Envy* (Oxford: Oxford University Press, 1991), 273.
9 Margot Heineman, 'How Brecht Read Shakespeare', in Jonathan Dollimore and Alan Sinfield, eds., *Political Shakespeare* (Manchester: Manchester University Press, Second Edition, 1994), 241.
10 Catherine Belsey, *Why Shakespeare?* (Basingstoke: Palgrave Macmillan, 2007), 125.
11 Jonathan Bate, *The Genius of Shakespeare* (Oxford: Oxford University Press, Kindle Edition, 2013).
12 Gregory Bateson, *Mind and Nature* (London: Fontana, 1979).
13 Gregory Bateson, *Steps to an Ecology of Mind* (St Albans: Paladin, 1973).
14 R. D. Laing, *The Divided Self* (Harmondsworth: Penguin, 1965).
15 Ibid., 195n.
16 Romeo and Juliet, Act 3, scene 5.
17 Elaine Showalter, 'Representing Ophelia: Women, Madness and the Responsibilities of Feminist Criticism', in Martin Coyle, ed., *Hamlet* (Basingstoke: Palgrave Macmillan, 1992), 118.
18 Ibid., 120.
19 Terry Eagleton, *William Shakespeare* (Oxford: Basil Blackwell, 1986), 72.
20 Mikhail Bakhtin, *Speech Genres and Other Late Essays* (Austin: University of Texas Press,1986), 69.
21 Stephen Mullaney, 'Mourning and Misogyny: Hamlet and the Final Progress of Elizabeth 1', in Kate Chedgzoy, ed., *Shakespeare, Feminism and Gender* (Basingstoke: Palgrave Macmillan, 2001), 173.
22 G. W. Pigman, *Grief and English Renaissance Elegy* (Cambridge: Cambridge University Press, 1985), 2.
23 Catherine Belsey, *Why Shakespeare?* (Basingstoke: Palgrave Macmillan, 2007), 112.

24 Stephen Greenblatt, *Hamlet in Purgatory* (Princeton: Princeton University Press, 2001).

25 Nicholas Hytner, *Interview with Ben Power* (Programme notes for National Theatre Production of Hamlet, 2010).

26 Mikhail Bakhtin, *Speech Genres and Other Late Essays* (Austin: University of Texas Press, 1986), 69.

CHAPTER 4

"*Being weak, seem so*"

Power, status and identity loss in *King Lear*

When the Earl of Gloucester bemoans *"Love cools, friendship falls off, brothers divide; in cities mutinies, in countries discords, palaces treason, the bond cracked between son and father,"* he draws attention to all those interconnected levels at which a world might be experienced as falling apart. In feudal society where blood ties are the indispensable bedrock of power and the intermeshing of household and society is taken as a given, one serious episode of family discord can herald social and political catastrophe.

Assumptions about the reliability and loyalty of kin underpin a sense of social order and, when these are experienced as treacherous, there is no safe footing. Thus themes of order and disorder permeate the play. In the opening scene, there are many signifiers of a world that seems to be in order. Patriarchy is firmly in place, succession a finely balanced matter of distribution between males, gender inequities meticulously observed as are the differences between an illegitimate son (subject to mocking jokes that reinforce the norm of marital sex) and a son gotten *"by order of law."* Wealthy suitors obediently queue up for Lear's only unmarried daughter. The semblance of order continues as far as the second half of Lear's opening speech when he presents the 'logic' of passing on to the next generation the onerous cares of office. Suddenly and explosively, the 'irrational' language of love and vulnerability intrudes and creates mayhem, confusion and fury. It is as if Lear suddenly realises that he has daughters and not sons, with all the complexity this entails for succession in a patriarchal society.

Themes of order and disorder are repeated at many levels, from politics to individual identity as certainties are swept away. Order and disorder do not, however, contain any fixed or absolute meanings because they are context-bound and relational. They will be valued or not according to position in the social hierarchy. A breakdown of the established order terrifies some – Lear, Gloucester and Kent – but offers welcome opportunities for others – Gonoril, Regan and Edmund. If patriarchy was the foundation of social order, then Shakespeare has, in *King Lear*, taken the "astonishing risk of unmasking patriarchal power."[1] This power has, for Lear the status of such unquestioned truth that even relatively minor challenges to it are experienced as psychic annihilation.

To a large extent the family story of Lear and his daughters is paralleled by that of Gloucester and his sons; fathers who are fearful of old age, filial betrayal of parents by their children, vicious sibling rivalry and each father eventually reconciled, however ambiguously, with their 'good child.' Both fathers are obsessed by the 'degeneracy' of their children. Lear rails: "*twas this flesh begot/Those pelican daughters*" and Gloucester bemoans: "*Our flesh and blood is grown so vile, my lord,/That it doth hate what gets it.*" Further comparisons between the two families, such as the catastrophic failure of fathers to read the motives and emotional states of their own children can be seen as embedded in patriarchal power and in the restricted relationships that it incubates. One crucial difference, however, between the family stories is that the Gloucesters' demonstrates some order and sequence, with a conservative ending in which the 'bad' illegitimate son is vanquished and slain by the 'good' legitimate son who survives and is vindicated. By contrast, in the Lear family story all sense of shape and sequence is denied.

The play undermines many assumptions about our social worlds, such as the security of blood ties or a sense of superiority over animals. Illusions about civilisation and law are ruthlessly deconstructed to lay bare their dependence on power and hierarchy. The play contains plentiful expressions of nihilism or despair: "*When we are born, we cry that we are come/To this great stage of fools.*" But while there is certainly little that is redemptive, the play need not be seen as pessimistic. What hope there is lies in individual acts of kindness and altruism, in fleeting visions of better worlds and in the capacity to confront and endure extremes of suffering and privation; a bleak message certainly, but not a pessimistic one. Gloucester embraces the void at the 'cliff edge' only to reconnect with the pain of living. His response is to take up a stance of endurance: "*Henceforth I'll bear/Affliction till it do cry out itself/Enough, enough.*"

Although many of Shakespeare's tragedies end with a restoration of order, this is withheld in *King Lear,* even though we are led to believe it could happen because a flimsy rescue plot runs tantalisingly alongside the main action. As well as hope for a happier outcome, audiences might also be tempted to impose narrative coherence by thinking of Lear as being on a journey through suffering towards insight and enlightenment. This was the humanist view favoured by twentieth century critics. The text, however, hardly supports this interpretation. Although certain contexts show Lear arriving at some shattering revelations, others lead him to retreat into rigid certainties, vanity and self-delusion.

In this chapter, before exploring the family relationships themselves, I first discuss three wider dimensions that fit with a systemic approach: the 'decentred self,' the intersections between gender, nature and power and the devices of language.

'Decentred' selves and their contexts

The idea of subjectivity as socially constructed and of identity as fluid and contested rather than fixed and stable are, as I have argued, key aspects of systemic thinking. Nowhere in Shakespeare's tragedies is the idea of the 'decentred self' explored as intensely as it is in *King Lear*.[2] Here, Shakespeare's portrayal of selves that are context-bound and non-essential can startle us with its modernity. His subtle grasp of the relationship between power and identity is brought to life through those interactions where shifts in power subvert and undermine fixed constructions of self.

Experiences of fragmentation and loss of selfhood are directly expressed in the text but are also embedded in the portrayal of states of confusion and the oscillation between feigned and 'real' madness, between unintelligibility and gibberish on the one hand and mordent, insightful and coherent reflections on the other. The notion of a 'core self' is constantly subverted. States of confusion are most frequently voiced by the two old men whose worlds are in turmoil. Gloucester bemoans the fact that maintaining his sanity only increases his suffering.

"The king is mad. How stiff is my vile sense,

That I stand up and have ingenious feeling

Of my huge sorrows! Better I were distraught;

So should my thoughts be fencèd from my griefs,

And woes by wrong imaginations lose

The knowledge of themselves." (xx.271–276).

However, this longing for the ease of madness through loss of self is offset by a portrayal of Lear's madness which is anything but one of comforting oblivion. Struggling to regain a sense of himself and his identity, Lear desperately calls for recognition: "*Doth anyone here know me?. . ./Who is it that can tell me who I am? /Lear's shadow?*" Lear's shocking realisation that his identity has been contingent on his status and power and has nothing essential about it is one that many people in positions of power today struggle to grasp: "*To say 'ay' and 'no' to everything I said 'ay' and 'no' to was no good divinity. . . . Go to, they are not men of their words. They told me I was everything;' tis a lie, I am not ague proof.*" (xx.98–103).

Lear is forced to question the identity he has relied upon within his political, social and familial world. The emotions he now experiences contradict everything he previously expected of himself. In other words, his map of the world no longer fits the territory he occupies. The bleakness and desolation of the physical landscape he inhabits mirrors this psychic state. The idea of 'decentring' can also apply to a person's relationship to their cherished ideas. Trauma, abuse, betrayal, decline or dislocation create enough challenges to a sense of self or to the reliability of intimate relationships; but the upending of previously unquestioned belief systems can be equally painful.

There are many examples of this in *King Lear*. In his treatment of the themes of power, property and inheritance, Shakespeare invites us to reflect on how much power contextualises what passes for justice and how its implementation is contingent on position and is thus unreliable: "*A dog's obeyed in office. . . . The usurer hangs the cozener. Through tattered rags small vices do appear; robes and furred gowns hide all.*" (xx.152–159)

Loss of power and suffering creates the opportunity for empathy as Lear's own unhoused state evokes a powerful realisation of what others suffer: "*Poor naked wretches, wheresoe'er you are,/That bide the pelting of this pitiless night,*" and how he has been insulated from knowledge of the conditions others suffer: "*O, I have ta'en/ Too little care of this.Take physic, pomp,/Expose thyself to feel what wretches feel.*" This moving realisation about injustice and inequity is echoed in Gloucester's speech to Tom, where his own suffering and encounter with an impoverished 'other,' likewise provokes new thinking:

"*Let the superfluous and lust-dieted man*

That stands your ordinance, that will not see

Because he does not feel, feel your power quickly.

So distribution should undo excess,

And each man have enough." (xv.65–69)

These statements point to alternative and radical understandings of the world which have a transformative potential that is however left unresolved at the end of the play. That they are spoken by the two old men whose worlds are in turmoil is significant. Their insights come and go as they are likely to in this world of colliding ideologies. Even early in the play when Lear appears most firmly set on his disastrously destructive path there are moments of self-reflection. For example, before leaving Gonoril's house, he instructs himself: *"Keep me in temper. I would not be mad"* and, in the middle of the fool's provocations, he bursts out, in relation to Cordelia: *"I did her wrong."*

Just before Lear's showdown with his daughters, when Regan and Cornwall are pointedly reluctant to meet with him, there is a telling example of how the colliding worlds of unquestioned authority and the rising power of aggressive individualism create challenges to identity as power shifts from the first to the second. In this speech, Lear oscillates between acknowledging Cornwall's power and thus accommodating to him and outrage at this challenge to his own sense of entitlement, leading to demands for instant attention and gratification.

Lear *"Deny to speak with me? They're sick, they're weary?*

They travelled hard tonight? – mere insolence,

Ay, the images of revolt and flying off.

Fetch me a better answer"

Gloucester *"My dear lord,*

You know the fiery quality of the Duke,

How unremovable and fixed he is

In his own course."

Lear *"Vengeance, death, plague, confusion!*

What 'fiery quality'? Why, Gloucester, I'd

Speak with the Duke of Cornwall and his wife."

Gloucester "*Aye my good lord*"

Lear "*The king would speak with Cornwall; the dear father*

Would with his daughter speak, commands, tends service.

'Fiery'? The Duke? – tell the hot Duke that Lear –

No, but not yet. Maybe he is not well.

Infirmity doth still neglect all office . . .

I'll forebear

And am fallen out with my more headier will,

To take the indisposed and sickly fit

For the sound man. – Death on my state,

Wherefore should he sit here? This act persuades me

That this remotion of the Duke and her

Is practice only. Give me my servant forth.

Tell the Duke and's wife I'll speak with them,

Now, presently. Bid them come forth and hear me,

Or at their chamber door I'll beat the drum

Till it cry sleep to death." (vii.257–279)

The polyphony of voices within this speech is rich and multi-levelled. It illustrates Mikhail Bakhtin's idea of "double-voiced" discourse in which we see both "open polemic" and hidden "dialogicality."[3] Lear responds both to Gloucester's actual speech as well as anticipate his further (unvoiced) advocacy of accommodation to the reality of power. He incorporates this voice – "*I'll forebear*" – and then roundly rejects it. Hearing himself urge caution – "*my more headier will*" – provokes in him the opposite reaction: "*Death on my state, Wherefore should he sit there?*" Lear is being asked to accommodate to the state of mind of another person – the fiery duke, which for him can only be associated with the loss of power. Likewise, self-reflection evokes rage that he should even have to restrain himself. Alongside a realistic appraisal of the duke and Regan's dishonesty is a desperate childlike fear of abandonment leading to the threat to beat down their bedroom door. Rank, social position and familial connections sit in uneasy tension, demonstrated by his uncertainty about how to address either the duke or Regan or whether to use 'command' or 'request' words. Exploring this type of contradictory communication illuminates the way such momentous shifts in the configuration of power enter uneasily into discourse. Focussing on these contradictions seems more relevant than a lineal story of Lear's journey towards personal enlightenment, a reading which the play seems to resolutely refuse.

Nowhere is this refusal more evident than in the ending, with the deaths of Cordelia and Lear sabotaging the prospect either of closure or recuperation. We come tantalisingly close, with the dying Edmund's revelation that he can *"perchance do good"* by revealing his own plot to murder Lear and Cordelia, but this communication is delayed by no less than fifty-four lines, by which time it is too late to save them. Decentring the heroic subject also means that the possibility of anyone else stepping forward to take the reins of power appears quite absurd. The restoration of Lear's relationship with Cordelia is ripped away by her death but the final scenes between father and daughter, touching as they are, also reveal a great deal about processes of gender and power

Gender, nature and power; "His little world of man"

Lear's 'discovery' of his dependence on women and his uncontrolled rage when he cannot control first Cordelia and then her sisters is one of the play's central dynamics. He erupts into tirades against nature as he is forced to confront the terror, first of not being nurtured in old age and then of all areas associated with the feminine: sexuality, procreation, life and death. Women asserting their sexual maturity is one of the underlying themes. Cordelia is punished by Lear for claiming that she cannot love a father more than a husband and sexual partner. Gonoril and Regan, having for strategic reasons chosen to conceal this in their own rhetoric, are shown, once they have the power to do so, as spiralling into an orgy of lust and cruelty. This 'perversion' of all that is conventionally 'feminine' opens up the way for the re-appearance of Cordelia as an 'idealised virgin body,' quiescent and stripped of her independence of spirit.[4] Her sisters' emergence as 'monstrous' exactly parallels Lear's confrontation with the limits of his own power and control. As Gregory Bateson has argued, the 'epistemological error' of believing in unilateral power and control is compounded by responding to its loss through efforts to exert control in the same old way.[5] If emotional attachments are experienced only in terms of control over others, then loss of that control leads to an urge to punish those who resist it.

Two elements – beliefs about women's power over nature and belief in male entitlement to wield power – converge in the storm scene, which is imagined as both feminine and masculine. Bleakness, desolation, abandonment by the nurturing female are evoked in gendered metaphor *"For many miles about/ There's not a bush."* Since women should be appendages of men, when they cannot be controlled, nothing can. Following the failure of his attempt to control his daughters, Lear tries to out-control the storm, appearing like a demented orchestral conductor ordering the storm to do what it is already doing: *"Blow wind and crack your cheeks."*

This omnipotent striving to subdue unruly nature is eloquently described to Kent by the first gentleman, highlighting at the same time the greater wisdom of the non-human world:

> Kent "*Where's the King?*"
>
> First Gentleman "*Contending with the fretful element;*
>
> *Bids the wind blow the earth into the sea*
>
> *Or swell the curlèd waters 'bove the main,*
>
> *That things might change or cease; tears his white hair,*
>
> *Which the impetuous blasts, with eyeless rage,*
>
> *Catch in their fury and make nothing of;*
>
> *Strives in his little world of man to outscorn*
>
> *The to- and-fro-conflicting wind and rain.*
>
> *This night wherein the cub-drawn bear would couch,*
>
> *The lion and the belly-pinchèd wolf*
>
> *Keep their fur dry, unbonneted he runs;*
>
> *And bids what will take all.*" (viii.3–14)

Lear's terror of women's power is revealed by his semi-divine assumption of power over fertility: *"Crack nature's mould, all germens spill at once."* His rejection of Cordelia is not just from his court but from life itself: *"Better thou hadst not been born than not to have pleased me better"* and his vicious attack on Gonoril specifically curses her fertility: *"Into her womb convey sterility/Dry up in her the organs of increase."* The absence of mothers in either the Lear or the Gloucester family intensifies these extreme distortions of womanhood and female sexuality. Janet Adelman's interpretation is that the play's power derives from its "confrontation with the landscape of maternal deprivation . . . the excision of the mother ends by releasing fantasies far more frightening than any merely literal mother could be."[6] Coppelia Kahn argues more benignly that the tragedy of masculinity lies in the cost of repressing vulnerability and the capacity for feeling which we call feminine. Lear, she argues, progresses in the play towards accepting the feminine in himself by developing empathy and through an acceptance of the fragility of male authority.[7] Although Kahn does not over-romanticise Lear's subsequent reconciliation with Cordelia, this idea of Lear's gender 'progress' is unconvincing. The reunion with Cordelia suggests that he moves comfortably into her 'nursery,' even if it is now a prison, but that he still needs reassurance that he has her at his command "*Have I caught thee*?" He does not relate to her as a separate person and she colludes with his regressive fantasy.

Systemically we can appreciate that, while there are certainly examples of empathy from Lear; his care for the fool in the storm is one example, once he is again in the presence of a nurturing female, the power of gender patterns reasserts itself. Certainly the only suggestion that Cordelia makes, that they should meet with her sisters, is quashed by Lear in favour of his own romanticised image of the two of them singing like birds in their prison cage. Alongside emotional longing for his daughter, the assumption that the world according to Lear is the same for everyone suddenly makes a re-appearance. It has, after all, a long history. It has already been illustrated in his encounter with Tom:

> Lear "*What, has his daughters brought him to this pass?*" . . .
>
> Kent "*He hath no daughters, sir*"
>
> Lear "*Death, traitor! Nothing could have subdued nature*
>
> *To such a lowness but his unkind daughters.*" (xi.56–63)

Lear and Gloucester are examples of the emotional obtuseness that can come from unquestioned patriarchal power. Both reject precisely those children most likely to have a genuine emotional connection to them; Shakespeare highlights their obliviousness to feedback and their lack of knowledge of the most basic characteristics of their own children; Gloucester has to ask Edmund about Edgar's handwriting when shown the incriminating letter. Kent can hardly contain his astonishment at Lear's misrepresentation of Cordelia:

> "*Answer my life my judgement,*
>
> *Thy youngest daughter does not love thee least.*"

While the favoured children of Lear and Gloucester are ill prepared for the injustice visited upon them, their least favoured offspring have developed acute skills in reading the states of mind of others, even if they put this knowledge to malign use. Gonoril and Regan know their father better than he knows them and indeed at times he is barely able to distinguish between them: "*Yet have I left a daughter.*" Those with power are less likely to feel the need to observe the states of mind of those subordinate to them. Gloucester, quite incapable of interpreting his own sons' behaviour, is more perceptive when it comes to the Duke of Cornwall, his patron: "*You know the fiery quality of the Duke.*" Edmund who, as an outsider, needs to "*study deserving,*" is better placed to understand the workings of power; he is quite clear about the arbitrary nature of social rules – "*the plague of custom*" – an insight that his father and Lear only arrive at through the extremes of suffering and madness. Edgar, unlike Cordelia, who has no illusions about her siblings, – "*I know you what you are*" – is portrayed as being as gullible as his father. Confident perhaps about his own privileged status he never questions Edmund's account of his father's anger nor the advice to flee. Gender and power thus intersect in complex ways, creating possibilities either for insight or obtuseness, for moments of clarity and agency or terrifying experiences of helplessness and fragmentation.

Language and fragmentation

Transformations of power and their challenges to selfhood are embedded in the language of the play. In *King Lear*, language operates at the extremes and often constrains protagonists into false polarities from which madness or exile can seem the only escape. Paradoxical communication and its connection to psychotic states throw into relief many of the ways that language can be used to obscure and confuse as much as to clarify.[8] Tom communicates through feigned madness, the fool through barbed humour and Cordelia, having spoken truth to power, – "*so young, my lord, and true*" – leaves the field.

"Truth" in the play, Terry Eagleton observes, 'becomes an inversion of whatever Lear says it is. The King of France states that Cordelia is '*most rich being poor*' and Kent that "*freedom lives hence, and banishment is here.*"[9] These linguistic reversals and paradoxes occur throughout the play; prison can be a site of freedom, vision can mean blindness: "*I stumbled when I saw*" and loss of sight can be the route to a more reliable vision: "*I see it feelingly.*"

In *King Lear*, language oscillates wildly between public and private domains, with the signifier "*nothing,*" set in motion in the 'succession scene,' crossing both domains. Its use, argues Alessandro Serpieri, emphasises the impossibility of Lear's attempt to "assimilate the non-hierarchical *qualitative* system of love to the hierarchical *quantitative* system of power."[10] This can "only lead to the pretence of love, to love's perversion and its degeneration."[11] Gonoril and Regan embark upon a competitive scale of superiority in the domain of affection, which is followed by a series of negations by Cordelia: "*Nothing, my lord.*"

Lear appears to believe that he can give up the trappings of power and still exist. But since "whoever is excluded from the medieval hierarchy of signs *is 'nothing'*; he will possess nothing and be reduced to crawling."[12] The word *'nothing'* recurs throughout the play as Lear and Edgar each confront the personal catastrophe of loss of position and existential annihilation:

> Edgar "*Poor Tuelygod, Poor Tom!'*
>
> *That's something yet. Edgar I nothing am.*"

For Lear the sense of psychic annihilation is named as a bodily experience.

> Lear "*Doth any here know me? Why, this is not Lear,*
>
> *Doth Lear walk thus, speak thus? Where are his eyes?*"

Much of the fool's commentary has the function of reminding Lear of his 'nothingness' and of highlighting the absurdity of his position; he cannot expect to be anyone when he has chosen to be no-one. "*Now thou art an O without a figure. I am better than thou art, now. I am a fool; thou art nothing*" (iv.184–186).

Distinctions in language between hierarchy and its absence continue to be made throughout the play, as, for example, between the panoply of rank and the anonymity of nakedness. Lear stands over Tom, gazing at and, memorably in Ian McKellen's performance, almost picking at his naked body as if it is an utterly new phenomenon, as if realising for the first time that this is what we all are.[13] "*Is man no more than this? . . . Unaccomodated man is no more but such a poor, bare, forked animal as thou art*" (xi.92–97).

Despite all the crazy, poetic and potentially emancipatory language spoken in the hovel by Lear, Tom and the fool there is still no escape from the symbolic order of language. Even madness fails to protect Lear from painful and disturbing realisations. The poetry, metaphor and hallucinogenic images in *King Lear* show language at the extremes, fitting with the extremes of emotion that erupt so suddenly. Characters often have difficulty expressing themselves, as if reality is changing so quickly around them that language cannot keep up. Lear and Edgar in particular demonstrate the way that language outruns the confines of the body. As Edgar puts it: "*The worst is not/ As long as we can say 'this is the worst'.*" "By naming an ultimate limit, speech transcends it in that very act."[14] In the storm scene, it is as if language can transcend physical suffering by simultaneously describing and prescribing the forces of nature:

> "*Blow, wind, and crack your cheeks! Rage, blow,*
>
> *You cataracts and hurricanoes, spout*
>
> *Til you have drenched the steeples, drowned the cocks.*" (ix.1–3)

Seemingly accurate and innocent language can suddenly be deadly. When Lear is staying with Gonoril, Oswald's description of Lear as "*My lady's father*" provokes a tirade. The correct descriptor from his point of view would have been 'the King.' The grim reality of loss of status is heightened by his identity now being conferred in relation to his daughter and the referents now being those of hospitality and household rules rather than rights and entitlement. The word 'King' has become an empty signifier; it is clung to but no longer represents any material reality. When Regan suggests that Lear might apologise to Gonoril for his behaviour, Lear makes this a political issue: "*Ask her forgiveness? Do you mark how this becomes the house?*" But the house no longer signifies the majesty and entitlement it once did. The shifting nature of power reaches into the language of relationships. Regan, when Gloucester bemoans Edgar's 'treachery,' pointedly changes family referents: "*What, did my father's godson seek your life?/He whom my father named, your Edgar?*" For his older daughters Lear's designation shifts from "*dearest father*" to "*the old man*" to "*the lunatic king*" and Lear and Gloucester express disapprobation of their offspring by denying the blood tie altogether. Lear says of Cordelia: "*We have no such daughter*" and Gloucester of Edgar: "*I never got him.*" Language use, as well as actions, sets a volatile frame for family relationships.

Family relationships

The profound reversal in intergenerational power in each family, set in violent motion by Lear's abdication and Edmund's plotting, reverberates through all family relationships, creating polarities of love and loyalty on the one hand and hatred and treachery on the other. These polarities are played out by the siblings and spouses in each family but the same differences are also discernible in the contributions of more 'minor' characters such as Kent and the servants, adding texture to the moral quandaries they face.

Gonoril's frustrated 'cri de coeur': *"Idle old man,/That still would manage those authorities/That he hath given away"* could be a timeless lament from members of many a family business in transition. The 'ordinariness' of this dilemma is, however, soon replaced by the murderous processes it unleashes. In the 'succession scene,' the political tensions between giving away land, renouncing the cares of office and yet still retaining authority and status are mirrored in the ambiguous process of 'giving away' a daughter and yet retaining her primary love and loyalty. Given that these aspirations are mutually incompatible, we can wonder why Lear sets up the charade he does. If the scene is intended to give Cordelia the opportunity to outdo her sisters in protestations of love, it would have been based on Lear's absolute certainty that this daughter, being his favourite, would respond exactly as he wanted her to. As well as refuse to play the game that her sisters play, Cordelia is aware that her father is attempting to bind her closer to him at the very moment she is to leave him through marriage.

Lear's behaviour has often been understood in individualistic terms as, variously, lack of self-knowledge, narcissism, terror of abandonment in old age or decline into dementia. While all of these can be valid, it is important to think beyond character flaws or illness to the ways that any of them come to be enacted in the particular contexts of power and its loss. Those in power, as I have discussed, have less need to engage with the viewpoints of others or to develop the skills of observing their own, let alone other people's, states of mind. Lear might never before have encountered any barriers to his 'unfettered will.' Stephen Greenblatt argues that Lear's own anxiety about his future was projected onto others through his little game:

> a ritual whose intended function seems to have been to allay the retiring monarch's anxiety by arousing it in others . . . Lear wants his children to experience the anxiety of a competition for his bounty without having to endure any of the actual consequences of such a competition.[15]

Old age is a time when questions about the reliability of kin can arise in the starkest of ways. Anxieties about the old being supplanted by the ruthless ambitions of the young are explicitly named within the Gloucester family and, according to Stephen Greenblatt, were widespread in the late middle ages and early modern period. Despite veneration of old age, the old, without control of their property, were vulnerable and fearful of being unhoused and unfed.[16] Lear's unilateral demands mask his desire, in the light of Cordelia's impending marriage, to ensure his care by her, *"to set my rest/On her kind nursery."*

Since he sets about this goal in a way that produces its exact opposite, so every other communication in the scene is caught up in a paradox. He intends to divide the kingdom into three parts, but one third is "*more opulent*" than the rest. He cannot reach a negotiated agreement about his future living conditions because, as an absolute monarch, he cannot recognise the rights of other parties to the negotiation. Handing over to Albany and Cornwall involves one transactional language, to Gonoril and Regan another. Cordelia, in response to these confused modes of communication, uses the cool language of duty rather than the warm language of love. Paradoxes are at their height at times of transition. Cordelia is in the state of not-yet-married, just as Lear is in the state of not-yet-not-king.

Cordelia perhaps responds as she does because, as her father' favourite, she has leeway to challenge him that her sisters do not. But she mistakes the impact that disrupting Lear's piece of theatre will have. All the sisters were longing to tell Lear (as Regan later does) that these are "*unseemly tricks*" but only Cordelia thinks she can afford to challenge him. Her sense of rectitude – "*I am sure my love's/ More richer than my tongue*" – blinds her to the danger she is in. Being the youngest and the favourite has the disadvantage that more is expected of her than of her sisters and her marriage would be experienced as a more devastating loss. Her sisters collude with the game precisely because they know they are neither loved nor favoured: "*What shall Cordelia do? Love and be silent.*"

"Tigers not daughters"

Savagely rejected by her father and by one of her suitors, Cordelia's recourse is to maintain her moral position. In the only scene between the three sisters, she confronts Gonoril and Regan, making it clear that Lear would be living with her if she remained in his favour and taking a lofty tone which does nothing to endear her to them:

> "*And like a sister am most loath to call/ Your faults as they are named.*"

Although Gonoril and Regan can hardly contain their triumph and send her off with Regan's vicious put-down: "*And well are worth the worst that you have wanted,*" they have no illusions that anything has changed within the family dynamics. Their understanding of their father, his whims and wilfulness, provides a nuanced distinction between the effects of old age itself and behavioural patterns over time:

> Gonoril "*The best and soundest of his time hath been but rash; then must we look to receive from his age not alone the imperfection of long-engrafted condition, but there-withal unruly waywardness that infirm and choleric years bring with them.*" (i.284–288)

Oppressed over time by their father's propensity to divide and rule and by his unabashed preference for Cordelia, Lear's abdication and her banishment is liberating for Gonoril and Regan. However, they are too cynical not to realise that they too could easily fall victim to his *"unconstant starts."* After Cordelia's departure, they acknowledge that his treatment of her and of Kent was too harsh and they predict similar behaviour towards themselves, since he will continue to try to exercise authority as he has always done. *"He hath ever but slenderly known himself"* is Regan's astute judgement, born, it is clear, from long years of experience. The sisters know that the arrangement Lear has imposed is doomed to failure; he will not want it to work since neither of them is Cordelia, the daughter he chose. Their decision is thus to maintain a united front: *"Let's hit together."*

'Hitting together' is exactly what Gonoril and Regan achieve in the short term, and this reaches its apotheosis in Scene 7 when, with exquisite choreography, they resist their father's attempts to manipulate and split them. The practice of 'divide and rule,' as in the competition of the first scene, no longer has any traction. Lear does his best to revive it, saying to Regan about Gonoril: *"her eyes are fierce, but thine/Do Comfort and not burn."* He challenges evidence of the sisters' collaboration but without much conviction:

> Lear "*Oh Regan, wilt thou take her by the hand?*"
>
> Gonoril "*Why not by the hand, sir? How have I offended?*"

The fool's cruel observation about the changing locus of authority – *"there's not a nose among a hundred but can smell him that's stinking"* – sets the scene perfectly for Lear's confrontation with his daughters. Here, the audience witnesses power shifting in the moment-to-moment process of their interactions, intensified by reiteration of the linguistic devices of the first scene. Once emotional appeals fail, the 'contractual obligation' becomes Lear's only source of power: *"But kept a reservation to be followed/ With such a number*." This might be reasonable had it been negotiated but it was a hasty dictate occasioned by Cordelia's banishment. Gonoril and Regan's suggestion that, if he resides in their households, their servants can look after him would also be reasonable if it did not ignore the context. Turning the tables on Lear is, however, nothing to do with reason, but about raw power.

In this scene, Lear reaches the limit of his ability to dictate terms unilaterally. Thereafter his use of authority and power takes the form of parody as the 'trial' of his daughters vividly illustrates. The confrontation over how many followers Lear can have at either daughter's home, is a battle over who has the power to decide. This scene echoes the first in the way that 'love' is reduced to quantification, with Lear's declaration that the daughter who loves him most will allow him the greatest number of men: "*Thy fifty yet doth double five and twenty. And thou art twice her love.*" For Lear, his followers are the only remaining symbol of his status. Criticism of their behaviour is a personal attack on him: "*My train are men of choice and rarest parts.*" The importance of followers as markers of status is reinforced by Lear's attack on Oswald – "*Out varlet from my sight*" – and his repeated question: "*How came my man i'th' stocks?*" Cornwall is quick to remind Lear of who now wields power: "*I set him there sir; but his own disorders/Deserved much less advancement.*"

As they engage in a symmetrical escalation over the number of men Lear is or is not entitled to keep, it becomes obvious that Gonoril and Regan have their father utterly at their mercy. He has tried and failed to divide them. The twin axes of reason and emotion are evoked by the participants in an inversion of usual gendered representations as Lear becomes increasing overwhelmed by impotent rage and distress. Regan and Gonoril, having assumed control can use reason to devastating effect:

> Gonoril "*What need you five-and-twenty, ten, or five,*
>
> *To follow in a house where twice so many*
>
> *Have a command to tend you*"
>
> Regan "*What needs one?*" (vii. 419–422)

Those without power are more likely to resort to emotional rhetoric rather than reason; hence the raw appeal of Lear's outburst: "*Oh reason not the need!*" when he finally realises that he is 'outnumbered' and defeated. The association of weakness and vulnerability with femininity: "*O, let not women's weapons, water drops/ Stain my man's cheeks*" is vividly evoked by the high falsetto Paul Scofield produces at the end of this speech in Peter Brook's film.[17] Lear initially pleads for his daughters to recognise his vulnerability: "*But for true need,*" moves into self-pitying pleas to higher powers: "*You see me here, you gods, a poor old fellow*" and rebounds again into rage and invective: "*No you unnatural hags/ I will have such revenges on you both. . . .*" No discourse can be sustained because each threat or plea evokes a vision of terrifying helplessness. Lear has reached the limits of his confrontation with the opposing polarities of control and vulnerability and, in this paradoxical world, madness seems to be the only recourse: "*Oh fool, I shall go mad.*"

At this point in the play, the private language of personal bonds and duties gives way to that of brutal power politics and warfare. A transfer of power, voluntarily embarked upon, has now been redefined as violent usurpation which demands retribution: "*These injuries the King now bears will be revenged home. There's a part of a power already landed.*" Both Lear and Gloucester are now cast as traitors, with the greater fury displaced onto Gloucester. Soon after Lear, their common 'enemy' is neutralised, the sisters turn on each other and this throws their different relationships with their husbands into sharp relief. The "*division betwixt the Dukes*" is named but never explained; however, the conflict between their values and approaches becomes increasingly evident. Regan and Cornwall can be seen as 'partners in crime,' encouraging each other, with evident relish, in escalating acts of cruelty. Gonoril and Albany, on the other hand, never act in concert and their own interests and values rapidly diverge as the play progresses. While both sisters are presented by Shakespeare as monstrous, it is worth reflecting on some nuances in their otherwise unremittingly 'diabolical' portrayal.

The audience witnesses Lear's vicious and largely unprovoked verbal assaults on Gonoril. As ever there are ambiguities: in instructing Oswald to "*put on weary negligence*" she humiliates her father in front of his knights. Depending on how the knights are portrayed, she either has good cause to complain about their behaviour or exaggerates it. In Peter Brook's film, both Lear and his knights wreak absolute havoc, overturning furniture and hurling it into the palace courtyard.[18] But the nature of her complaining is civilised. She does not abuse him and she even appeals to his better self: "*These dispositions that of late transform you/ From what you rightly are.*" Whatever she says, however, the context of the relationship counts more than the content of her speech. It is when Albany enters that Lear, thinking perhaps that he has a male ally, launches into the most vitriolic abuse of Gonoril: "*And from her derogate body never spring/ A babe to honour her.*" Albany witnesses all this but makes no move to defend his wife other than a few placatory gestures to Lear. Even when she asks him directly "*Do you mark that, my lord?*" he replies equivocally: "*I cannot be so partial, Gonoril,/ To the great love I bear you.*"

That Gonoril has first-hand experience of being diminished and disrespected by two men, might just have some bearing on her later behaviour, when she rounds on Albany for being "*milk livered*" and "*a moral fool.*" Clearly she has studied at the Lear school of invective. In scene 16, when Albany condemns her behaviour towards her father, she attacks his masculinity: "*Marry your manhood, mew.*" There is an echo here of her father's readiness to respond to any evidence of her strength or power as an assault on his masculinity: "*I am ashamed/ That thou hast power to shake my manhood thus.*" Her line: "*Fools do those villains pity who are punished/ Ere they have done their mischief*" could be read as the hyper-alertness to threat learnt by those with long histories of being abused or humiliated. What drives Gonoril to murder her sister and to plan her husband's death is, however, her infatuation with Edmund, whose "*Yours in the ranks of death*" she might have hoped would signify a man finally prepared to put her first and help her escape "*my hateful life.*" This provides a credible background to her terror of losing him to the newly widowed Regan. Regan's portrayal is even less nuanced; often played as drunk on either alcohol or sadism, her presentation as 'empty surface' is prefigured in her speech in the 'succession scene' which is impoverished linguistically compared to her older sister's:

> "*I find she names my very deed of love – /Only she came short.*"

In the rivalry over Edmund, Regan is shown to be as driven by envy of Gonoril as much as by any passion of her own: "*Why should she write to Edmund? . . . And more convenient is he for my hand/ Than for your lady's.*"

Witnessing the abuse of Gonoril by her father, we can create a narrative about her resentment and vengefulness. Her story reflects the power of past patterns to influence the present. Regan's demonstrates the headiness and excitement *in* the present that comes from seizing power. While Gonoril's desires, values and actions are presented as in sharp contrast to her husband's, thereby emphasising her individuality, Shakespeare has chosen to portray Regan as totally enmeshed with Cornwall. They act in concert, encouraging and escalating each other's rhetoric and actions.

> Cornwall "*Fetch forth the stocks!*
>
> *As I have life and honour, there shall he sit till noon.*"

Regan "*Till noon? – till night, my lord, and all night too.*" (vii.126–128)

Cornwall "*Cunning,*"

Regan "*And false.*" (xiv.47)

Regan is also provided, especially in scene 7, with perfectly timed, brief and poisonous interjections which highlight the heady release resulting from such profound transfers of power:

Kent "*Why, madam, if I were your father's dog/You could not use me so*"

Regan "*Sir, being his knave, I will*" (128–130)

Regan "*I pray you, father, being weak, seem so*" (358)

Lear "*I gave you all*"

Regan "*And in good time you gave it*" (407–408)

Gonoril apparently continues to feel oppressed by a man who despises her, but Regan expresses the sheer fun and pleasure of being out from under the yoke of her father's tyranny. In her relationship with Cornwall, there are no openings, as there are between Gonoril and Albany, for disagreement or alternative moral positions. In their brutal mutilation of Gloucester, they act in complete harmony. This provides a vacancy for a position of moral protest. It emerges in the form of Cornwall's own servant, a man "*that he bred*" who, with extraordinary courage, challenges his patron to desist:

"*Hold your hand, my lord.*

I have served you since I was a child

But better service have I never done you

Than now to bid you hold" (xiv.69–72)

Justifying his disobedience to Cornwall, this servant redefines the very nature of service as being to teach his lord a moral lesson. He thus challenges the feudal social order, which both Cornwall and Regan immediately reassert, calling him "*dog,*" "*villein*" and "*peasant.*"

Putting morality above feudal loyalty and his own safety, the unnamed servant, stabbed by Regan, pays for his intervention with his life. However, in the process, he has not only fatally wounded Cornwall but also opened up space for other members of the servant class to voice disgust and protest.

Second servant "*I'll never care what wickedness I do If this man come to good*"

Third Servant "*If she live long*

And in the end meet the old course of death

Women will all turn monsters." (xiv.97–100)

The significance of these actions and responses are sometimes overlooked by those critics who try to find 'goodness' in the play but tend not to consider servants; turning instead to Cordelia to glimpse "beyond the chaotic horror, something of infinite sweetness that we cannot fully comprehend."[19]

Masters, mistresses and servants

The 'family' of masters and servants in *King Lear* is often ignored even by those critics most concerned to present the play as implicitly committed to equality, mutuality and co-operation, rather than division, domination and exploitation. In *King Lear,* however, Shakespeare eschews any such polarisation and virtually always offers exceptions, however small, to dominant narratives. From the servants' revolt at Cornwall's cruelty, to the tender application of *"flax and whites of eggs"* to Gloucester's bleeding face,[20] servants offer glimpses of human kindness, courage and attentiveness that provide another dimension again to the actions of the 'good' characters of Kent, Cordelia and Edgar or the morally outraged but ineffectual Albany. They add texture to the play's work in undermining or rupturing cherished ideologies. As moral orders collapse from 'above', alternative moral positions are glimpsed from 'below.'

Cornwall's servant's action was an anomaly since servants have a vested interest in being seen as loyal, as the disguised Kent recognises: "*I do profess to be no less than I seem, to serve him truly that will put me in trust.*" He proves this to Lear immediately by humiliating Oswald and Lear is quick to respond: "*I thank thee, fellow. Thou serv'st me, and I'll love thee.*" Lear's other servants who have an interest both in being maintained in their numbers and in seeing their master's status respected, are quick to draw his attention to their inferior conditions in Gonoril's household:

Servant ..."*to my judgement your highness is not entertained with that ceremonious affection as you were wont. There's a great abatement appears as well in the general dependants as in the Duke himself also, and your daughter.*" (iv.53–55)

Servants are of necessity acute readers of power relations and their treatment is in turn a marker of the workings of power. Additionally, servants, as we have seen, may take up positions on behalf of their masters or mistresses. This is demonstrated in the otherwise absurd fight between Kent and Oswald, instigated by Kent to teach Oswald to show due deference to the king: *"You . . . take Vanity the puppet's part against the royalty of her father."* Kent, whose role seems primarily to act as a defender of the feudal order, performs a caricature of a simple bluff fellow, hurling insults at the bewildered Oswald but also revealing a heartfelt sense of his own loss of status as well as Lear's. Oswald's presumptions and apparent lack of respect for social distinctions – *"That such a slave as this should wear a sword"* – thus have a double significance; they are seen to disrespect both Lear himself and his servant. In this scene, much as in Lear's 'trial' of Gonoril and Regan, the clash between the ideologies of unquestioned feudal authority and of aggressive individualism (with its attendant opportunists such as Oswald) is played out through parody.

Kent's response to being put in the stocks by Cornwall is to draw attention to the insult it purveys to his master, the no-longer-king whom continuing to name as such carries political intent:

> Kent "*Call not your stocks for me. I serve the King, On whose employment I was sent to you. You should do small respect.*" (vii.124–126)

Gloucester's remonstration that Lear will *"take it ill"* is countered by Regan in another reminder that reconfigurations of power also apply to servants:

> "*My sister may receive it much more worse*
>
> *To have her gentleman abused, assaulted*
>
> *For following her affairs.*" (vii.141–143)

Oswald is presented as a different kind of servant to the disguised Kent, taken into the confidence of his mistress, as Regan says: *"I know you are of her bosom."* He is fiercely loyal to her but with a constant eye for his own advantage, perhaps having designs on her of his own This scenario for male servants has already been described by Edgar/Tom: *"A serving man, proud in heart and mind, that curled my hair, wore gloves in my cap, served the lust of my mistress' heart and did the act of darkness with her"* (xi.76–78).

Sex and violence

As well as alluding to the rupturing of social hierarchies, Tom's speech draws upon the trope of predatory and dangerous female sexuality, so strong in the portrayal of Gonoril and Regan and so floridly captured in the psychotic language of Lear:

> *"Down from the waist*
>
> *They're centaurs, though women all above.*
>
> *But to the girdle do the gods inherit*
>
> *Beneath is all the fiend's There's hell, there's darkness*
>
> *There's the sulphury pit, burning, scalding*
>
> *Stench, consummation."* (xx.119–124)

This speech immediately follows Lear's encounter with Gloucester and his reminder of Gloucester's adultery: "*What was thy cause? /Adultery? Thou shall not die for adultery.*" Its juxtaposition illustrates the way that representations of male fear and revulsion at women's sexuality are reinforced and intensified by being repeated in the two families. Violence as well as uncontained and unregulated sexuality is also a theme that crosses between both families. The most violent acts are perpetrated by the younger generation in each family against the patriarch in the other. It is Cornwall and Regan who put out Gloucester's eyes, having kindly spared Edmund's supposed squeamishness: "*The revenges we are bound to take upon your traitorous father are not fit for your beholding.*" It is Edmund, not Gonoril or Regan, who orders the deaths of Lear and Cordelia; although they are said to *seek his death*, he acts on these desires. This displacement and distancing of murderous intra-familial and intergenerational feelings, rather than being located only in the dysfunctional dynamics of the individual families, brings into more intense focus the extremes to which parent/child enactments of revenge, rage, love and loyalty can go.

"Is this the promised end?" Closure or inconclusiveness?

King Lear treats the audience to a series of reversals where every 'taken for granted' category of gender, generation, custom and social position is upended. Alongside this, however, is Shakespeare's tantalising encouragement of the fantasy of restoration of an ordered world, a fantasy which is then snatched away. Three consecutive scenes highlight these conflicting narrative possibilities and their tone could hardly be more different. By scene 16, Oswald has provided Gonoril with a vivid description of her husband Albany's state of mind:

"*Madam within; but never man so changed*
I told him of the army that was landed;
He smiled at it. I told him you were coming;
His answer was 'The worse.' Of Gloucester's treachery
And of the loyal service of his son
When I informed him, then he called me sot,
And told me I had turned the wrong side out.
What he should most defy seems pleasant to him;
What like, offensive." (xvi. 3–11)

Albany's world is, it seems, in as confused a state as Lear's and Gloucester's. Appalled that his wife flouts the laws of filial loyalty – "*That nature which contemns it origin,*" – and that she confounds propriety both as a woman and as a daughter, he castigates her:

"*What have you done?*
Tigers not daughters, what have you performed?
A father, and a gracious, agèd man,
Whose reverence even the head-lugged bear would lick,
Most barbarous, most degenerate have you madded." (xvi.38–42)

After the news of Cornwall's death, Gloucester's mutilation and Edmund's treachery, the scene ends with Albany apparently swearing vengeance:

"*Gloucester, I live*
To thank thee for the love thou showed'st the King,
And to revenge thy eyes." (xvi.93–95)

Although four scenes later he leads the attack on the army protecting Lear and Cordelia, the possibility that Albany might avenge Gloucester and Lear's ill treatment creates in the following two scenes the possibility for healing within family relationships.

In these scenes we could be back in the domain of fairy tales where the spurned good daughter will effect a rescue, aided and abetted by the disguised loyal servant.[21] The possibility of rescue is first raised in scene 8 when Kent sends the first gentleman to Dover with a letter for Cordelia and is kept in play by Lear's conveyance there. The flimsiness of this plot is, however, expressed by the unusually stultified language of scene 17, from the clumsy explanation for France's departure to the trite sentimentality of the first gentleman's depiction of Cordelia as an unworldly saint: "*There she shook/The holy water from her heavenly eyes.*"

In the following scene, Cordelia's discourse is suffused with the language of healing:

> "*All blest secrets,*
>
> *All you unpublished virtues of the earth,*
>
> *Spring with my tears, be aidant and remediate*
>
> *In the good man's "distress!"* (xviii.16–19)

This can of course be seen as intensifying the moral differences between Cordelia and her sisters, but there are other levels at play. Cordelia expresses love and loyalty but takes it to the extreme by her virtual obliteration of self. She acts as if the absolute domain of love can triumph over material reality. Her final speech in scene 18, when she has been advised that the "*British powers are marching hitherward,*" recreates the confusion between personal and political domains that proved so lethal in the opening scenes:

> "*O dear father,*
>
> *It is thy business that I go about...*
>
> *No blown ambition doth our arms incite*
>
> *But love dear love, and our aged father's right.*" (xviii.26–29)

This expressed motivation for joining battle leads Cordelia to disregard the political context, especially the likelihood that an invading foreign army will be resisted, as Albany makes clear:

> "*It touches us as France invades our land;*
>
> *Yet bold's the King, with others whom I fear,*
>
> *Most just and heavy causes make oppose.*" (xxii.27–29)

While realpolitik organises even the indecisive Albany, it fades away in the opposing camp. The airbrushing of France himself leaves dramatic space for the moving reunion between Lear and his youngest daughter and for their subsequent imprisonment together. However, Cordelia's certainty leads her to eschew strategy to preserve 'genuine love.' In the eve-of-battle scene, positioning herself solely in the domain of private emotion means occluding the physical danger she and her father are in. The virtual obliteration of Cordelia's identity as queen of a foreign country and her re-entry into her father's world where she can only serve his emotional needs is encapsulated in the bizarre stage direction at the beginning of scene 23: "*The powers of France pass over the stage (led by) Queen Cordelia with her father in her hand.*" The audience can be so moved by the poignancy of Cordelia's reunion with Lear that we too forget the wider context of the play as Shakespeare juxtaposes scenes of bleakness, cruelty and despair with those which seem to offer hope, healing and redemption, hinting at a "*promised end*" in which 'good' will triumph. But in the process he exposes these as naïve illusions.

Ambiguity is further heightened by the way that the two parent/child reunion scenes are juxtaposed. In the battle scene, each parent is 'led' by a child. Each reunion is, however, witnessed or narrated in subtly different ways. Cordelia's 'healing narrative' contrasts with the morally instructive discourse of Tom/Edgar when, leaving Gloucester at the supposed cliff edge, he states his reason for maintaining the subterfuge: "*Why I do trifle thus with his despair/Is done to cure it.*" After the choreographed 'fall' he counsels his father: "*Bear free and patient thoughts.*" Later on, after the defeat of Cordelia's army, Edgar employs biblical language, reinforcing his position as a moral arbiter: "*What, in ill thoughts again?/Men must endure/ Their going hence even as their coming hither.*" At this stage Edgar has still not revealed himself to his father. He takes control of the decision about when to disclose his identity and narrates the moment when he does so. By contrast, in the reunion between Lear and Cordelia, she eagerly awaits *his* recognition and proceeds to enact the loving and sacrificial female role that her father has always expected of her:

> Lear "*You have some cause; they have not*"
>
> Cordelia "*No cause, no cause*" (xxi.72–73)

The audience has only Edgar's report of how he revealed his identity:

> *"Never-O father!-revealed myself unto him*
>
> *Until some half hour past, when I was armed.*

Not sure, though hoping, of this good success,
I Asked his blessing, and from first to last
Told him my pilgrimage; but his flawed heart –
Alack, too weak the conflict to support –
'Twixt two extremes of passion, joy and grief
Burst smilingly." (xxiv.189–196)

Being confronted with Edgar, previously a bedlam beggar, now armed and asking his father's blessing to kill his other son, might indeed have left Gloucester keen to depart this earth. Cordelia, still respectful of her father's authority, despite his infirmity, puts emotional attachment above instrumentality. Edgar, having his father totally under his control, is more judgemental and more expedient. Gendered narratives assert themselves with Cordelia yielding power to her father and Edgar exerting it over his. Cordelia relies on the doctor's advice and, once she and Lear are captured, she does what her father tells her. Although an earlier version of *King Lear* has Cordelia and Edgar marrying at the end, Shakespeare provides them with very different fates. Cordelia is hanged and her death even provides a heroic narrative for Lear in the midst of his despair: "*I killed the slave that was a-hanging thee.*" Edgar kills his brother in a duel and is likely to succeed to the kingdom.

Neither Cordelia nor Edgar has lines to express their reaction to their fathers' betrayal of them, but each performs very differently the part of the 'child' who has been wronged. By providing alternative narratives of reconciliation and forgiveness, Shakespeare reminds us that they do not lie in individual personality traits nor in some abstract idea about reconciliation, but are enacted within specific relationship contexts where 'noble' self-sacrificing narratives may not be all they appear to be.

Conclusion

King Lear is a tragedy that undermines stable meanings and confounds false dichotomies such as mind and body or sanity and insanity in a way that is both disturbing and liberating. Its radical potential lies in the way that it interrogates and undermines the beliefs that hold hierarchy in place. It also lies in the fleeting visions the play provides of a more just and equitable world. The sense that these alternative visions are out of reach is reinforced by the belief some protagonists convey that, through the strength of their emotions and the power of their words, they can transcend their material contexts. Lear and Gloucester in the storm and Dover cliffs scenes show the same desire to slip free from material or bodily bonds: "*This tempest in my mind/ Doth from my senses take all feeling else*" and "*I have no way and therefore want no eyes.*"

At the end of *King Lear*, Albany and Edgar are left in a state of bewilderment with Albany desperately searching for someone to take up the reins of power only to have Lear die and Kent presumably bent on suicide. His conclusion that they must now

> "*Speak what we feel, not what we ought to say*
>
> *The oldest have borne most. We that are young*
>
> *Shall never see so much nor live so long*" (xxiv.319–321)

is ambiguous to say the very least.

Two aspects of the play's inconclusiveness are relevant for therapists. We have to hold in tension our hopes for better outcomes for those who are suffering but also maintain a respect for the 'dark side' that undermines hope. For psychoanalysts this tension is mainly contained within the individual psyche; for systemic therapists, as well as consider how the past influences individual world views, the impact of the context is all-important. This context includes the therapeutic conversation. Systemic therapists are alert to moments when individuals or families are able, however briefly, to act in ways that challenge the dominant narrative. These moments occur in *King Lear,* as I have argued, in individual acts of kindness, courage or self-sacrifice and through the insertion of potentially healing narratives. In the play they conspicuously fail to have any impact on the outcome but we can all be effected by our desire that they will. The temptation to turn these 'golden moments' into a coherent narrative may however exist more in our own heads than in the context. Among the many riches that *King Lear* offers us is the challenge to hold in parenthesis our own desired 'promised ends.' In aiming for intelligibility and meaning-making, we also need to pay attention to those aspects of language and experience that resist tidy categorisation and whose meanings are contested, fractured and evolving. If experiences of fragmentation and madness arise in the gap between the signifying systems of different worlds, this teaches us to be humble about those aspects of human experience that, however hard we try to understand them, are always beyond our grasp.

Notes

1 Felicity Rosslyn, *Tragic Plots: A New Reading from Aeschylus to Lorca* (Aldershot: Ashgate, 2000), 131.
2 Jonathan Dollimore, *Radical Tragedy* (Basingstoke: Palgrave Macmillan, Third Edition, 2004), 50.
3 Mikhail Bakhtin, *Problems of Dostoevsky's Poetics* (Minneapolis: University of Minnesota Press, 1984), 196–197.
4 Janet Adelman, *Suffocating Mothers: Fantasies of Maternal Origin in Shakespeare's Plays, 'Hamlet' to 'The Tempest'* (New York and London: Routledge, 1992).
5 Gregory Bateson, *Steps to an Ecology of Mind* (St Albans: Paladin, 1973).
6 Janet Adelman, *Suffocating Mothers: Fantasies of Maternal Origin in Shakespeare's Plays, 'Hamlet' to 'The Tempest'* (New York and London: Routledge, 1992).
7 Coppelia Kahn, 'The Absent Mother in King Lear', in Kiernan Ryan, ed., *King Lear* (Basingstoke: Palgrave Macmillan, 1993).
8 Gregory Bateson, *Steps to an Ecology of Mind* (St Albans: Paladin, 1973).
9 Terry Eagleton, *William Shakespeare* (Oxford: Basil Blackwell, 1986), 78.
10 Alessandro Serpieri, 'The Breakdown of Medieval Hierarchy in King Lear', in John Drakakis, ed., *Shakespearean Tragedy* (London: Longman, 1992), 89.
11 Ibid., 88–89.
12 Ibid., 90.
13 Royal Shakespeare Company, Courtyard Theatre, Stratford upon Avon, 2007.
14 Terry Eagleton, 'Language and Value in King Lear', in Kiernan Ryan, ed., *King Lear* (Basingstoke: Palgrave Macmillan, 1993), 89.
15 Stephen Greenblatt, *Learning to Curse* (New York: Routledge, 1990), 123.
16 Ibid., 124.
17 King Lear, directed by Peter Brook (Columbia Pictures, 1971).
18 Ibid.
19 Anthony Nuttall, *Shakespeare, the Thinker* (New Haven and London: Yale University Press, 2007), 312.
20 This account only appears in the Oxford World Classics quarto text. It does not appear in the Folio text.
21 Catherine Belsey, *Why Shakespeare?* (Basingstoke: Palgrave Macmillan, 2007).

CHAPTER 5

"And yet how nature, erring from itself"

Racism, gender and intimate violence in *Othello*

Two quotations from Othello and Desdemona illustrate their different places in the social world of Venice and their individual ways of narrating this difference. Desdemona says: *"I saw Othello's visage in his mind,"* and Othello says *"For she had eyes and chose me."* For Othello, his image in Desdemona's eyes initially acts as reassurance that she accepts him despite the exclusionary norms and practices of Venice. Desdemona, at the same time as flouting these norms, reveals, by her occlusion of Othello's outward appearance, how much she continues to be captured by them. These different constructions of the relationship are a vital subtext; they form a key part of its currency and they intensify the fears and misunderstandings that ultimately destroy it. They are reflected through many other images of inner and outer 'realities' that the protagonists respond to in ever more divergent ways as the play progresses.

Othello is suffused with references to what is seen and what is hidden, to what lies behind an 'honest' surface, to claims to 'know' the secret thoughts and practices of others, to the demand for *"ocular proof"* of betrayal. Referents for inner and outer domains, to outside appearances and hidden internal states are also couched in the language of blackness and whiteness, thus creating many levels at which representations of race and processes of racism can be explored.

Of all Shakespeare's plays, *Othello* most clearly challenges audiences to engage with the politics and practices of representation. It cannot be produced, acted in, watched or read without some shadows of its performance history looming, sharpened by changing understandings of race and racism from Shakespeare's own time through the eras of colonialism and post-colonialism. As well as reflect the historical processes through which racism has been evaded, occluded or highlighted, the appropriation of *Othello* as cultural icon intensifies the play's particularly reflexive quality, inviting the audience to question our own participation or collusion in the unfolding drama. This participation exists in the physical as well as the psychological domain since "performance history offers more examples of audience interruption of *Othello* than of any other Shakespeare play."[1]

The play's capacity to perturb and incite in this way lies partly in its blurring of boundaries between performers and audience, most notably in Iago's tendency to invite the audience into a state of complicity, compelling us to engage with his perspective however much we are repelled by it. Iago has more lines and more soliloquies than Othello, and in most modern productions his character dominates, thus positioning Othello as the object of his manipulations.

Audience complicity is also intensified by what Lynda Boose calls a 'pornographic aesthetic' in *Othello*.[2] The audience is titillated by a voyeuristic imagining of Othello and Desdemona's bedroom, revealed in the final act as a site of sexual violence. Each moment of sexual consummation between Othello and Desdemona is disrupted, first by the call to the Senate and then by Cassio's drunken rampage; so a sense of frustrated voyeurism is heightened. Boose also refers to the regular iteration of the words 'look,' 'watch,' and 'see,' which have been, "throughout the play directed towards an increasingly sexualised image, yet an image that, until that final act, has been available only through the participatory act of imagining it."[3] In a reversal of Desdemona's position as 'unseen' observer to Brabantio and Othello's conversations, Othello listens 'unseen' to Cassio and Iago as they discuss Cassio's supposed sexual dalliance with Desdemona.

Othello's insistence on 'objective proof' of betrayal paradoxically leads him further into the realms of fantasy and confusion in which relationships are increasingly distorted and misinterpreted. Pronouncements of love, hatred, loyalty and derision emerge in ways that seem quite inappropriate to the occasion, often signifying the opposite of what the context seems to call for. The manipulation and destruction of relationships in *Othello* is underscored by the manipulation and misappropriation of language, opening up semantic as well as emotional confusion.[4] In *Othello,* these core tensions are given a richer texture by the iteration of other imagery. Among them is the language of place. Metaphors of 'place'; of being out of it, searching for it, or being falsely secure within it suffuse the text as do rank and position and the effects of losing them. When Othello receives notification from Venice that he is to be recalled and *"Cassio shall have my place,"* this displacement is connoted as both political and sexual.

Processes of displacement thus occur at many psychic and relational levels and can also be seen as a unifying theme of Iago's resentment, whether it is social, sexual or psychological. Many varieties of loss of place or usurpation of place form the backdrop to depictions of states of confusion and uncertainty, the overwhelming emotional impact of which is akin for Othello to being *"set upon the rack."* This uncertainty thrives on the play's many enigmas, contradictions and evasions, which place the audience, primed by Iago, into an uneasy state of collusion. As many commentators have pointed out, this is the standard form of comedy.[5] It helps explain why no matter how many times I see *Othello* performed, I still find myself longing for a different outcome where, as in comedy, all can be revealed in time for it to be healed. In this way the tragic nature of the play is actually heightened by its comedic structure.

Othello is often described as a play in which characters engage in story telling of different kinds, what Stephen Greenblatt describes as 'narrative self-fashioning.' While Iago's stories develop as a result of conscious improvisation, the identity of the more fragile Othello depends on constant performance of his story.[6] All these stories are situated within the orbit of the story that Venice tells about itself, within its world of waxing and waning powers and its linked unease about the tropes of 'civilisation' and 'barbarism.' The state's power to determine which stories will prevail is vigorously reasserted at the end of the play when, despite Othello's dying efforts, it is clear who will narrate his downfall.

Othello is set almost entirely within the confined and yet unstable space of Cyprus, the island of Aphrodite, goddess of love. This space is geographically and metaphorically situated between the Venetian state and the Turkish enemy who represent 'otherness' and a constant underlying threat to reason and discipline: *"are we all turned Turks?"* Even this space is ambiguous; on the one hand it is a military garrison, far removed from the sophisticated urban life of Venice. On the other hand, the action in Cyprus unfolds around a wide-ranging and adventurous hero, Othello, now confined within a domestic space. Anthony Nuttall describes him as "a hero who went into a house."[7] Thus, both Othello and Desdemona are displaced and much of their seemingly destructive interaction can be understood as their increasingly frantic attempts to re-establish the security of attachment and identification.

As I have argued, many of Shakespeare's plays reflect the subtle ways that power enters into discourse and shapes intimacy. Protagonists can be seen to employ covert as well as overt practices of power as they strive to maintain their positions in relationships. The richness of *Othello* lies in the variety of ways in which this dynamic is played out. Contexts of race, religion, gender and class create a vibrant dynamic that suffuses the relationship between, on the one hand, the omnipotent posturing of Iago and, on the other, the uneasiness of Othello, anxiously reading himself against the norms and expectations of others. Desdemona, while incontrovertibly a victim of violence at the end of the play, is, for much of it, actively claiming agency and entitlement for herself. It is partly the extremes to which these processes lead that give the play its powerful emotional drive.

Race and performance dilemmas

While performance history is not a focus of this book, in the case of *Othello* it seems important to explore it briefly since questions of casting, staging and performance have been so contested. These stem both from the play's subject matter and its singularly reflexive and 'audience aware' qualities. It is also beset by a tendency for the roles of Iago and Othello to be seen as in opposition to each other so that a dominant performance in one weakens the impact of the other. One of the paradoxes of *Othello's* performance history is the inverse relationship between the occluding or foregrounding of race and the respective dominance of the roles of Othello and Iago. This paradox highlights a history in the previous century of casting the most well-known white actors in the key role (Paul Robeson and John Kani being notable exceptions), whether it be Othello or Iago. When white actors played Othello, the theme of a noble man brought down by the 'fatal flaw' of jealousy tended to prevail, in which case his character could dominate. But, while racial stereotyping was rampant, as in Lawrence Olivier's performance, racism itself was sidelined.[8]

In recent years, with racism more likely to be placed at the forefront, the role of Iago, embodying that very racist practice, has tended to dominate.

This can pose a challenge for black actors to find ways of portraying Othello as other than Iago's increasingly frenetic dupe. Michael Neill argues that

> even as aesthetic and political pressures converged to make the casting of white actors in the lead role appear increasingly undesirable, black actors themselves were repeatedly disabled by fear of the racial stereotyping that might ensue from a full commitment to the emotional excess and extravagant theatricality of the part.[9]

On the other hand, black actors playing a restrained and dignified Othello run the risk of being over-shadowed by Iago and the play thus becomes more a study of Iago's villainy than of racial conflict. This dominance of Iago creates such challenges to new interpretations of the play that Toni Morrison, discussing her re-imagining of *Othello* through Desdemona's childhood with an African nurse, Barbary, declared firmly: "the first rule is: 'No Iago!' "[10]

Foregrounding race has met with different kinds of resistance from some critics who reject its inevitably political overtones in favour of the universals of "spite, gullibility, innocence and green-eyed rage."[11] Part of the problem is a tendency to isolate one theme as being what a play is 'really about.' Thus, productions that foreground race are responded to as if they rule out other dimensions, thus limiting directorial creativity. Adrian Lester, who played the part in the 2013 National Theatre production, rebuts simplistic attributions of Othello's actions to his colour:

> He doesn't kill his wife because he's black, he isn't jealous because he's black. So you take off that preoccupation, the tragedies of Othello and Desdemona and Iago live a little more because they have their own colour, and not the one colour we've washed the play with for so many flipping years.[12]

Contemporary critics can seem almost relieved when race is sidelined. Susannah Clapp writes of the same production: "It pulls off, almost casually, a major reinterpretation, batting away the notion that Shakespeare's drama is dominated by racism."[13] However, the assumption that viewing the play in the context of race means stifling all other emotional or contextual perspectives is mistaken. Another comment from Adrian Lester about Othello's tendency towards self-consciousness and bombast in his speech is enlightening:

> It is as if he's hearing the sound of his voice as he speaks. So I thought "why can't I be unselfconscious and get into the character?" But then I realised

> it's because the character is self-conscious, at which point I thought "just embrace it." He's trying to be this person who has the right to be in charge.[14]

It seems almost wilful to detach this insight from the context of racism, which produces the conditions for precisely this kind of self-monitoring.

I argue that considering racist discourses in the play by no means implies that this is the only lens through which it should be viewed. Racism and other inequities such as gender or class have a tendency to seep into the fibre of intimate relationships, distorting and restricting their possibilities but never, of course, dictating exactly how they will be enacted. There is enough crude racist language in the first half of the play to convince even the most hardened sceptic of its importance; but the extent to which this can be obscured in critical reactions is striking. A recent discussion between psychoanalysts and a renowned Shakespearean actor and director about the character of Iago manages the quite extraordinary feat of never once mentioning race.[15]

Insiders and outsiders

Intersecting with race and with equally nuanced texture and dimensions, the tension between 'insider' and 'outsider' status is a crucial element in *Othello*. 'Uncanny' insider knowledge is juxtaposed with a fatal ignorance of others and their motivations. All positions of insider or outsider are, however, unstable, just as are their signifiers. Othello, whose name is not used until Act 1, scene 3, and is dropped again at the end in favour of 'The Moor,' is an outsider who becomes a quasi-insider on the basis of his military success. Of the other characters, Brabantio, Desdemona, the Duke, Lorenzo, Gratiano and Rodrigo are Venetian and share an insider's sense of class privilege. Cassio, a Florentine, is a well-educated outsider who also exudes a sense of his own entitlement. Iago has an ambiguous status both as an insider (a Moor-killer, a self-appointed expert on Venetian manners and mores, an intimate confidant to the audience) and an outsider (a Spaniard, of lowly status, an "*ancient*"). His claim to be representative is partly convincing because his is the voice of 'common sense,' the constant repetition of the already 'known,' the 'culturally given.' Indeed, the term "*probal to thinking*," used by both Brabantio and Iago conveys just this assumption that their views are mainstream. "Iago's warped response to Othello is not an idiosyncratic aberration (except perhaps in its neurotic intensity) but the attitude shared by Brabantio and Venice in general."[16]

While Shakespeare provides a number of possible motives for Iago's hatred of Othello, none, other than his displacement as lieutenant by Cassio, is more than briefly alluded to and he has Iago tease and tantalise the audience with what might be fuelling it; that Othello has slept with Emilia, that Cassio has slept with Emilia and that he (Iago) really loves Desdemona. This has led, in Coleridge's famous phrase, to a caution against "the motive-hunting of motiveless malignity."[17] However, although no-one in life, let alone in drama, can venture to state what anyone else's 'true' motives are, these unconvincing offerings from Iago can lead audiences or critics in two different directions.

The first, mostly embraced by psychoanalysts, is to search deeper into the inner world of Iago, to his perverted state of mind, his unconscious envy of, or denied sexual longing for, Othello, his desire to enviously attack and destroy all happiness and beauty or his wish to attack the 'primal scene' of intercourse between his own parents. These unconscious 'motivations,' while they do illuminate the processes of projection and displaced envy so powerful in *Othello,* still focus attention on the psychopathology of Iago himself. This has the effect both of diminishing the impact of wider contexts including race, gender and class and of minimising the other relationships in the play.

The alternative is to explore the contexts and the relationships that make it possible for Iago's machinations to achieve such devastating success. In the first scene, Iago 'explains' to Rodrigo his hatred of Othello:

"Three great ones of the city...

Off-capped to him; and, by the faith of man

I know my price, I am worth no worse a place.

But he — as loving his own pride and purposes –

Evades them with a bombast circumstance,

Horribly stuffed with epithets of war;

And in conclusion

Non-suits my mediators. For 'Certes,' says he,

'I have already chose my officer'." (I.i.7–16)

Being passed over for the office of lieutenant in favour of Cassio, a mere *"arithmetician"* and all *"prattle without practice,"* with far less military experience than the battle-hardened Iago, is a slight that continues to rankle throughout the play. The offence seems to be intensified by Iago's clear implication that Othello, despite being a respected general, is not entitled to make this decision. He explains that acceptance of Othello's authority was only an opportunistic stance; *"I follow him to serve my turn upon him."* Iago and Roderigo easily agree that Othello has no real legitimacy or entitlement to his position:

> Roderigo "*What a full fortune does the thick-lips owe! If he can carry't thus?*"

Many of the problematics of race and 'status contradiction' are encapsulated in this exchange, revealing the fragile nature of the authority vested in an outsider like Othello. It is immediately after this exchange that Iago expresses his desire to *"poison his delight"* which could refer either to Brabantio or to Othello himself. For Iago, Othello has overstepped himself twice; first in daring to choose his own lieutenant and second in daring to sleep with a white woman, and not just any white woman but the daughter of a senator who is at the heart of the very establishment from which Iago has just been excluded.

The theme of acceptance and legitimacy is echoed in the contrast between the alacrity with which Othello took at face value Brabantio's acceptance of him – *"Her father loved me, oft invited me"* – and Brabantio's rapid shift from a contemptuous dismissal of Roderigo, to embracing common cause with him against the 'other' who no longer has a name:

> "*Where did'st thou see her – O unhappy girl*
>
> *With the Moor sayst thou?-Who would be a father?* . . .
>
> *O would you had had her!* (1.i.162,174)

This shift from charging Roderigo *"not to hang about my doors"* to speaking as one gentleman to another: *"On, good Roderigo; I will deserve thy pains"* refers to shared class and racial interests that for Brabantio seem self-evident:

> "*The Duke himself,*
>
> *Or any of my brothers of the state*
>
> *Cannot but feel this wrong as 'twere their own;*
>
> *For if such actions may have passage free*
>
> *Bondslaves and pagans shall our statesmen be.*" (1.iii.95–99)

While the Venetian state clearly values Othello, this does not mean it accepts him. Its heavy reliance on him in its military adventures highlights the republic's weakness and points to an ambivalence towards Othello, which his marriage to Desdemona throws into sharp relief. It is unlikely that the other Venetian senators held very different opinions to Brabantio but the need for Othello's services prompts from the duke the more nuanced if equally toxic comment about difference: "*If virtue no delighted beauty lack/Your son-in-law is far more fair than black.*"

In the face of Brabantio's crude reminders of his 'otherness' – "*such a thing as thou*" – Othello draws attention to his service to the Signory, his own royal blood and his previous reluctance to consider marriage. This 'good story' that Othello tells about his love for Desdemona is counteracted by Iago's mercenary motive for Othello's marriage:

> *Faith, he tonight hath boarded a land-carrack:/ If it prove lawful prize, he's made for ever.*

Presumably because of his social class and genteel manners, Othello uses Cassio as a go-between in his wooing of Desdemona, rather than rely on the rougher Iago. Cassio, before he is reduced to depending on Iago for his reinstatement, rarely misses an opportunity to remind him of their difference in class, education and status. "*He speaks home, madam: you may relish him more in the soldier than in the scholar*" and "*The lieutenant is to be saved before the ensign.*"

Othello's awareness that he is only accepted as long as he has "*performed some service to the state*" might lead to anxieties about only being as good as his last battle. The fact that no military action happens after they arrive on Cyprus is therefore significant. Even in the rapturous meeting with Desdemona in Cyprus, there is a sense from his words that this is a summit to be savoured and, in his handling of the fracas involving Cassio, a fear that he will be seen as unable to control his men.

The more insecure Othello becomes, the more he relies upon Iago the 'insider' as a cultural interpreter who 'knows' Venetian mores and the more powerful and reassuring are the bonds of male soldierly solidarity. As the play progresses, these emotional attachments, based on life-saving acts earlier hinted at by Iago "*And I – of whom his eyes had seen the proof/At Rhodes, at Cyprus and on other grounds,/Christened and heathen*" and reaching their apogee in the exchange of vows between them in Act 3, all lay the ground for Othello's distorted and alienating justification for murdering his wife: "*Yet she must die, else she'll betray more men.*"

The comforting sense of 'insider-ness' created by male bonds involves an element of shared titillation and voyeurism, reflecting representations of women in the male imagination from the field of war. Notions of hierarchy, military duty, sexual excitement and sexual anxiety are all exploited to the full in the following exchanges:

Iago "*How 'satisfied' my Lord?*

Would you the supervisor grossly gape on?

Behold her tupped?"

Othello "*Death and Damnation! O!*" (3.ii.396–398)

Iago " . . . *I do not like the office:*

But sith I am entered in this cause so far,

Pricked to't by foolish honesty and love,

I will go on: I lay with Cassio lately. . ." (3.ii.412–415)

Othello "*I will chop her into messes – cuckold me?*

Iago *o tis foul in her*

Othello "*With mine officer*"

Iago "*That's fouler.*" (4.i.193–196)

The actor playing Othello could even risk a complicit snigger in the first dialogue before the full impact of Iago's words hits him. Simon Russell Beale describes how, playing Iago, he wanted to convey the message to Othello: "you know you are enjoying this."[18] However, focussing too heavily on Iago's wiles masks the extent to which Othello himself seeks out his ensign for comfort as well as for the evidence that can end his agonised state of uncertainty. It also reduces our appreciation of the other key relationships in the play.

Gender and power in couple relationships

Although the relationships, of Othello and Iago and Othello and Desdemona sit at the heart of *Othello*, the rich texture of the play requires that we pay attention to the other two: Iago and Emilia and, most importantly, Emilia and Desdemona. Each relationship throws into sharp relief the dynamics of the others.

Othello and Desdemona

Once they arrive in Cyprus, Othello and Desdemona have few opportunities to work out what on earth is going on between them. This would be standard in comedy; here it only intensifies the tragic process. They are only alone together in the 'brothel scene' and the 'death scene.' Unlike the intimate scenes between Othello and Iago, mostly in private and twice as long, Desdemona and Othello's relationship is not one where such conversations, or 'meta-communications,' take place. Even when they were courting, Cassio was their intermediary. Othello never asks Desdemona directly about her relationship with Cassio until he has decided to kill her and she never asks Othello why her attempts at pleading Cassio's case upset him so much. While the time frame of the play has been much debated, we are presented with a couple who hardly know each other and have little awareness of each other's state of mind.

At the outset of the play, the disapproval and crude racism surrounding Othello and Desdemona serve to intensify the audience's appreciation and admiration of their love, commitment and courage. "Othello and Desdemona glory in their free choice" writes Felicity Rosslyn. "Before everything goes wrong, Shakespeare lends this couple the unqualified tenderness of the truly well matched, united in body and spirit."[19] The sense of free choice is underpinned by ideals of racial equality and sexual freedom As tensions in the relationship emerge, orchestrated by Iago to be sure, but, crucially, driven by their own dynamics, the racist language is muted and the emphasis on Desdemona's 'innocence' and purity intensifies. This has the effect of exaggerating Othello's irrationality and brutality, widening the gulf between them so that the mutuality of the early scenes disappears. In the relationship itself it could be seen as a move from an apparent symmetry – exemplified by Desdemona publicly asserting her right to make a free marital choice and by Othello calmly defending his right to woo her – to the complementarity of abuser and victim. When Desdemona tries to restore symmetry, first by challenging Othello in the 'handkerchief scene' and then in speaking to the emissaries from Venice, these are taken up by Othello as challenges to which he responds with violence.

At this crucial turning point in the relationship, Desdemona, hitherto spirited and determined, seems to enter into a dream-like state of passivity and disorientation. Despite this apparent resignation however, she can still be seen as taking up an active moral stance; exonerating Othello's violence and intensifying her commitment to duty and responsibility, trying ever harder to understand his motives and refusing to criticise him.

In the story of Othello and Desdemona it is worth reflecting on what each has given up for the sake of this relationship and in what ways and with what effects do these 'losses' keep appearing in their interactions. Desdemona relinquished her status and social position, her father's love and approval and what might have been a pleasant and privileged, if restricted life in Venice. Like Othello, she was not keen to marry, having shunned "*the wealthy curled darlings of our nation*" and she clearly does not wish to give up the flirtatious, 'merry' and teasing side of her that, in the ambience of Venice, probably involved a degree of dissemblance. This comes to the fore just before Othello lands on Cyprus.

> Desdemona "*Come on assay –. There's one gone to the harbour?*"
>
> Iago "*Ay, Madam*"
>
> Desdemona "*I am not merry; but I do beguile.*
>
> *The thing I am by seeming otherwise.*
>
> *Come, how wouldst thou praise me?*" (2.i.120–124)

On Othello's side, he gave up his hard-won autonomy and freedom:

> "*But that I love the gentle Desdemona,*
>
> *I would not my unhousèd free condition*
>
> *Put into circumscription and confine*
>
> *For the seas' worth.*" (1.ii.25–28)

The cool, controlled and disciplined self that Othello presents to the Venetian world is inevitably unsettled by his passion for Desdemona.

> *And heaven defend your good souls that you think*
>
> *I will your serious and great business scant*
>
> *For she is with me.*" (1.iii.264–266)

Othello's self-worth has been developed though his prowess as a warrior, an identity which conflicts with the desire to lead a full and emotionally committed life. Emotional and sexual commitment involves acceptance both of marital 'bonds' with their uncomfortable echoes of slavery, and of a sexual passion that sits uneasily with disciplined self-control. Iago's words capture this dichotomy: "*his soul is so enfettered to her love.*"

Outside of his soldierly identity, Othello's only sense of security is that of Desdemona's loyalty and fidelity; when he starts to doubt this, an unbearable sense of loss is evoked so that his only recourse is to espouse certainty, however agonising: *"She's gone. I am abused and my relief/ Must be to loathe her."* Although the sight of Desdemona unsettles this certainty, as he reflects on the discrepancy between outward appearances and 'inner realities' – *"If she be false, O then heaven mocks itself/I'll not believe't"* – the need for certainty overrides the misgivings created by Desdemona's innocent appearance. To feel safe, what trust Othello has is transferred to the male soldierly bond, ironically, as we have seen, with Iago himself.

Seeds of unease and lack of trust between Othello and Desdemona can, however, be seen from the play's outset. Their relationship is constructed as an act of rebellion and deception on an easily duped father: *"how got she out?"* The boldness of Desdemona's choice of a man who, while acknowledged to be heroic and noble, is considered unsuitable as a marriage partner, becomes contaminated by imputations of perversity. Othello's qualities of charm and charisma are reconstructed by Brabantio as witchcraft and sorcery, with Desdemona being drugged or subject to *"practices of cunning hell."* The relationship begins with Othello's 'exoticised' narrative, to which Desdemona responds with a mixture of wonderment, vicarious excitement and empathy for his travails. Othello, argues Janet Adelman, narrates

> not his heroic exploits among men but his sufferings in the vast and desolate landscape of maternal abandonment. Thus, re-understood, abandonment becomes the burden of his tale and helps explain both his terrible hunger for Desdemona and the terrible speed with which he believes that she too has abandoned him.[20]

The fragility of 'wooing by story-telling' is ruthlessly captured by Iago as *"mark me with what violence she first loved the Moor, but for bragging and telling fantastical tales. To love him still for prating?"* (2.i.217–219). Othello's own summary that *"She loved me for the dangers I had passed/ And I loved her that she did pity them"* provides a poignant but highly constraining frame for a relationship.

This image of a strong and charismatic but intensely vulnerable man could be the prototype for a dynamic typical of violent relationships.[21] It involves a man investing his female partner with the power to nurture, sustain and unconditionally love him. This supports a fragile sense of self, but it has the corollary that challenging or subverting his control will be seen as transgressive, neglectful or unfaithful. In other words, she must not demonstrate an independent mind. Indications that Desdemona will do exactly that are present from their earliest interactions. Othello's description of how she did *"with a greedy ear/, Devour up my discourse"* could be seen as containing an element of anxiety as does his slight unease that Desdemona has arrived in Cyprus before him: *"It gives me wonder great as my content/. To see you here before me."*

When Desdemona asserts her right to accompany Othello to Cyprus and thereby claim her sexual fulfilment, she does so as an insider, confident on the basis of her social status that she can command the duke's attention:

> *"That I did love the Moor to live with him,*
>
> *My downright violence and storm of fortunes*
>
> *May trumpet to the world....*
>
> *... if I be left behind*
>
> *A moth of peace, and he go to the war*
>
> *The rites for why I love him are bereft me."* (I.iii.246–255)

This evokes an uneasy apologia from Othello who, seemingly reading himself against the discourses of black male sexuality held by most Venetians, is eager to reassure the duke that he does not want Desdemona there *"To please the palate of my appetite/Nor to comply with heat the young affects/In my defunct and proper satisfaction."* Othello can be feted for his military prowess, but when sex is mentioned by Desdemona he has to disown it. He is thus in a bind; in reading himself against a narrative of rampant black male sexuality, as a *"black ram,"* he has to construct himself as virtually impotent. When that rhetorical strategy confronts the racist narrative evoked by Iago that Desdemona must be a sexually licentious woman because her very desire for Othello is perverted, the relationship's fragility is compounded.

An anxiety that, in desiring Othello so fiercely, Desdemona has virtually proved that she is adulterous is linked by Stephen Greenblatt to a strand of Christian doctrine which contends that too ardent sexual love between husband and wife is in itself adulterous and sinful. He argues that this underlies the confessional tone utilised by Othello as he murders Desdemona.[22] Unease about adultery would be intensified for Othello by Brabantio's poisonous and insulting parting shot: *"Look to her, Moor, if thou hast eyes to see/She has deceived her father, and may thee."* Othello initially counters these fears by emphasising his desire to enjoy and appreciate his wife's independent spirit in all its variety:

> *"Tis not to make me jealous*
>
> *To say my wife is fair, feeds well, loves company,*

Is free of speech, sings, plays, and dances well –

Where virtue is, these are more virtuous." (3.iii.186–189)

The other side of this narrative emerged earlier in the same scene as Desdemona describes Cassio's role in their courtship. He not only acted as a go-between, using his gentlemanly attributes to mediate and soften Othello's *"rude speech"* and inexperience of the world outside the battlefield, but Desdemona also highlights the way he countered her own doubts and misgivings:

"*What? Michael Cassio,*

That came a-wooing with you, and so many a time

When I have spoke of you dispraisingly

Hath ta'en your part." (3.iii.71–74)

In this scene, where tensions between the pair are first made overt, Desdemona, having already inserted herself into a 'male world' by listening to Othello's conversations with her father, performs this 'insertion' again when the male world of the military garrison threatens her intimate relationship with Othello. The loss of her previous status and the constraints of the soldierly culture provide the background to Desdemona's pleading for Cassio, attempting to demonstrate that she is indeed *"our captain's captain"* and can bend Othello to her will, using 'male' 'soldierly' language as she does so: *"Come, come you'll never meet a more sufficient man."*

Because Act 3, scene 3, immediately precedes the 'temptation scene' between Othello and Iago, its dramatic impact is muted in many productions to highlight the impact of what follows, as Iago lets loose his poisonous rhetoric. It can however be played as a full-blown row between the couple, with Desdemona accusing Othello of *"mamm'ring on"* and Othello responding with *"Prithee no more"* and *"grant me this/: To leave me but a little to myself."* Already, after the heady excitement of their reunion, Othello has been putting Desdemona off, citing his work, letting her know he will not dine at home. The earlier brief scene shows Othello in professional rather than private mode and he indicates that the transition between the two domains is stressful. He has already warned Desdemona that *"'tis the soldier's life/ To have their balmy slumbers waked with strife."* For Desdemona, undertaking the commission for Cassio is a means of demonstrating that by marrying Othello she still has influence and can wield power. She makes it clear that this influence needs to be demonstrated at a different level to the 'wifely' function of catering to her husband's needs: "*Nay when I have a suit. . . /It shall be full of poise and difficult weight/And fearful to be granted.*"

Rather than being an innocent and subservient Desdemona whose happy relationship with Othello is destroyed by Iago, she is quite prepared to challenge both Othello and their relationship. It is clear from Emilia's earlier account to Cassio that Desdemona could have anticipated Othello's likely reaction since, making a demarcation between public duty and private emotions, he has warned her not to interfere:

> "*The general and his wife were talking of it,*
>
> *And she speaks for you stoutly. The Moor replies*
>
> *That he you hurt is of great fame in Cyprus*
>
> *And great affinity; and that in wholesome wisdom*
>
> *He might not but refuse you. But he protests he loves you*
>
> *And needs no other suitor but his likings.*" (3.i.44–48)

As well as demonstrating Desdemona's desire to assert influence, it can also be seen as another example of 'status contradiction' where Othello's authority now encounters Cassio's entitlement, buttressed by common class identification between him and Desdemona. In dismissing her pleas, Othello can be shown as trying to demonstrate that he will not be 'enslaved' by his marriage. At this moment of potential fracture in the relationship, each draws upon contexts that give them a sense of security and agency. Othello draws upon his rank and position and Desdemona her entitlement to respect and influence.

In Murray Carlin's play, Desdemona is portrayed as the first of the 'white liberals,' treating Othello as a slave who has to obey her to satisfy her pride and honour.[23] Where, however, Desdemona's stance fatally merges with Iago's plot is that her commitment to obedience and duty – which sits in tension with her desire to assert control – leads her to exert this control on behalf of another (Cassio) rather than for herself. In fact, during the whole interchange Desdemona only refers to actions on behalf of men, rather than make any demand for herself.

Othello and Desdemona end their dialogue with her avowals of duty: "*Be as your fancies teach you: /Whate'er you be, I am obedient*" and his declarations of love "*Excellent wretch, perdition catch my soul/ But I do love thee!*" Othello also, however, refers to love's contingency and his own fragility: "*and when I love thee not/Chaos is come again.*" In their next encounter, Othello refuses to allow Desdemona to comfort him. Iago's machinations have already unsettled him; as often in couple relationships when power struggles emerge, we see signifiers of control and dominance co-exist with desires for nurturance and closeness:

Othello "*I have a pain upon my forehead here*"

Desdemona "*Let me but bind it hard, within this hour/ It will be well*"

Othello "*Your napkin is too little.*" (3.iii.287–290)

The conflict between Othello and Desdemona reaches its apotheosis in the 'handkerchief scene.' Again, audiences, primed by the centrality of Iago and aware of his appropriation and misuse of this talisman, may be less alert to the tensions in the relationship that it exposes. Already the handkerchief has become a contested signifier between the couple, with Desdemona seemingly sceptical of Othello's claims for its magical qualities. In contrast to her reaction to Othello's exotic narrative in Act 1, scene 3, this time he only alienates her:

Othello "*To lose't or give't away were such perdition*

As nothing else could match"

Desdemona "*Is't possible?*"

Othello "*Tis true; there's magic in the web of it:*

...The worms were hallowed that did breed the silk,

And it was died in mummy, which the skilful

Conserved of maidens' hearts"

Desdemona "*I'faith, is't true?*"

Othello "*Most veritable; therefore look to't well*"

Desdemona "*Then would to God that I had never seen't!*" (3.iv.66–76)

For Desdemona, now she possesses the man, the object is redundant. For Othello it remains an essential symbol of their union as well as his past.

In the following dialogue the handkerchief becomes the focus of a symmetrical escalation in which each party disqualifies the discursive frame drawn upon by the other. Desdemona, unable to directly ask the question: "What is this all about?" resorts to equivocation and then attempts to recover herself by returning to the toxic subject of Cassio:

Desdemona "*Why do you speak so startingly and rash?*"

Othello "*Is't lost? Is't gone? Speak, is't out o'th way?*"

Desdemona "*Heaven Bless us!*"

Othello "*Say you?*"

Desdemona "*It is not lost; but what an if it were?*"

Othello "*How!*"

Desdemona "*I say it is not lost*"

Othello "*Fetch't. Let me see't*"

Desdemona "*Why, so I can, sir; but I will not now;*

This is a trick to put me from my suit –

Pray you, let Cassio be received again"

Othello "*Fetch me the handkerchief; my mind misgives*"

Desdemona "*Come, come: You'll never meet a more sufficient man –*"

Othello "*The handkerchief!*"

Desdemona "*I pray, talk me of Cassio –*"

Othello "*The handkerchief!*"

Desdemona – "*A man that all his time*

Hath founded his good fortunes on your love,

Shared dangers with you"

Othello "*The handkerchief!*"

Desdemona "*I'faith, you are to blame.*"

Othello "*Swounds!*" *Exit* (3.iv. 78–95)

Beneath this verbal escalation with its crazy dissonances, a clash of two worlds and two belief systems can be seen. For Othello the handkerchief belongs simultaneously to the domain of empirical proof (i.e. of Desdemona's infidelity) but is also replete with mystical significance, with its connection to his mother and to a world he has lost. For Desdemona, while the handkerchief once represented her attachment to Othello and acted as a symbol of his 'exotic' world, it is now a troubling symbol of an aspect of her husband that she prefers not to engage with. Not understanding the emotional significance of the handkerchief nor aware of its new status as 'evidence for the prosecution,' Desdemona, by stubbornly persisting with her pleas for Cassio, fatally misreads the context.

In demanding her recognition of the importance of the symbolic handkerchief, Othello could be seen as desperately trying to find a way back to Desdemona. In Act 4, scene 2, when at his most verbally abusive, he continues to try to evoke her pity. This time he draws upon a common trope in gender politics, closely associated with domestic violence. That is how men's emotional dependence on women is equated with beliefs about women's power, in turn associated with the power of nature. The threatened loss of Desdemona is enough to conjure up for Othello an utterly terrifying image of the loss of the life force itself and he unleashes a flood of self-pity:

(He groans)

"*But there, where I have garnered up my heart*

Where either I must live or bear no life

The fountain from the which my current runs

Or else dries up – to be discarded thence

Or keep it as a cistern for foul toads

To knot and gender in!" (4.ii 57–62)

However, this hyper-charged and semantically fragmented emotional appeal evokes from Desdemona a terse and rational response: "*I hope my noble Lord esteems me honest.*" Her cool reply has to be seen in the context of an encounter in which nothing she says can challenge his position of certainty. The "*smallest fear or doubt of her revolt*" has become 'absolute fact.' Desdemona's denials are further proof of her guilt and duplicity; she is "*the cunning whore of Venice.*" The speed with which 'false evidence' points inexorably in one direction is a common feature of comedy; since this is a tragedy, the process has to be psychologically and relationally credible.

The threat of loss is so terrifying that Othello's whole identity and sanity is at stake, but at the same time it is what he has always known and always anticipated. He has already produced an explanation for Desdemona's supposed infidelity: "*Haply for I am black . . . or for I am declined/Into the vale of years.*" This level of the 'already known,' reinforced by Desdemona's pleas for the younger, better spoken and white Cassio makes plausible the alacrity with which Othello accepts Iago's malign rhetoric and hardens his heart against any protestations from Desdemona. The trajectory of his self-abasing and self-pitying narrative in which loss of Desdemona is conflated with loss of status and of his heroic and military identity startles even his manipulative ensign

Othello "*Farewell! Othello's occupation's gone.*"

Iago "*Is't possible my lord?*"

Again, centring the play primarily on Iago's psychopathy detracts from Othello as subject. When love acts as a protection from chaos, its loss or threatened loss is so painful that loathing is "*my relief.*" Whilst lamenting the loss of his potency and military identity, the soldier Othello responds, as soldiers are primed to do, by resorting to violence.

On Desdemona's part, her progress from combativeness and self-confidence to an almost fugue-like state and a seemingly passive acceptance of her fate can be troubling for audiences and can easily lead either to sentimentality or to irritation. Janet Adelman suggests that, in Desdemona, Shakespeare has created a woman who can be presented as "independent not only of the crime Othello imagines but also of the fantasies that infect it" since she refuses "to turn whore to suit Othello's needs."[24] If the play is read in this way, however, the focus on Othello's inner world leads us away from Desdemona's own subjectivity. Since the audience 'knows' that Desdemona is not guilty of adultery with Cassio, the dramatic change in her position that occurs in Act 4, scene 2, from "*by heaven you do me wrong*" to "*'Tis meet I should be used so, very meet.*" needs to be explored. As Emilia says "*Here's a change indeed.*" The effect of being abused, hit and publicly humiliated could certainly lead Desdemona to shift from submission to Othello through wifely duty to submission to him through fear.

Desdemona also knows only too well the rules and norms for women in the society she lives in, as she so clearly acknowledges in Act 1, scene 3. If fulfilling her duty to her husband is in itself a source of self-esteem, then intensifying this in the face of humiliation is not a sign of weakness but a way of claiming agency in the only way she can. Her position is complex and contradictory; in almost anticipating death at Othello's hands – "*if I should die before thee, prithee shroud me/ In one of these same sheets*" – she might be taking back some power and control in a context of no choice, since Othello is stronger than she and she is unprotected. However, the choice of the wedding sheets may also be an attempt to win Othello back by reminding him of their sexual consummation and her virginity. Again, as the literature on domestic violence shows us, it is very hard for women to give up the belief that they can repair relationships. Desdemona searches under the surface of Othello's cruelty for an internal explanation: his behaviour is due to madness: *"he she loved proved mad,"* or disability *"you're fatal when your eyes roll so . . . why gnaw you so your nether lip/ Some bloody passion shakes your very frame."* When nothing deflects Othello, Desdemona evokes a moral discourse, taking a position above the fray. She has in no way reconciled herself to dying – nowadays she is played as struggling and fighting to stay alive – but she keeps up her dignity to the end, claiming innocence: *"falsely, falsely murdered," "A guiltless death I die,"* even denying that it is Othello who has killed her: *"Nobody – I myself,"* and, hard to say without irony, *"Commend me to my kind lord – Oh farewell."*

For Othello's part, the murder scene evokes an extraordinary series of contradictory declarations; the lofty detached confessional tone: *"Have you prayed tonight?," "Sweet soul, take heed/ Take heed of perjury: thou art on thy death bed,"* the wish to reduce Desdemona to inert monumental alabaster so that she can be loved as an asexual being, all sit uneasily alongside continuing abuse: *"Out strumpet. . . . Down Strumpet."* The desperate desire to tell a good story about himself is still evident as Othello evokes a bizarre moral discourse even as he murders his wife: *"I that am cruel am yet merciful:/ I would not have thee linger in thy pain."* This juxtaposition of a violent and vengeful self with a benign and almost reluctant executioner breaks down in the face of his panic at Emilia's arrival:

> "*What's best to do?*
>
> *If she come in, she'll sure speak to my wife—*
>
> *My wife, my wife! What wife? I have no wife.*" (5.ii.97–99)

Othello recovers enough to claim that *"I did proceed upon just grounds,"* but after the agony of discovering the truth, his desire for a good story about himself only resurfaces just before his suicide, when he says: *"I have done the state some service, and they know't"* and with a self-alienated account, while stabbing himself, of killing a *"malignant and a turbaned Turk . . . a circumcisèd dog."*

Both Othello and Desdemona, from their different positions of perpetrator and victim, give accounts of themselves that draw upon moral discourses, prime among which are those relating to selflessness, obedience, duty and service. Neither displays an ability to reflect on their own actions nor to understand the actions of others. They have idealised each other and paid the price. They are both innocents when it comes to the workings of power.

Iago and Emilia

The same could not be said of the other married couple, Iago and Emilia. Despite the inequality and abusiveness of their relationship – Iago never misses an opportunity to humiliate his wife – they have in common an ability to deconstruct the workings of power and indeed those very concepts of service, duty and obedience that Othello and Desdemona draw upon so uncritically. Iago knows just how enslaving is the practice of *"obsequious bondage"* and how service has to be utilised and turned to one's own advantage. He also views sexual relations as a commercial exchange, from his comment about Othello having *"boarded a land carack"* to his jibe to Desdemona that:

> "*She that was ever fair and never proud,*
> *Had tongue at will and yet was never loud,*
> *Never lacked gold and yet went never gay.*" (2.i.146–148)

Unlike Othello and Desdemona, Iago's suspicion of Emilia's adultery is presented, not as a personal catastrophe, but as an opportunity for revenge:

> "*... it is thought abroad that twixt my sheets*
> *He's done my office. I know not if't be true,*
> *But I, for mere suspicion in that kind,*
> *Will do as if for surety.*" (1.iii.376–379)

Emilia suffers constant abuse from her husband and has few illusions about his character. She is not above trying to please him, as she does by stealing the handkerchief, despite suspecting the uses to which it might be put, and she is complicit with Iago in besmirching Bianca's reputation. Her language in castigating Othello after Desdemona's murder is just as racist as her husband's. Emilia is constructed as a woman who has learnt to act according to patriarchal rules but is as adept as her husband in dissecting the dynamics of power. Her view of men is cynical and unflattering:

> "*Tis not a year or two shows us a man:*
> *They are all but stomachs, and we all but food;*
> *They eat us hungerly, and when they are full*
> *They belch us.*" (3.iv.99–102)

Emilia's analysis of the double standards within marriage in a patriarchal society is unrivalled in all of Shakespeare's canon:

"*Let husbands know,*

Their wives have sense like them; they see and smell

And have their palates both for sweet and sour

As husbands have. What is it that they do

When they change us for others? Is it sport?

I think it is And doth affection breed it?

I think it doth. Is't frailty that that thus errs?

It is so too. And have we not affections

Desires for sport, and frailty, as men have?

Then let them use us well: else let them know,

The ills we do, their ills instruct us so." (4.iii.88–98)

Again, in contrast to Othello and Desdemona, infidelity, or the imputation of it, can at least be named between her and Iago: "*Some such squire he was/ That turned your wit the seamy side without/And made you suspect me with the Moor.*"

At this stage, Emilia, with her close-hand experience of and cynicism about Iago, has still apparently not comprehended the full extent of his perfidy. When, however, she directly defies and denounces Iago – for which she pays with her life – she speaks truth to power with courage and utter clarity. Iago's threats and misogynous abuse – "*Villainous whore!,*" "*Filth, thou liest*" – are exposed as attempts to silence her as she loses whatever fear she has:

Iago "'*Swounds, hold your peace*"

Emilia "'*Twill out, twill out! I peace?*

No, I will speak as liberal as the north;

Let heaven and men and devils, let them all,

All, all, cry shame against me, yet I'll speak"

Iago "*Be wise and get you home*"

Emilia "*I will not.*" (5.ii.217–222)

When Emilia speaks these brave and moving words, she is, like Desdemona, challenging her husband on behalf of another, rather than for herself. In this case it is love, loyalty and grief for Desdemona that moves her to such eloquence.

Desdemona and Emilia

As we have seen, a shift in the play occurs when Emilia, initially silenced, subservient and compliant compared to the socially superior, self-assured and outspoken Desdemona, begins to find a voice. As Desdemona is emotionally and physically abused by Othello, Emilia, witnessing perhaps a reflection of her own abuse by Iago, names the oppressive practices at work and begins to fight back on behalf of both of them. Desdemona did this for her when she challenged Iago's silencing and abusive rhetoric: "*Do not learn of him, Emilia, though he be thy husband.*" Again both women stand up to men mainly on behalf of another. Never constrained by the need to idealise her own husband, Emilia challenges Desdemona's depiction of Othello as a man incapable of jealousy: "*Is not this man jealous*?" As Desdemona becomes more despairing, Emilia becomes increasingly outspoken and invites Desdemona to take a different, and a more subversive view on male/female sexual relationships. It is possible therefore to see Desdemona and Emilia as two sides of women existing within the constraints imposed by their society but also acting with agency and morality. Emilia acts as a 'second self' for the floundering Desdemona, "providing a voice for that sturdy resistance to patriarchal tyranny that she exhibited in the confrontation with Brabantio but which her love for her husband forces her to suppress."[25] Whether it is love for her husband or his bullying that constrains Desdemona is another matter, but this is the point at which Emilia comes into her own. The dialogue between the two women in Act 4, scene 3, is one in which we see Desdemona for the first time exploring the possibility of a different way to think. She perhaps begins to realise how trapped she has been within a rigid frame of female duty and moral conduct, which has not protected her one iota from Othello's accusations of whoredom. At this late stage in the play we are not given any kind of 'awakening' on Desdemona's part but the beginnings of a different kind of questioning and the imagining of alternatives – "*This Lodovico is a proper man.*" The 'Willow song' constitutes the beginnings of an inner dialogue about male and female infidelity: "*Let nobody blame him, his scorn I approve/Nay that's not next. . . . If I court more women, you'll couch with more men . . . /Oh these men, these men"* (4.iii.47–55). For the first time in the play, Desdemona engages in an intimate and humorous female conversation:

Desdemona "*Dost thou in conscience think – tell me Emilia –*

That there be women do abuse their husbands/ In such gross kind?"

Emilia "*There be some such, no question*"

Desdemona "*Wouldst thou do such a deed for all the world?*"

Emilia "*Why, would not you?*"

Desdemona "*No by this heavenly light*"

Emilia "*Nor I neither, by this heavenly light:*

I might do't as well i'th' dark"

Desdemona "*Wouldst thou do such a thing for all the world?*"

Emilia "*The world's a huge thing: it is a great price For a small vice.*" (4.iii.56–64)

Emilia's responses are both playful and pragmatic as well as displaying some of the same cynical traits as her husband; her famously proto-feminist speech ends with: *"The ills we do, their ills instruct us so."* This provokes Desdemona into rapid withdrawal from talk of sexual tit-for-tat, perhaps re-awakening a desire to save her relationship with Othello.

Desdemona "*Good Night, good night. God me such uses send*

Not to pick bad from bad, but by bad mend."

Emilia too perhaps rebounds from this sharing of confidences with Desdemona into the safety of familiar discourses which divide women. She rounds upon the courtesan, Bianca, who dares to name women's shared sexual oppression:

Emilia "*O,fie upon thee, strumpet!*"

Bianca "*I am no strumpet/*

But of life as honest as you that thus/

Abuse me"

Emilia "*As I? Foh! Fie upon thee!*" (5.i.119–124)

While the conversation between Desdemona and Emilia cannot be seen as transformative for either of them, it offers, as so often in Shakespeare, a glimpse of other worlds, of alternative possibilities, of conversations that might have continued, of unexpected humour and subversiveness and of tantalising disruptions to the play's tragic denouement.

Conclusion

An individual whose psychopathology seems as obvious as Iago's provides a systemic therapist both with a challenge and with a stronger imperative to interrogate the surrounding relationships. The power of one person, however resourceful or wicked, to influence events is always contextualised by the positions of others. In 'marginalising' Iago and his plot, this analysis of *Othello* focuses on the play's other key relationships and, in doing so, explores how themes of displacement, oppression and silencing erode the creative potential in relationships and restrict the longed-for possibilities of a good life.

For Othello and Desdemona, the very processes of idealisation – of each other and, for Othello, of his status and military identity – foreclose possibilities for dialogue that might have saved them. They retreat into a narrower set of discursive positions where duty, service and servitude exert an ever more powerful hold. Desdemona, despite having her abuse by Othello publicly witnessed, never asks for help from her relatives.

That the potentially liberating conversation with Emilia takes place so late resonates powerfully with this closing down of psychic space. Othello's emotional dependency on Desdemona likewise never finds its way into language but is displaced into ever more grotesque attempts to diminish her, finally acting as her judge and executioner. With the revelation of her and Cassio's innocence, he rebounds into self-loathing, self-abasement, self-alienation and suicide.

The relationship of Iago and Emilia demonstrates a much more pragmatic coming-to-terms with human failings, cruelty and malevolence, providing the ground for an uncompromising deconstruction of the workings of power. The relationship between Desdemona and Emilia reveals love and altruism in all their poignancy and it is, above all, in this relationship that a potentially transformative conversation occurs only to be truncated and foreclosed. In *Othello*, as well as its preoccupation with what is seen, what is unseen and what is vicariously imagined, the audience is also kept in suspense by the unspoken. Othello is given no language to object to exclusionary and racist language and Desdemona has no language to challenge violence.

Unlike in comedy, a conversation that could unravel a web of deceit is withheld and, when it finally takes place, it is already too late. Thus, almost more than in any other Shakespeare tragedy, we are kept in a prolonged state of tension about the unsaid, the not-yet-said and the never-to-be said.

Notes

1 Laurie Maguire Othello, *Language and Writing* (London: Bloomsbury, 2014), 178.
2 Linda Boose, '"Let it be Hid": The Pornographic Aesthetics of Shakespeare's Othello', in Lena Cowen Orlin, ed., *Othello* (Basingstoke: Palgrave Macmillan, 2004).
3 Ibid., 23.
4 Laurie Maguire, *Othello, Language and Writing* (London: Bloomsbury, 2014).
5 Susan Snyder, *The Comic Matrix of Shakespeare's Tragedies* (Princeton: Princeton University Press, 1979).
6 Stephen Greenblatt, *Renaissance Self-Fashioning* (Chicago: University of Chicago Press, 1980), 245.
7 Anthony Nuttall, *Shakespeare the Thinker* (New Haven: Yale University Press, 2007), 279.
8 Lawrence Olivier, *Othello* (National Theatre Company, London, 1964).
9 Michael Neill, Othello, *The Moor of Venice* (Oxford: Oxford Worlds Classics, Oxford University Press, 2006), 57.
10 Tony Morrison in conversation with Peter Sellars, Barbican theatre, July 2012.
11 Patrick Marmion, *Evening Standard*, 7 February 2002.
12 Adrian Lester, interview in *Daily Telegraph*, April 2013.
13 Susanna Clapp, review in *Observer*, 27 April 2013.
14 Adrian Lester, interview in *Daily Telegraph*, April 2013.
15 Simon Russell Beale, *Iago on the Couch* (British Psychoanalytical Society DVD, 2009).
16 Kiernan Ryan, *Shakespeare* (Basingstoke: Palgrave Macmillan, Third Edition, 2002), 85.
17 Samuel Taylor Coleridge, annotation on copy of Othello, in preparation for a series of lectures delivered in winter 1818–1819.
18 Simon Russell Beale, *Iago on the Couch* (British Psychoanalytical Society DVD, 2009).

19 Felicity Rosslyn, *Tragic Plots: A New Reading from Aeschylus to Lorca* (Aldershot: Ashgate, 2000), 120.
20 Janet Adelman, *Suffocating Mothers: Fantasies of Maternal Origin in Shakespeare's Plays, 'Hamlet' to 'The Tempest'* (New York and London: Routledge, 1992), 65–66.
21 Gillian Walker and Virginia Goldner, 'The Wounded Prince and the Women Who Love Him', in Charlotte Burck and Bebe Speed, eds., *Gender, Power and Relationships* (London: Routledge, 1995).
22 Stephen Greenblatt, *Renaissance Self-Fashioning* (Chicago: University of Chicago Press, 1980), 241.
23 Murray Carlin, *Not Now, Sweet Desdemona: A Duologue for Black and White within the Realm of Shakespeare's Othello* (Oxford: Oxford University Press, New Drama from Africa, vol. 2, 1969).
24 Janet Adelman, *Suffocating Mothers: Fantasies of Maternal Origin in Shakespeare's Plays, 'Hamlet' to 'The Tempest'* (New York and London: Routledge, 1992), 64.
25 Michael Neill, *Othello, the Moor of Venice* (Oxford: Oxford Worlds Classics, Oxford University Press, 2006), 29.

CHAPTER 6

"Wrenched with an unlineal hand"

The dynamics of violence in *Macbeth*

Amira Kurosawa's film, *Throne of Blood,* captures the extent to which the language and texture of *Macbeth* is suffused with the multiple meanings and metaphors relating to the word 'blood.'[1] In the play, the first 'human' line is: "*What bloody man is that?*" A great deal of blood is graphically spilt: "*. . . who would have thought the old man to have had so much blood in him*" and it signifies both violent acts and the necessity for violent responses: "*It will have blood they say; blood will have blood.*" But 'blood' also carries the connotation of kinship bonds and, after the murder of his father, Donalbain neatly draws the different meanings together: "*The near in blood/The nearer bloody.*"

Blood in the sense of lineage is one means of incorporating acts of violence into a context of structure and order "Blood is symbolic of aggression, but blood, as in blue blood or the blood royal carries the symbol of legitimacy and succession."[2] In the English history plays Shakespeare explored the question of whether or not violent seizure of power from an anointed monarch could, with enough narrative effort, be sanitised over time and transformed within a generation into a 'natural succession.' In *Macbeth* the themes of usurpation and illegitimacy – "*borrowed clothes*" – intersect constantly with this question of time and with the crucial issue of 'lineality'; the ability to produce heirs. Violent actions in the present can be justified in terms of the future security and status they might produce for children, as Banquo reflects in his own "*cursèd thoughts.*"

In Justin Kurzel's film of *Macbeth*, children both 'real' and imagined are everywhere, opening with the funeral of the Macbeths' infant child and featuring, as well as Fleance and the young Macduffs, a number of phantom children foregrounding the crucial question of generativity.[3] As the texture of the play itself is suffused with the imagery of parents and children, of rightful inheritance and of avenging the murders of both parents and children, so the fact that Macbeth himself is marooned and isolated from this trajectory is intensified, since, in Macduff's memorable words, "*he has no children*." Macbeth has neither avenged the death of a father nor has he a son to avenge him.

Revenge narratives create dynamics of violence which, while no less bloody than Macbeth's arbitrary and 'illegitimate' seizure of power, are imbued with a sense of purpose, coherence and entitlement because they highlight intergenerational bonds. Children too grow up with the obligation to avenge their parents. Consequently, children usually meet the fate of their parents. *Macbeth* is one of very few Shakespeare plays that features the direct voice of a child; young Macduff emerges in all his questioning humanity, challenging adult deception and interrogating the workings of power, thus heightening the poignancy of his gruesome death. "Children are included in acts of genocide . . . they are imagined, consciously or unconsciously as future agents of retribution or revenge."[4] Fleance's escape from this fate is the first in a number of external factors that ensure that Macbeth, having attained the throne, can never be "*safely thus*."

The lack of a succeeding generation that could provide for a real or an imagined future means that, even early in the play, both Macbeth and Lady Macbeth convey a hovering sense of the sterility and senselessness of their actions, a feeling that constantly threatens to invade and engulf them and that they collectively struggle to keep at bay. Childlessness should certainly not, however, be seen either as a cause of the Macbeths' behaviour nor as a state that has only psychological implications; it effects participation in all levels of social and political life within a feudal society. Macbeth's lack of dynastic potential also serves to foreground the themes of ruthless individualism and the negation of human bonds that Shakespeare explores so powerfully in this play.

Macbeth might lay a claim to be one of the most modern of Shakespeare's protagonists:

> He belongs to that very species that has been hovering at the edge of Shakespeare's consciousness for so long, the Machiavel . . . he shows us what it might mean to be modern and to break all the bounds of piety at a stroke.[5]

The play can also be seen as a "fierce arraignment of one of the mainsprings of modern Western society ... the ideology and practice of individualism."[6] Unlike many of Shakespeare's other eponymous heroes, Macbeth shows an acute and agonised awareness of exactly what he is doing and exactly where it will lead. In *Macbeth* and *Hamlet*, which feature two of his most self-reflexive creations, Shakespeare explores opposing aspects of the relationship between thought and action. In each play there is a 'supernatural' intervention that initiates or calls for acts of regicide. Macbeth starts by committing a murder which leads to his psychological and moral disintegration as the play progresses; it is Hamlet's reluctance to commit the same act that is popularly, if simplistically, considered to lead to his unravelling. In each play the problematic nature of a classical revenge tragedy is laid bare. In *Macbeth*, the portrayal of ambition and cruelty, remorse and vengeance point to the unremittingly circular processes involved in maintaining power that has been attained violently and which can only be sustained by further acts of violence. This prospect is grappled with by both Macbeth and Lady Macbeth but also, crucially, by Malcolm, so that focussing these dilemmas on the person of Macbeth alone greatly diminishes their scope and impact. At times all three protagonists can be said to be 'living in the future' with the capacity to predict or imagine long-term consequences, even if they do not choose to act differently.

In *Macbeth*, time and its ambiguous meanings are at the core of the drama. These are dramatised through the witches' interventions, constructing a sense that time can either be cheated, experienced as frozen and empty or as driving relentlessly and impersonally onwards in a way that renders people impotent to make choices. As I will argue, the question of time and of indeterminacy is inextricably linked to the themes of generativity and to the compelling power of intergenerational bonds.

Generativity and infertility

Infertility, or childlessness, is a key emotional subtext of the play. As Duncan approaches Macbeth's castle, and comments on it as a *"pleasant seat,"* Banquo elaborates on its hospitable climate for breeding: *"the temple haunting martlet does approve,"* making in its masonry a *"pendant bed and procreant cradle/ Where they most breed and haunt, I have observed/The air is delicate."* The pathos of Banquo's poetic speech lies not only in its contrast with the horror that is to come but also in Shakespeare's juxtaposition of abundant nature alongside human sterility. A poem written centuries later by Gerard Manley Hopkins about his own creative struggle evokes the same contrast:

> "... *birds build – but not I build; no, but strain*
>
> *Time's eunuch, and not breed one work that wakes.*"[7]

Shakespeare leaves it to the audience to imagine how their childless state has arisen for the Macbeths, but some critics, keen to emphasise their innate wickedness, have drawn attention to her infertility as a punishment. Freud asserted that it is Lady Macbeth's "own fault if her crime has been robbed of the better part of its fruits."[8] While this judgemental stance represents one extreme, Andrew O'Hagan, in his review of Justin Kurzel's film, warns against the opposite, which is to use it as an excuse:

> The urge in the film is always toward a modern explanation of what makes good people do bad things, thus . . . feelingful depictions of Lady Macbeth with her lost child. We see her weep while her husband burns Macduff's children at the stake, but not for any evil she has done or even at any evil Macbeth has done. We must assume that the water in Cotillard's eyes is prompted by the innocence of children generally and the memory of her own dear child.[9]

I argue here that, while approaching the Macbeths childlessness in purely psychological terms has severe limitations, exploring it in a relational and social context is crucial. Lady Macbeth herself makes no mention of it except to say that she has "*given suck*." She could be played as full of rage, transforming frustrated maternal impulses into violence: "*Come to my woman's breasts/And take my milk for gall, you murd'ring ministers*." Alternatively she could be shown as having dealt with the loss of her own child by turning Macbeth into her child, committing herself to the fulfilment of what she knows is his deep desire to be king, offering to take charge: "*you shall put/This night's great business into my dispatch . . . leave all the rest to me,*" tutoring and cajoling him by turns to act and expressing concern for his self-image if he does not:

> "*Wouldst thou have that*
>
> *Which thou esteem'st the ornament of life*
>
> *And live a coward in thine own esteem,*
>
> *Letting 'I dare not' wait upon 'I would'*
>
> *Like the poor cat i'th'adage.*" (I.vii.41–45)

In their interchanges, metaphors relating to babies certainly abound:

> "*I have given suck, and know*
>
> *How tender 'tis to love the babe that milks me;*
>
> *I would, while it was smiling in my face,*
>
> *Have plucked my nipple from his boneless gums,*
>
> *And dashed the brains out.*" (I.vii.54–58)

Macbeth, however, responds to this horrific image in pragmatic terms – "*If we should fail?*" – suggesting that such hyperbole might be a predictable part of their dialogue. In response to Lady Macbeth's fierce exhortations he replies: "*Bring forth men-children only/For thy undoubted mettle should compose/Nothing but males.*"

While this could suggest that Macbeth still had hopes of producing an heir, this is nowhere evident in any of his other reflections on the future. In Shakespeare's day, the effects of Elizabeth's childlessness were profound. Male monarchs such as her father simply set about finding another woman with a more promising womb. Lady Macbeth's desperate fight to secure for her husband the kingship he desired could be presented as a way of making herself indispensable to him and thus less replaceable.

Macbeth himself cannot imagine, beyond killing Duncan, a future that will not bring him further angst and turmoil: "an action intended as creative, self-definitive is in fact destructive self-undoing."[10] Its futility rests on the knowledge that he is not creating a future beyond himself:

> "*They hailed him father to a line of kings.*
>
> *Upon my head they placed a fruitless crown*
>
> *And put a barren sceptre in my gripe,*
>
> *Thence to be wrenched with an unlineal hand,*
>
> *No son of mine succeeding. If't be so,*
>
> *For Banquo's issue have I filed my mind,*
>
> *For them the gracious Duncan have I murdered,*
>
> *Put rancours in the vessel of my peace*
>
> *Only for them, and mine eternal jewel*
>
> *Given to the common enemy of man*

To make them kings, the seed of Banquo kings.

Rather than so, come Fate, into the list,

And champion me to th' utterance." (3.i.59–71)

The idea that an act of regicide might be justified for the sake of future generations is echoed by Banquo, reflecting on his own desires, his own future and that of his heirs: "... *merciful powers/Restrain in me the cursèd thoughts that nature/Gives way to in repose.*"

This 'restraint' does not always work: "... *yet it was said/It would not stand in thy posterity,/But that myself should be the root and favour/ Of many kings.... May they not be my oracles as well/And set me up in hope?*"

Before killing Duncan, Macbeth has invited Banquo into a discussion about his prospects: "*Do you not hope your children shall be kings,/When those that gave the Thane of Cawdor to me/Promised no less to them?*" He later suggests that they "*speak/Our free hearts to each other,*" opening up the possibility of a dialogue between two equals sharing a common dilemma. Just before the murder, the conversation is more circumspect but revealing, especially as it is Banquo who raises the subject:

Banquo "*I dreamt last night of the three Weird sisters;*

To you they have showed some truth."

Macbeth "*I think not of them. Yet when we can entreat an hour to serve*

We would spend it in some words upon that business,

If you would grant the time"

Banquo "*At your kind'st leisure.*" (2.i/21–27)

This exchange, laced as it is with mutual suspicion, still opens up the possibility of a more prosaic plot line with the two men, already quasi-conspirators in their shared experience of the sisters, mutually exploring the possibility of regicide. But the chasm that the witches' words have opened up between the men; "*Your children shall be Kings*" ... "*You shall be King*" is unbridgeable. Indeed, Fleance is as much of a threat as Banquo and has to be included in the assassination plans: "*Goes Fleance with you*?" When the murderers bring the news that "*Fleance is scaped,*" Macbeth's response is visceral:

"*Then comes my fit again;*

I had else been perfect –

Whole as the marble, founded as the rock,
As broad and general as the casing air;
But now I am cabined cribbed confined, bound in
To saucy doubts and fears." (3.iv.21–25)

The solid images of marble and rock, contrasting with the fragility of "*borrowed clothes*" conjure up the longing for a secure throne with a sense of permanence and duration beyond the lifespan of the occupant; the image of the casing air is also that of possibilities for limitless expansion. The permanent removal of Banquo and his heir would perhaps have allowed Macbeth to indulge in the fantasy that he was indeed founding a dynasty. Fleance is, however, not only alive, but carries with him his father's dying words: "*Fly good Fleance, fly, fly, fly –. Thou mayst revenge.*" The ghostly image of Banquo that disrupts the feast can be seen not as a product of Macbeth's guilt or remorse as much as the power Banquo still has over him: "*Hence horrible shadow/ Unreal mock'ry, hence!*" He is powerful after death because he can unleash the next generation onto Macbeth.

The reverse situation occurs with Macduff's family. Here, the father escapes and Macbeth, as soon as he learns the news, determines to wipe out Macduff's entire line:

"*The castle of Macduff I will surprise,*
Seize upon Fife, give to th'edge o'th'sword
His wife, his babes and all unfortunate souls
That trace him in his line." (4.i.165–168)

Shakespeare could easily have set Macduff up as an exemplary opposite to Macbeth, since his anguished and deeply feeling response to the murder of his family invites us to think of him as a different kind of man. Indeed Coppelia Kahn denotes Macduff as a "touchstone of manhood . . . set in the context of procreation and the family." When he fights Macbeth, it is not only to save the state and to avenge his family but "to defend the continuation of human life itself as it devolves on love between man and women, procreation, nurturance and pity."[11] However, what we are actually presented with is a much more nuanced, complex and troubled picture of relationships in the family from Fife. Macduff's abandonment of his wife and children is never fully explained and his wife is outraged by it. She dies an angry as well as a terrified woman and is far from being forgiving. Ross' pleadings on behalf of Macduff have no impact on her because they carry no credibility:

> Ross "*You must have patience madam*"
>
> Lady Macduff "*He had none –*
>
> *His flight was madness: when our actions do not,*
>
> *Our fears do make us traitors...*
>
> *He loves us not. /He wants the natural touch.*" (4.ii.3–9)

Ross' image of the *"wild and violent sea,"* upon which humans are helplessly tossed and exposed to unnamed horrors, is closer to Lady Macduff's experience in the moment, but he quickly recoils from it, perhaps to make it easier for himself to abandon them: *"Things at the worst will cease, or else climb upward/ To what they were before."* Lady Macduff will have none of this reassurance; she faces full on the implications of what being without the protection of their father will mean for her children: *"Fathered he is, and yet he's fatherless."* The dialogue between her and her son which follows centres on how to live in this state of 'fatherlessness,' literal or metaphorical. *"How will you live? As birds do mother."* Although the content is manifestly different, there is a resemblance to the opening scenes between the Macbeths, where an intense private intimacy exists alongside the violence, chaos and unpredictability of the external world. Young Macduff also interrogates the norms of the adult world in language that echoes those recurring inversions of meaning – *"fair is foul and foul is fair"* – first introduced by the witches.

> Son "*Who must hang them?*" (traitors)
>
> Lady Macduff "*Why, the honest men.*"
>
> Son "*Then the liars and swearers are fools; for there are liars and swearers enough to beat the honest men and hang them up.*"

This undermining of linguistic polarities is taken up by his mother – *"to do harm/ Is often laudable, to do good sometime/ Accounted dangerous folly."* As the murderers close in on him, young Macduff offers a moving example of young children trying, even *in extremis,* to protect and defend their parents, morally and physically:

First Murderer (of Macduff) "*He's a traitor*"

Son "*Thou li'st thou shag-eared villain*"

First Murderer "*What you egg! Young fry of treachery!*" *(Kills him)*

Son "*He has killed me mother,/ Run away I pray you.*" (4.ii.86–91)

As well as being an example of a child's intense desire to protect a vulnerable parent, thus further highlighting the power of the generational bond and the threat it poses to those without children, this brief scene illustrates the responses to violence that can easily be overlooked if the focus is only on the wickedness of the perpetrator. It opens up space to imagine the exiled Malcolm, Donalblain and Fleance and the impact on them of the violence perpetrated on their fathers. Additionally, in this mother/son interaction we are offered, as we so often are with Shakespeare, a vivid counter narrative to a common interpretation of *Macbeth*. This is one of 'masculinised' women dominating their men who in turn struggle to escape emasculation, a narrative typical of psychoanalytically based readings.

Gender

Psychoanalytic interpretations of *Macbeth* centre mainly on masculinity and femininity and on maternal and paternal functions. Janet Adelman explores the fantasies of destructive maternal forces represented both by the witches and by Lady Macbeth, which so influence Macbeth and from whose power he seeks to free himself.[12] Peter Hildebrand argues that *Macbeth* is a play about mother/son incest – *"a deed without a name,"* as he claims the witches allude to it, with Lady Macbeth representing Macbeth's forbidden but desired mother.[13] All these interpretations rely on transcendent norms of masculinity and femininity; they engage somewhat uncritically with gender tropes, for example the idea that manhood resides in – rather than being socially constructed as – a disavowal of vulnerability and dependency. Shakespeare himself typically provides a more nuanced view, in which stereotypes of manhood are set up only to be undermined.

Conflicting views of how to be a man emerge within the context of relationships and through dialogue. In Act 4, scene 3, after Macduff receives the devastating news of the murder of his wife and children, Malcolm makes the assumption that masculine duty requires the bereaved father to leap into violent action: *"Let's make us medicines of our great revenge,/ To cure this deadly grief. . . . Dispute it like a man."* Macduff replies: *"I shall do so;/But I must also feel it as a man."* Even the substitution of *"as"* for *"like"* is suggestive of a shift between an identity that must be performed and a feeling sense that can be incorporated into an identity.

In Act 5, scene 9, Malcolm himself takes up the position that he had earlier provoked in Macduff; that men should express feeling rather than be constrained by abstract rules of heroic conduct. He questions the assumption that Siward's son, having died a 'noble' death, should not be mourned:

> Siward "*Had I as many sons as I have hairs,*
>
> *I would not wish them a fairer death.*
>
> *And so his knell is knolled*"
>
> Malcolm "*He's worth more sorrow,*
>
> *And that I'll spend for him.*" (5.vii.77–81)

Gender patterns at their extremes are most typically observed in the relationship between the Macbeths. Lady Macbeth works exceptionally hard to realise her husband's desire to be King. She is certainly portrayed as ruthless but not as monstrous as, for example, Gonoril and Regan. She makes her own decisions and lives with them, just as men do.[14] While some critics comment on Lady Macbeth's disavowal of 'the feminine principle,'[15] or her 'emasculating behaviour,'[16] there are no exhortations within the text for her to be 'more womanly.' Macbeth's enemies only refer to her as *"fiend-like"* and Macbeth's sole comments on her gendered self are admiring rather than critical, praising her *"undaunted mettle."*

The only person who speaks of women as women is Lady Macduff when she contrasts her own understanding of love to that of her husband's:

> "*For the poor wren,*
>
> *The most diminutive of birds, will fight,*
>
> *Her young ones in her nest, against the owl.*
>
> *All is the fear, and nothing is the love.*" (4.ii.9–12).

Ross' response is to try to silence her:

> "*My dearest coz,*
>
> *I pray you school yourself. But for your husband,*

He is noble, wise, judicious and best knows

The fits o'th' season."

Lady Macduff is enjoined to be a loyal and uncomplaining wife, a state of passivity and exemplary female 'goodness' she knows will absolutely not save her: "*Why then, alas, do I put up that womanly defence,/ To say I have done no harm?*"

Unsurprisingly, as feminist writers have argued, the requirement to work at the 'project' of maleness tends to take up more discursive space than that of femaleness.[17] There are many more examples in Shakespeare of male than female behaviour being subjected to 'gender monitoring'. If masculine ideals are set up in opposition, not only to vulnerability but to any experience of doubt, moral scruple or uncertainty, this requires constant 'gender vigilance,' but the performance of it is always situational. When murdering Duncan is the matter at hand, Lady Macbeth seeks to extinguish weakness in her husband: "*when you durst do it, then you were a man,*" although he is expressing reasonable doubt rather than fear. Macbeth has already shown himself to be amenable in relation to this gender monitoring: "*Prithee peace:/I dare do all that may becomes a man,/ Who dares do more is none,*" virtually inviting further challenge to his manhood. By time of the banquet scene, exhortations to manliness arise in response to Macbeth's bizarre and erratic behaviour: "*Are you a man?*" "*. . .What, quite unmanned in folly?*" Again Macbeth enters compliantly into this discourse: "*Ay and a bold one*" . . . "*What man dare, I dare*" . . . "*I am a man again.*"

A counterpoint to the rigid and stereotyped gender tropes that both Macbeth and Lady Macbeth articulate emerges from the three "weird sisters" who offer the most potent challenge to gendered norms. As women with beards they appear androgynous and, as "*imperfect speakers,*" they are subversive, undermining stable meanings, employing riddles, and allegory, speaking in contradictions and inversions: "*When the battle's lost and won . . . Fair is foul and foul is fair.*" The witches invoke a "celebration of liminality"[18] heightening the ritualistic and indeterminate textures of the play with its ambiguity about what is real and material and what is imaginary and insubstantial:

> As the most fertile force in the play, the witches inhabit an anarchic, richly ambiguous zone both in and out of official society: they live in their own world but intersect with Macbeth's. They are poets, prophetesses and devotees of female cult, radical separatists who scorn male power and lay bare the hollow sound at its heart. Their words and bodies mock rigorous

> boundaries and make sport of fixed positions, unhinging received meanings as they dance, dissolve and re-materialize.[19]

They mock ambition and selfishness – *"loves for his own ends, not for you"* – and they pay no heed to male authority: *"Speak I charge you!"(witches vanish).*

After Macbeth has consulted them for the second time, the weird sisters disappear as active participants in the play, as does Lady Macbeth. This erasure of women leaves a wholly masculine world at the end, extinguishing women even as progenitors of males. Macduff being *"not of woman born"* is, however, revealed as a myth based upon which, as the sisters predicted, Macbeth allowed himself a false sense of security. In first setting up and then exposing this illusion, the sisters have laid bare the fantasy that there can exist a male world which is separate and not interdependent with women, a fantasy that is intensified in the construction of 'sick' Scotland as female and 'healing' England as male.

Time

The weird sisters, who *"look into the seeds of time"* identify, when speaking to Banquo, precisely the dilemma both he and Macbeth face, which is between short-term gain and the sense of long-term security that could result from loyally serving one's time:

> *"Lesser than Macbeth "and greater"*
>
> *Not so happy yet much happier*
>
> *Thou shalt get kings though thou be none."* (i.iii.65–67)

This emphasis on begetting kings rather than being king opens the question of whether having an heir allows for the possibility of waiting for events to take their course rather than obeying the impulse to *"jump the life to come."*

The weird sisters, as supernatural beings, stand outside time. They can thus observe the vicissitudes, the *hurly burly* of human struggles. They stimulate imagination about the future while their ambiguous forms and their theatricality act as a further vehicle for the imagination. Paradoxically for the fearful Macbeth they also act as a repository of certainty, as holders of the keys to the future. His fantasy that the future can be subject to control is however constantly undermined by the sisters. On his second visit,

Macbeth expresses the hope that they will be able to reassure him that he *"Shall live the lease of nature, pay his breath/ To time and mortal custom."* The most deadly question is kept until near the end:"

tell me, . . . shall Banquo's issue ever/Reign in this kingdom?" The vision that unfolds in front of him is, of course, unwelcome: *"Filthy hags/Why do you show me this?"* Even the more 'comforting' news that *"none of woman born shall harm Macbeth,"* while employed as a talisman later in the play, evokes the opposite desire; to rely more on his own agency rather than on prophecy:

> "*But yet I'll make assurance double sure,*
>
> *And take a bond of fate: thou shalt not live,*
>
> *That I may tell pale-hearted fear it lies*
>
> *And sleep in spite of thunder.*" (4.i.96–99)

In having evoked at the outset, a vision of the future and in voicing Macbeth and Banquo's unspoken desires and ambitions, the sisters invite both protagonists into positions of reflexivity where they are required to grapple with the future consequences of either action or inaction. Banquo in a similar way to Hamlet's struggle over his father's ghostly appearance, is preoccupied with the thought that the sisters represent evil spirits leading him astray:

> "*And oftentimes, to win us to our harm,*
>
> *The instruments of darkness tell us truths,*
>
> *Win us with honest trifles, to betray's*
>
> *In deepest consequence.*" (1.iii.125–128)

Macbeth's dilemma is different. The sisters' predictions shock him because they identify thoughts he already has; his *"royal hope."* Additionally, he is offered immediate 'proof' of their veracity through Cawdor's demise. If the future is so accurately predicted, then will it come, as he says, *"without my stir"*? In this case he need not compromise his moral responsibility. The state of profound confusion and uncertainty into which the sisters plunge Macbeth appears to relate to the unleashing of murderous desire that had perhaps not until then been articulated, even to himself. But, while the sisters point to a time frame which is indeterminate and imprecise,

Shakespeare provides an immediate spur in the form of another family narrative. Duncan makes the 'innocent' announcement that he will *"establish our estate upon/ Our eldest, Malcolm."* This occurs immediately after he has lavished praise on Macbeth and Banquo and made an ambiguous promise that is again suggestive of a longer time span: *"I have begun to plant thee, and will labour/ To make thee full of growing."* This metaphor however can find no resonance for the childless Macbeth. While Duncan's speech is replete with 'noblesse oblige,' with the expectation that Macbeth's loyal service will be transferred to Malcolm and that Malcolm in turn will reward him: *"signs of nobleness, like stars/Shall shine on all deservers,"* this benign paternalistic language is in stark contrast to the description of Macbeth's brutal conduct on the battlefield which brought him such accolades and honours.

The phrases *"o'erleap"* and *"jump the life to come"* carry multiple meanings; of usurping legitimate rulers, of striking first to protect a position, of taking actions that might disrupt a preordained plan and, significantly, of transgressing social norms. Although public narrative refers to the legitimacy of rulers – *"our duties are to your throne and state"* – in Macbeth's private agonising, this features less strongly. The rules that he fears breaking are those of kinship: *"as I am his kinsman and his subject,"* hospitality: *"as his host/Who should against his murderer shut the door/ Not bear the knife myself"* and offence against Duncan's particular qualities as king – *"his virtues/Will plead like angels."*

After the murder of Duncan, Shakespeare increases the intensity of the dilemma around what circumstances and what mindset might lead people to go beyond the bounds of civilised norms and to betray social bonds; to carry out what Malcolm calls *"confineless harms."* There is a relatively long scene – hardly necessary for the plot – between Macbeth and the two murderers whom he hires to assassinate Banquo and Fleance. Here, he tries to make the case that they should kill Banquo because of the latter's supposed ill treatment of them. It is clear that these two men have needed some persuasion; their compliance cannot be taken for granted. Justifying murder on the grounds of the victim's bad behaviour is, ironically, an argument Macbeth never made in the case of Duncan and the two murderers seem unimpressed. Instead, they each speak of the unbearable state of their own lives; their willingness to commit murder is justified by their suffering and deprivation in general.

Second Murderer "*I am one, my liege*

Whom the vile blows and buffets of the world

Hath so incensed, that I am reckless what I do

To spite the world."

The first murderer adds

"*And I another,*

So weary with disasters, tugged with fortune,

That I would set my life on any chance,

To mend it or be rid on't." (3.i.108–114)

Minor characters, as well as offsetting the focus on the heroic protagonists, add to our appreciation of the emotional and ethical quandaries they are struggling with. The two murderers reveal a world of suffering and oppression that undermines any fantasy that there was order and stability before Macbeth's seizure of power, thus again opening up a wider time frame. What Macbeth introduces as a specific grudge to be held against Banquo becomes instead a reflection on the desperation induced by a world of human injustice and deprivation. It challenges those interpretations of Macbeth that rely on his individual psychology by highlighting another dimension, which for the murderers is that of seizing any opportunity that might make a difference, not out of strategy but out of desperation. Macbeth's long speeches of justification are thus irrelevant to them. This adds a third level to the interplay between savage individualism – "*For mine own good/All causes shall give way*" – and the demands of the human community, "*the milk of human kindness.*" Rather than "*jump the life to come*" which implies a vision of the future, the two men simply want any means of escape from an utterly miserable and seemingly frozen present.

Recklessness and chance are to come into closer focus as Macbeth loses control over events. From needing to consciously force himself into action and stifle his conscience, Macbeth now elevates action above thought as he is increasingly portrayed as mindless automaton. Kiernan Ryan's somewhat deterministic reading, echoing Marx, is that "The handmaidens of Hecate underscore the fact that Macbeth does indeed fashion his own doom but, does so under conditions which he has neither created nor chosen himself, and over whose ultimate ramifications he has no control at all."[20] This reading obscures the way that the other protagonists also grapple with similar questions of choice and agency.

This struggle between individual agency and a sense of events evolving over time and under their own momentum is not only highlighted through the person of Macbeth but it is powerfully enacted in the dialogue between Malcolm and Macduff in Act 4, scene 3. This exchange, in which Malcolm warns of his own capacity to be a more terrible despot even than Macbeth, is usually understood to result from mutual suspicion between the two men and from Malcolm's need to test Macduff's loyalty. Macduff's potential for betrayal has been introduced in the scene immediately preceding this when the murderers taunt his young son as they kill him: "*Young fry of treachery*." From the shocking intrusion of violence into intimate domestic life, the canvas is widened to include the effects on the whole society of Macbeth's tyrannical and violent rule where "*our country sinks beneath the yoke*." Beneath the fear and paranoia induced by violence and despotism lie other reflections about how tyranny infiltrates all human relationships so that "*A good and virtuous nature may recoil/In an imperial charge*." The effect on Malcolm is that he mistrusts Macduff's avowals of loyalty:

> "*Let not my jealousies be your dishonours,*
>
> *But mine own safeties; you may be rightly just,*
>
> *Whatever I shall think*." (4.iii.29–31)

Malcolm's next speeches appear melodramatic and excessive, even in the cause of testing his friend. They can, however, be seen as an exploration of the limits of power, and of abuses of power as well as a commentary on the perpetuation and intensification of cycles of violence:

> Malcolm "*It is myself I mean– in whom I know*
>
> *All the particulars of vice so grafted,*
>
> *That when they shall be opened, black Macbeth*
>
> *Will seem as pure as snow, and the poor state*
>
> *Esteem him as a lamb, being compared*
>
> *With my confineless harms*." (4.iii.50–55)

The young and inexperienced Malcolm is as likely to be testing himself as Macduff. His descriptions of the "*cistern of my lust*" may be comically countered by his subsequent confession that "*I am yet unknown to woman*," but the fantasy he creates of his own potential for tyrannical, unjust and oppressive rule in which he will *"Pour the sweet milk of concord into Hell/ Uproar the universal peace, confound/ All unity on earth"* points to a deeper concern. That is how the overthrow of a tyrant is just as likely to result in an escalation of violence as it is a peaceful restoration of order. The question *"If such a one be fit to govern, speak: I am as I have spoken"* seems designed, as well as to provoke Macduff, to address the crucial question of whether there can be any limits to human cruelty and avarice. Macduff's response to Malcolm is first to indulge him – *"Scotland hath foisons to fill up your will"* – and then, as Malcolm escalates his rhetoric, reassures him that there are indeed limits and that he would not sanction a king who behaves as Malcolm claims he will.

It seems to be Macduff's willingness to state a limit that reassures Malcolm as much as an acceptance of his loyalty. In this process, Macbeth, a man whom they had previously trusted is held up as a benchmark of ruthlessness and cruelty but also as an attractor: *"Devilish Macbeth/By many of these trains, hath sought to win me/ Into his power."* As Macbeth does in Act 1, Malcolm projects his imagination into the future; as well as having suffered the trauma of his father's murder, he envisions further trauma; a kind of flash-forward in which he forces himself to face the meaning of unfettered power and its consequences. The firm reassuring voice of Macduff whose *"modest wisdom plucks me/ From over-credulous haste"* has the effect of grounding Malcolm within the present: *"What I am truly/ Is thine, and my poor country's to command."* This crucial dialogue, while echoing similar fears about the future, provides a stark contrast with that of the Macbeths.

Macbeth and Lady Macbeth; relationship positions

Jeanette Winterson notes that "the only successful marriage in Shakespeare is that of the Macbeths. At least they talk to each other."[21] Of all the relationships in Shakespeare's drama, this one has probably been the most thoroughly analysed. The Macbeths' relationship can indeed be understood as, at some level, modern and intimate[22] but in a society organised around feudal bonds and in the absence of children they have to find ways of addressing (or avoiding) the crucial question of 'how are we going to live?'.

In exploring the Macbeths' relationship, I will focus on the interplay between their dialogues and their soliloquies, which provide a particularly rich 'double description' of their interactions. What is especially striking about the differences between them is that doubts and moral scruples are generally reserved for 'inner talk,' especially in the case of Lady Macbeth.

In our first encounter with her she voices her concern about her husband's resolution:

> *"... yet do I fear thy nature*
>
> *It is too full o' th' milk of human kindness*
>
> *To catch the nearest way. Thou wouldst be great,*
>
> *Art not without ambition, but without*
>
> *The illness should attend it."* (I.v.14–18)

That *"illness"* refers to action rather than to intention is illustrated by her ambiguous words, *"wouldst not play false/And yet wouldst wrongly win."* Into the gulf between ambition and outcome, Lady Macbeth is determined to insert the missing action and she therefore takes this *'illness'* upon herself. However, despite her reputation for ruthlessness, she has to work surprisingly hard to maintain her mission. The affective range she draws upon in her soliloquy encompasses *"remorse"* and *"compunctious visitings of nature"* and an inner voice crying *"Hold, hold!"* In dialogue, by contrast, only words likely to galvanise her husband into action – *"pour my spirits in thine ear"* – are selected out.

Reciprocally Macbeth relies on his wife to do just what she does. His anguished moral doubts when he eloquently evokes Duncan's goodness and the likely reaction of others to his assassination – *"his virtues/ Will plead like angels, trumpet-tongued against/The deep damnation of his taking off"* – are restricted to monologue and in dialogue he reverts to more prosaic language:

> *"We will proceed no further in this business.*
>
> *He hath honoured me of late, and I have bought*
>
> *Golden opinions from all sorts of people,*
>
> *Which would be worn now in their newest gloss*
>
> *Not cast aside so soon."* (I.vii.31–35)

This provokes a predictable response from Lady Macbeth which sets him again on the path to murder. Macbeth could certainly be played as showing relief as well as admiration for his wife when he concludes *"I am settled and bend up/Each corporal agent to this terrible feat."* She has performed her part, has dismissed her own doubts and soothed her husband's fears: *"If we should fail? We fail?/ But screw your courage to the sticking place/ And we'll not fail."*

As Macbeth heads toward Duncan's chamber, his 'dagger' speech pushes at the polarities between either asserting human agency or passively submitting to fate, and he ends with an ambivalent phrase that encapsulates both active and passive voices: "*I go and it is done.*" Lady Macbeth, by contrast, uses an active voice throughout: "*I have drugged their possets*" but again hints at the effort it takes to be resolute: "*That which made them drunk hath made me bold.*" She continues to perform a different linguistic repertoire between dialogue and monologue, keeping doubts and fears for the latter: "*Alack, I am afraid they have awaked/ And 'tis not done. . . . Had he not resembled/My father as he slept, I had done't.*" Just as there is an ambiguous overlap between this speech and Macbeth's actual entrance, so what follows is a series of fragmented interchanges in which each seems to struggle to connect with each other and with the external world. This is a brief moment in which the habitual patterning in their relationship is disrupted:

Lady Macbeth "*My husband?*"

Macbeth "*I have done the deed. Didst thou not hear a noise?*"

Lady Macbeth "*I heard the owl scream, and the crickets cry.*

Did you not speak?"

Macbeth "*When?*"

Lady Macbeth "*Now*"

Macbeth "*As I descended?*"

Lady Macbeth "*Ay.*" (2.ii.15–17)

This interlude perhaps highlights the ambivalent gulf between urging an act upon a reluctant other and the shocked realisation that they have actually done it. However, as Macbeth expands on his fears: "*I could not say 'Amen'/ When they did say God bless us,*" Lady Macbeth reverts to taking control: "*Consider it not so deeply . . . these deeds must not be thought/After these ways: so, it will make us mad.*" His fear again produces the prompt for her decisive action:

Macbeth "*Look on't again I dare not*"

Lady Macbeth "*Infirm of purpose;*

Give me the daggers . . . I'll gild the faces of the grooms withal,

For it must seem their guilt." (2.ii.51–56)

Left alone, and having firmly located 'action' in his wife, Macbeth's language once again reverts to the depersonalisation of the dagger speech:

"What hands are here?" and the scene ends with his final statement of regret: *"To know my deed, t'were best not know myself . . . Wake Duncan with thy knocking: I would thou could'st."*

However, as soon as the deed is in the public domain and he is on the path to kingship, Macbeth's expressions of moral scruple disappear. Achieving the crown seems to leave each of the Macbeths with a sense of inner depletion. What they have created between them is a complex 'dance' around different aspects of the key dilemma in the play; what it means to push beyond all moral bounds, why do it and what are the consequences? Freud's exploration of this process led him to describe the Macbeths as psychically one person.

> "It is he who, after the murder, hears the cry in the house:
>
> 'Sleep no more! Macbeth does murder sleep . . .' but we never hear that *he* slept no more, while the Queen, as we see, rises from her bed and, talking in her sleep, betrays her guilt. It is he who stands helpless with bloody hands, lamenting that 'all great Neptune's ocean' will not wash them clean, while she comforts him: 'A little water clears us of this deed'; but later it is she who washes her hands for a quarter of an hour and cannot get rid of the bloodstains . . . she becomes all remorse and he all defiance. Together they exhaust the possibilities of reaction to the crime, like two disunited parts of a single psychical individuality, and it may be that they are both copied from the same prototype."[23]

A close reading of the juxtaposition of dialogue and monologue suggests another way of viewing this process. A relational perspective highlights the extent to which two individuals may struggle with a similar dilemma but take up different positions in relation to it, relying on the other to hold the opposing position. Likewise, the attribution of essential character traits to each is challenged by an interactional view that describes how each person may give voice to or hold back some emotional expressions for the sake of the relationship. The extent to which Lady Macbeth maintains an overt stance of determination and resolution despite her own misgivings is perfectly illustrated by the following:

Lady Macbeth "*Nought's had, all's spent*

Where our desire is got without content

'Tis safer to be that which we destroy

Than by destruction dwell in doubtful joy." (3.ii.5–8)

When Macbeth enters her tone instantly changes:

> "*How now my lord? Why do you keep alone*
>
> *Of sorriest fancies your companions making,*
>
> *Using those thoughts which should indeed have died*
>
> *With them they think on? Things without all remedy*
>
> *Should be without regard. What's done is done.*" (3.ii.9–13)

In this scene, the exhortation to banish or at least publicly conceal troublesome thoughts and feelings intensifies in the face of Macbeth expressing the very same sentiments that she just has: "*Better be with the dead/Whom we to gain our peace have sent to peace.*" This moment of potential intimacy is discarded in favour of a mutual but tacit agreement that opts for concealment. She suggests that Macbeth should "*sleek o'er your rugged looks*" and he advocates making "*our faces / Vizards to our hearts, disguising what they are.*" This is the point at which Macbeth stops confiding in his wife; although he describes his fears "*Oh full of scorpions is my mind, dear wife – /. Thou know'st that Banquo and his Fleance lives,*" he stops short of explicitly revealing that he has already given orders for their murder. Their language around this possibility is circumspect.

> Lady Macbeth "*But in them nature's copy's not eterne*"
>
> Macbeth "*There's comfort yet, they are assailable./ Then be thou jocund.*"

Although Macbeth strongly hints at the imminent deaths of Banquo and Fleance: "*there shall be done/A deed of dreadful note,*" he recoils from making his wife complicit in its details: "*Be innocent of the knowledge, dearest chuck.*"

The effect of this secrecy is that the Macbeths move out of collaborative dialogue and into a context (reaching its climax in the banquet scene) where the gulf between inner terrors and outward show becomes unbridgeable. This event – "*our great feast– a solemn supper*" – is signified as an important ritual for Macbeth to be given further legitimacy after the crowning at Scone, an event where social hierarchies are marked and loyalty avowed: " *Our duties and the pledge.*" It thus forms part of a process in which at least some of the Lords acknowledge the new ruler despite private misgivings. It also marks the rupture with Macduff, who is conspicuously absent.

Lady Macbeth, fully aware of the banquet's significance, is determined to observe the social proprieties even while her husband is gibbering with terror at Banquo's ghost. This involves moving between furious asides to her husband to play his part – *"fie for shame"* – and ever more desperate attempts to reassure the guests that nothing is seriously out of order: *"my lord is often thus"* and, even more implausibly: *"Think of this, good peers/ But as a thing of custom: tis no other."* Macbeth and Lady Macbeth are thus portrayed as operating in parallel universes where her orientation towards 'normal' social and political practice cannot connect with the supernatural context he is immersed in:

> "*You make me strange*
>
> *Even to the disposition that I owe,*
>
> *When even now I think you can behold such sights*
>
> *And keep the natural ruby of your cheeks,*
>
> *When mine is blanched with fear.*" (3.iv.13)

After the peers have departed, the brief conversation that follows is the last one between the Macbeths and, as the disconnection between them increases, dialogue breaks down. Macbeth, deciding to seek out the weird sisters as a way to *"know/By the worst means the worst,"* moves into a trajectory of unreflective violent action in which he has no need of Lady Macbeth's pragmatism. He signifies this shift with the weary comment that:

> "*I am in blood*
>
> *Stepped in so far, that should I wade no more,*
>
> *Returning were as tedious as go o'er.*
>
> *Strange things I have in head, that will to hand,*
>
> *Which must be acted, ere they may be scanned.*" (3.iv.137–141)

This privileging of action over thought not only blocks Macbeth's fear, but also all expression of moral compunction; his preoccupation is not the past nor the present but is now only directed at the future; his questions thus have to be asked of the witches, not of his wife.

Lady Macbeth, no longer required to spur her husband on to bloody deeds, moves out of dialogue and her voice, paralleling her husband's state, becomes that of a sleepwalker. She is often described as in a state of guilt: "run mad with guilt" is how Peter Hildebrand describes her.[24] But what she actually says is more nuanced and complex than that. Once she is out of dialogue, the other voices, previously restricted to inner talk, are now brought into polyphonic speech so that she draws upon a range of different and indeed contrasting voices. She continues to echo her previous injunctions and reassurances to Macbeth: "*Fie, my lord, fie, a soldier and afeared? . . . look not so pale: I tell you yet again Banquo's buried: he cannot come out on's grave– what's done cannot be undone.*" (5.i.34–5, 60–61) These words come across as frozen in time and replicate her previous efforts to stiffen her husband's backbone. But she also expresses horror at the brutal murder she was complicit in: "*Who would have thought the old man to have had so much blood in him*" as well as disquiet at further acts of brutality: "*The Thane of Fife had a wife – where is she now?*" Speaking directly to the absent Macbeth, she reverts to reassuring him about their invulnerability: "*What need we fear who knows it when none can call our power to account?*"

Whereas it is possible to play Lady Macbeth in this scene as a guilty woman with traumatic memories coming back to haunt her, with the obsessive handwashing symptomatic of her mental unravelling, she could also be played in such a way as to heighten the contrast between all the different voices that are in play. The contrast between past and present is vividly illustrated in the handwashing; a ritual that once seemed so easy to perform: "*a little water cleans us of this deed,*" now seems utterly impossible: "*will these hands ne'er be clean?*" The significance of this is that, within the relationship with her husband, moral quandaries, fear, shame and disgust could be contained because he could be relied on to hold the alternative stance. Alone she has to encompass all the contradictions of her morally compromised position.

Rather than interact with her, Lady Macbeth's attendants and the doctor comment fearfully on her revelations – "*she has spoke what she should not*" – highlighting the sense of terror and dysfunction within the Scottish kingdom and evoking the earlier contrast between Scotland as a sick country and the English king as one to bring "*the healing benediction.*" The role of the doctor and the metaphor of healing acts as a transition from private to political domains, vividly illustrated in Act 5, scene 3, in which Macbeth reflects *on* rather than from *within* his intimate life. Lonely and afraid, detached from his wife, Macbeth – like Lady Macbeth – draws upon a polyphony of voices, moving between omnipotent and defiant posturing: "*The mind I sway by, and the heart I bear,/Shall never sag with doubt nor shake with fear,*" ridiculing his servants for their fears – "*Thou lily-livered boy*" – and then moving into an unsparingly honest confrontation with his future.

In this speech Macbeth returns briefly to the reflexive voice he drew upon before Duncan's murder:

> *"I have lived long enough: my way of life*
>
> *Is fall'n into the sere, the yellow leaf,*
>
> *And that which should accompany old age,*
>
> *As honour, love, obedience, troops of friends,*
>
> *I must not look to have – but in their stead*
>
> *Curses not loud but deep, mouth-honour, breath*
>
> *Which the poor heart would fain deny, and dare not....*" (5.iii.22–28)

Macbeth's last three lines in this speech echo perfectly Angus' statement in the preceding scene: "*Those he commands move only in command/Nothing in love*" and Malcolm's in the following scene: "*none serve with him but constrainèd things/Whose hearts are absent too.*" This highlights the key idea of the sterility of power which can be only sustained by violence rather than through human bonds. The trajectory set in motion by Duncan's murder, as well as amplifying Macbeth's status as usurper, is crucially about his inability to create loyal followers; Macbeth himself knows that this isolation as much as his crimes is what will defeat him: "*the thanes fly from me.*"

These final speeches also undermine the idea that Macbeth, any more than Lady Macbeth, has degenerated into a mental state that can be reduced to a 'diagnosis' of psychosis or paranoia. Shakespeare depicts states of mind in a much more complex, relational and contextual way than this. As discussed earlier, while many of his tragic heroes seemingly head towards an inevitable doom that sweeps the audience along in a lineal trajectory, in these final scenes he portrays a complex variety of states of mind, from passive acceptance to vigorous protest, from guilt and remorse to bravado and defiance.

Conclusion

On receiving the news of his wife's death, Macbeth's sublimely poetic speech, "*Tomorrow and tomorrow and tomorrow*" draws upon the theme of time being out of synchrony with life and its rituals and upon the sense of a reckoning with meaninglessness which has formed such a major part of the play's textual and dramatic structure. The awareness that there is no good reason to continue fighting but that it might as well be done because there is nothing much else to do emerges even more strongly later in the same scene:

> "*I 'gin to be aweary of the sun*
>
> *And wish th'estate o'th'world were now undone.*
>
> *Ring the alarum bell, blow wind, come wrack,*
>
> *At least we'll die with harness on our back.*" (5.v.49–53)

In the next scene, the urge towards suicide is discarded in favour of violence to others:

> "*Why should I play the Roman fool, and die*
>
> *On mine own sword? Whiles I see lives, the gashes*
>
> *Do better upon them.*" (5.vi.31–33)

Whereas for an Anthony or a Brutus suicide was considered to be the ultimate way to reclaim male *virtus*, Macbeth's way of 'doing masculinity' is now reduced to the sole action of continuing to fight against the odds. When he realises that the witches – "*those juggling fiends*" – have led him into a false premise which has completely undermined and diminished him – "*cowed my better part of man*" – he initially refuses to fight. Macduff, not to be deprived of his opportunity for revenge, provokes him by painting a picture of the public humiliation that will follow his capture, a provocation which elicits instant compliance from Macbeth: "*I will not yield/, then To kiss the ground under young Malcolm's feet. . ./ Lay on Macduff.*" Thus, the rituals of killing – Macbeth's decapitated head being displayed and relished, much as Macdonald's eviscerated body was celebrated – are reasserted as symbols of the transfer of power. In this way they also leave open the space, as Malcolm predicted, for their likely continuance into the future.

As well as being a play in which intimate and even tender dialogues co-exist with extremes of violence, *Macbeth* is one of Shakespeare's most successful political plays. It explores in profound and complex ways the question of the meaning and future consequences of violence, the folly of believing that seizure of power conveys security, what happens when a ruler "*cannot buckle his distempered cause/Within the belt of rule*" and the mindlessness that results from cycles of revenge and retribution. These are all highly relevant themes over time and across cultures and societies. Although the ending can be read conservatively as a restoration of legitimate rulers over a usurper, Shakespeare, as ever, provides enough counter-currents to undermine this view.

I have highlighted the theme, common in many of the tragedies but especially potent in *Macbeth,* that dialogue is the cradle of creative thinking and that isolated individuals are unlikely to find a reflective space in which to challenge themselves to act differently. While the Macbeths' dialogue leads to a closing down of thought and ultimately breaks down altogether, leaving both without an interlocutor, the crucial interchange between Macduff and Malcolm lays the ground for their own successful collective action. This particular scene, and the contribution of the two murderers in Act 3, scene 1, lend weight to an argument for a reading of the play in which the 'ambition' of the Macbeths has to be seen not only in individualistic terms but in the context of those social conditions in which violence exerts such a strong appeal. Beyond the individual lie the unremittingly circular processes that violence unleashes and which develop their own momentum over time.

For systemic therapists, time can act as a context which creates meaning and time itself acquires different meanings within different contexts. At the outset, Macbeth evokes the future to try and locate himself within an ethical framework in the present and he revisits the future at the end to remind himself of all he has lost. Duncan's complacent certainty about his own and his sons' future creates a sense of time as being predictable and as unfolding in a way that does not require him to reflect on any dilemmas his decisions may create for others.

The childless Macbeths, by contrast, have a quite different sense of time; action has to be taken urgently because nothing in the future can be relied upon and there is no new generation to provide for. As I have argued, their dialogues show the effects of their uncertainty about what can possibly give meaning to their actions. Rather than being the product of the ruthless ambition of either one of them individually, their murderous collaboration rests on each of them closing down the moral compunctions and fears they express when they are alone and opting instead to maintain a joint story-line. Additionally, in *Macbeth,* other protagonists take up or refuse those positions that the Macbeths struggle with, including the question of intergenerational bonds, the limitations to violent acts and how to challenge or support troubled male or female identities. The portrayal of these dilemmas is thus hugely enriched by their repetition in so many of the different interactions within the play.

Notes

1 *Throne of Blood*, directed by Akira Kurasawa (Toho Studios, 1957).
2 Peter Hildebrand, 'The Caledonian Tragedy', in Inge Wise and Maggie Mills, eds., *Psychoanalytic Ideas and Shakespeare* (London: Karnac, 2006), 49.
3 *Macbeth*, directed by Justin Kurzel (See-Saw Productions, 2015).
4 Margaret Rustin and Michael Rustin, *Mirror to Nature* (London: Karnac, 2002), 79.
5 Felicity Rosslyn, *Tragic Plots: A New Reading from Aeschylus to Lorca* (Aldershot: Ashgate, 2000), 142.
6 Kiernan Ryan, *Shakespeare* (Basingstoke: Palgrave Macmillan, Third Edition, 2003), 90.
7 Gerard Manley Hopkins, 'Justus quidem tu es, Domine', *Selected Poetry* (Oxford: Oxford University Press, 1996), 165.
8 Sigmund Freud, *Some Character Types Met with in Psychoanalytic Work, Collected Works*, vol. XIV (London: Hogarth, 1916).
9 Andrew O'Hagan, 'Macbeth without Evil', *New York Review of Books*, December 2015, 42.
10 Terence Eagleton, *Shakespeare and Society* (London: Chatto and Windus, 1970), 130.
11 Coppelia Kahn, quoted in Nicholas Tredell, *Shakespeare Macbeth* (Basingstoke: Palgrave Macmillan, 2006), 133–134.
12 Janet Adelman, *Suffocating Mothers: Fantasies of Maternal Origin in Shakespeare's Plays, 'Hamlet' to 'The Tempest'* (New York and London: Routledge, 1992).
13 Peter Hildebrand, 'The Caledonian Tragedy', in Inge Wise and Maggie Mills, eds., *Psychoanalytic Ideas and Shakespeare* (London: Karnac, 2006).
14 Felicity Rosslyn, *Tragic Plots; a new reading from Aeschylus to Lorca*, (Aldershot: Ashgate, 2000), 143.
15 Marilyn French, *Shakespeare's Division of Experience* (London: Jonathan Cape, 1982).
16 Michael Jacobs, *Shakespeare on the Couch* (London: Karnac, 2008), 101.
17 Charlotte Burck and Gwyn Daniel, *Gender and Family Therapy* (London: Karnac, 1995).
18 Lorraine Helms, 'Acts of Resistance: The Feminist Player', in Dymphna Callaghan, Lorraine Helms and Jyotsna Singh, eds., *The Weyward Sisters* (Oxford: Wiley-Blackwell, 1994), 138.
19 Terry Eagleton, *William Shakespeare* (Oxford: Basil Blackwell, 1986), 3.

20 Kiernan Ryan, *Shakespeare* (Basingstoke: Palgrave Macmillan, Third Edition, 2003), 91.
21 Jeanette Winterston, *Guardian*, 19 April 2016.
22 Margaret Rustin and Michael Rustin, *Mirror to Nature* (London: Karnac, 2002), 79.
23 Sigmund Freud, *Some Character-Types Met with in Psycho-Analytical Work* (London: Hogarth, 1916).
24 Peter Hildebrand, 'The Caledonian Tragedy', in Inge Wise and Maggie Mills, eds., *Psychoanalytic Ideas and Shakespeare* (London: Karnac, 2006), 57.

CHAPTER 7

"Let me have war, say I"

Man as a fighting machine in *Coriolanus*

In *Coriolanus* Shakespeare portrays the Roman ideal of *virtus* in its most extreme form. He then proceeds to interrogate and subvert this model of masculinity and autonomy, with its chimaera of freeing the subject from subservience to human, relational and social bonds. The play explores many of the ambiguities and contradictions created by emotional attachments – to people, to places and to values – and the conflicts exposed in the attempt to shed them. The complexities of gender and power are revealed in the drama between mother and son; but this drama is firmly located within the wider contexts of political power, leadership and legitimacy and in the dynamics of war and peace. Classified as a tragedy, *Coriolanus,* with its unprepossessing man/boy/demi-god protagonist, and with its use of exaggeration, hyperbole and its blatant manipulations, also has moments of the absurdity and farce that dramatic portrayals of narcissistic fascist leaders so often invite.

Rather than focus solely on the eponymous hero and the other principle characters, I argue that *Coriolanus* is a play where much relational and political understanding emerges from the mouths of the marginal players and from brief and seemingly insignificant moments of dialogue, The contributions of the citizens and officers of Rome and the serving men of Antium are particularly significant. As Kiernan Ryan writes, Shakespearean tragedy "devises predicaments that cannot be accounted for, let alone resolved, by pinning responsibility on the protagonist alone"[1] Given the hero's dominance over the plot, it is particularly important to hold this in mind in relation to *Coriolanus*.

In Coriolanus himself, Shakespeare has created a protagonist who offers few direct insights into his interior world. He does not provide, through soliloquies, the internal debates and moral and psychological quandaries of a Macbeth or a Hamlet. Coriolanus can in fact be portrayed as the antithesis of thinking; he is presented as a one-man war machine, a person whose identity is at times whittled down to the sole function of fighting. He even describes himself as a weapon: "*make you a sword of me*." He is at times imbued with a robotic quality; in the words of Menenius Agrippa, "*he moves like an engine*."

Those looking for a hero brought down by an innate character defect, which surfaces and then intensifies as the drama progresses, will not find it here. Coriolanus is depicted as harsh, overbearing and lacking in empathy from the very outset. Nor is there much evidence of the play unfolding in a way that can be seen as redemptive, since it ends with Coriolanus reverting to the same self-aggrandising rhetoric that he used at the beginning. Coriolanus' rise and downfall is, therefore, only credible when viewed as a process which is co-created between him and the other participants and between him and those ideological discourses which have shaped him and to which he seems so subservient.

In *Coriolanus* we have an ideal context within which to explore how a man becomes constructed as a war machine, how a heroic martial identity is sustained both relationally and socially, whose interests are served by it and, crucially, what its defects are. Coriolanus, begging to excuse himself from his public honouring and elevation, says: "*When blows have made me stay, I fled from words*." As this unusually self-revealing and rather endearing phrase suggests, the play teases away at the pitfalls of a transition from warrior to political leader. This is a particular challenge for someone who, rather than trusting the persuasive potential of words, has defined himself in terms of the language of force. However, a change in the political context leads Coriolanus to find his voice: "*so shall my lungs/ Coin words til their decay against these measles. . .,* " only to find that his words are most unwelcome. Those with power decide that the fewer words he uses the better and they prefer to emphasise his heroism and inherent physical superiority. "Coriolanus, perhaps even more than Antony, is constituted by the contradiction inherent in the martial ideal: though identified in terms of an innate superiority, he is in fact the ideological effect of powers antecedent to and independent of him."[2]

That 'his' power exists independently of him is, of course, just what one defined as a martial ideal cannot acknowledge. Coriolanus' cry at Corioles:

"Oh me alone! Make you a sword of me?" captures this contradiction perfectly. An 'autonomous' inanimate weapon has, in reality, to be launched by other humans, who in turn have to be instructed to do so. Throughout the play, these contradictions are manifested in the nuances and subtle shifts in language and positioning and in the way that, when dilemmas or ambiguity *could* emerge, their possibilities are quickly extinguished through the stances taken by others. This reaches its climax at the moment when Coriolanus pushes omnipotence to its limit by transforming his banishment *by* the people into *his* banishment of *them:*

> Brutus "*There is no more to be said, but he is banished*
>
> *As enemy to the people and his country.*
>
> *It shall be so!*"
>
> Citizens "*It shall be so, it shall be so!*"
>
> Coriolanus "*You common cry of curs, whose breath I hate*
>
> *As reek o'th'rotten fens, whose loves I prize*
>
> *As the dead carcasses of unburied men*
>
> *That do corrupt my air: I banish you!*" (3.iii. 118–124)

The making of a 'war machine'

Coriolanus bursts on to the scene in Act 1, fully performing 'hard man.' He abuses the citizens, mocks their hunger, sets out his own repressive credentials; *he* would never have agreed to grant the citizens their tribunes. He extols war as a means of creating surplus to satisfy the inconvenient needs of the citizens and taunts them with their cowardice. He then covers himself in blood, gore and glory at Corioles. Acting as the military arm of the *polis,* he delivers a stunning, almost preternatural victory and the adulation he receives for doing so is delivered in the most uncompromisingly essentialist language. From his mother Volumnia, to the senators, all agree that what he achieved is despite, rather than because of any help or support from others: *"Alone he entered . . . aidless came off."* The scale of his victory is intensified by Shakespeare's juxtaposing it with the cowardliness or indecisiveness of the other participants, from the citizen/soldiers to their commander-in-chief, Cominius. The crisis for Coriolanus emerges when this discourse of transcendence is troubled, not least by those who were most enthusiastic in promoting it.

In the construction of a Coriolanus there is an interweaving of family and societal influences; inevitably the world of intimate relationships is also firmly located within the political and ideological imperatives of the day. Few of Shakespeare's plays offer an opportunity to learn about a protagonist's childhood or about the parental as well as the social influences on its protagonist. The dynamics of the mother/son relationship, which underpin Coriolanus' desperate striving for autonomy and his refusal to accommodate to human bonds, can be partly located in Volumnia's particular child-rearing practices. Her aim appears to have been, through harsh and brutal means, to discourage any kind of dependency and to enhance his self-sufficiency at all costs. Volumnia has often been portrayed as an emasculating virago, using her son as a surrogate penis to gain vicarious power in a society where women's status depends entirely on their relationship to men. This is a common trope in political life of all ages.

Psychoanalytic commentators have been inclined to locate the development of Coriolanus' narcissistic and dependency-avoidant personality in the specific dynamics of this mother/son dyad. Janet Adelman explores Coriolanus' terror of dependency and locates it in Volumnia's denial of his oral needs.[3] She discusses his "transformations – from feeding to warfare, from vulnerability to aggressive attack, from incorporation to spitting out." These, she argues, hold the key both to Coriolanus' vicious response to the hunger of the citizens and to the many depictions of himself as a weapon. She describes him acting according to his mother's direction, so that he remains caught in the paradox that "the more he transforms himself into an autonomous fighting machine, the more he is trapped into carrying out a role predetermined by, and thus dependent on, his mother."[4] While Coriolanus might have been unable or unwilling to face this 'reality,' it was common knowledge among the citizenry: *"he did it to please his mother."* Thus, the feared notion that this indomitable warrior is really still his mother's child recurs as a leitmotif throughout the play, culminating, just before his death, in Aufidius' contemptuous dismissal of him as a *"boy of tears."*

There are many ways in which Volumnia could be described as a 'double-binding' mother.[5] Coriolanus is potentially trapped within two binds. First, to truly fulfil his mother's ambition for him as a warrior, he has to be ready to die in battle:

Virgilia "*But had he died in the business, madam, how then?*"

Volumnia "*Then his good report should have been my son; I therein would have found issue.*"

However, although Coriolanus certainly displays a willingness to risk his life, if he were to die, he would deprive his mother of the vicarious pleasure she gains from imagining him in battle: *"Methinks I see him stamp thus, and call thus/'Come on you cowards! You were got in fear,/Though you were born in Rome."*

The second paradox is that, although Volumnia desires her son to be an instrument of war, she also aspires to his political success. In fact, she has always assumed the first to be the route to the second:

> "*I have lived*
>
> *To see inherited my very wishes*
>
> *And the buildings of my fancy. Only*
>
> *There's one thing wanting, which I doubt not but*
>
> *Our Rome will cast on thee*." (2.i.194–178)

The skills involved in each are, however, very different.

Volumnia, an intelligent, ambitious, patrician widow whose only hope of achieving any power is via a man, could be seen to be just as trapped as her son; however, the effects of her strategies on him bear closer examination. Shakespeare never portrays Coriolanus as especially ambitious to be consul and, when he refuses to play the part required of him to obtain office, the very behaviour that his mother has conditioned him into from an early age is now highlighted by her as a defect.

> "*You might have been enough the man you are*
>
> *With striving less to be so.*
>
> *...You are too absolute*." (3.ii.19–20, 42)

One way that double-binding processes work to confuse the child/recipient is that the parent changes the context in which the matter under debate takes its meaning. The recipient can then feel constantly wrong footed. The scene at Coriolanus' house is a perfect example of this process in operation. In this wonderful sequence, the issue is whether he should adopt a more conciliatory posture towards the tribunes and citizens. Coriolanus whose 'essential' nature has been so lauded, now finds that fidelity to this 'nature' and the need to be strategic are set in opposition to one another, creating a conflict between the political and the essentialist aspects of *virtus*. He attempts to meta-communicate about the anomaly of his mother suddenly disapproving of all those aspects of him she had previously encouraged, reminding her of the class-ridden ideology she has inculcated in him:

> "*I muse my mother*
>
> *Does not approve me further, who was wont*
>
> *To call them woollen vassals....*
>
> *Why did you wish me milder? Would you have me*
>
> *False to my nature?*" (3.ii.7–15)

Volumnia counters with a series of lecture on how to be strategic, how to perform compliance and how not to act repressively until he is certain of having attained power.

> "*Lesser had been*
>
> *The tryings of your dispositions if*
>
> *You had not showed them how ye were disposed*
>
> *Ere they lacked power to cross you.*" (3.ii.20–23)

Volumnia's dialogue includes other rhetorical devices such as drawing his attention to her own more sophisticated brain:

> "*I have a heart as little apt as yours*
>
> *But yet a brain that leads my use of anger*
>
> *To better vantage.*" (3.ii.29–31)

This positions Coriolanus as mindless and he responds accordingly: "*What must I do?*"

As information is fed in about how combustible the political situation is, Volumnia, Menenius and Cominius all urge tactics on him; this reinforces the idea that they prefer Coriolanus as an instrument rather than a thinking participant. He lapses first into inarticulacy and then, as the pressure mounts, into hyperbole, entertaining and then roundly rejecting the idea of compromise, now equated with self-abasement. Volumnia then abandons the attempt to persuade her son to be strategic and reminds him of his dependence on her approval:

> "*I prithee now, sweet son, as thou hast said*
>
> *My praises made thee first a soldier, so,*

To have my praise for this, perform a part
Thou hast not done before." (3.ii.109–112)

These words induce initial compliance in Coriolanus followed by a stream of overblown images of prostitution, emasculation, femininity and 'infantilism.' Hearing himself utter these words, he again refuses to comply:

"*Away, my disposition; and possess me*
Some harlot's spirit! My throat of war be turned,
Which choired with my drum, into a pipe
Small as an eunuch or the virgin voice
That babies lull asleep!" (3.ii.113–117)

In this brief speech is encapsulated the tension between inner and outer dialogues, displaying its 'double-voiced' quality. Coriolanus, responding to his mother's strictures is also reacting to a set of internal signifiers, partly, of course, engendered by that very mother. In this speech, he typifies what Bakhtin calls the "hidden polemic" where the other's thought "does not personally make its way inside the discourse but is only reflected in it, determining its tone and its meaning" In Coriolanus' case this takes the form of parody and hyperbole.[6]

Volumnia then resorts to her final 'strategy'; she declares impotence and withdraws from the fray, "*At thy choice then,*" conjuring up perhaps the most terrifying prospect of all; Coriolanus must think for himself. However, for his 'own good,' there is only one way he can think. Volumnia also disowns her own part in creating such obduracy in him:

"*Thy valiantness was mine, thou suckd'st it from me/ But owe thy pride thyself.*"

This produces instant capitulation, albeit of a sullen, adolescent kind. "*Pray be content./Mother, I am going to the market-place/Chide me no more.*"

Taking this faux submissive stance which barely covers his belligerence, Coriolanus goes off to meet the tribunes, who know him well enough to have worked out exactly how to provoke him. This scene follows the earlier pattern of a grudging acceptance to play by the rules: "*Well mildly be it, then,– mildly!* A hesitant nod of acquiescence to the tribunes: "*I am content,*" is swiftly followed by a full-scale temper tantrum at their accusation of treason.

If, however, Coriolanus is caught up in paradoxical communication from his mother, he is no less so from the senators. At some points, when he is serving the Republic's interests, he is depicted as a demi-god:

> Cominius "*alone he entered*
> *The mortal gate of th' city, which he painted*
> *With shunless destiny, aidless came off*
> *And with sudden reinforcement struck*
> *Corioles like a planet.*" (2.ii.108–112)

Depicted thus, he is obviously serving the ideological purposes of the Senate, who wish to strengthen themselves by honouring him. They seem unaware that their overblown language of heroic individualism makes for an uneasy fit with their later language of restraint and compromise. "*I think twill serve if he/Can thereto frame his spirit.*" When Coriolanus refuses to play the game, the language is very different; personal, cajoling, leaving no doubt about who is in charge.

Cominius speaks to the erstwhile 'Mars' as if he were a greenhorn: '*Come come we'll prompt you*"; and Menenius Agrippa as if he were a child: "*Is this the promise that you made to your mother?*" Menenius is aware of the struggle Coriolanus the warrior has in engaging with any other form of identity: "*Consider this: he has been bred i'the wars/ Since a could draw a sword, and is ill school'd/ In bolted language.*" However, there was a time when he welcomed exactly this "*ill-schooling*" as a counterbalance to his own more emollient style. When his fatuous 'body politic' tale in Act 1, scene 1, failed to induce compliance in the citizens, Coriolanus' crude invective came as a welcome support:

> Menenius "*Rome and her rats are at the point of battle;The one side must have bale. (Enter Caius Martius) Hail noble Martius!*"
>
> Martius "*Thanks.What's the matter you, dissentious rogues ...?*" (1.i.158)

The useful weapon that was Coriolanus in Act 1 has by Act 3 become a loose cannon or an unguided missile. Rather than view this as deriving from internal character flaws or from maternal manipulation, it is more convincing to locate it in the way that different contexts (e.g. of political struggle rather than warfare) create new exigencies, new dilemmas and therefore new constructions of 'character' as well as of desirable behaviour. These changes of context have the capacity to both confuse and enrage Coriolanus.

It is also possible to see Coriolanus himself as seeking out a different path, even if he has barely articulated it, and even though he only does so by a refusal to play by the rules. Coriolanus' dislike of praise and honours is conveyed strongly in the early part of the play, but it is ambiguous. It can be understood at different levels; as rooted in his relationship with Volumnia: "*my mother,/ Who has a charter to extol her blood,/When she does praise me grieves me.*" It could be seen as a further mark of pride; that Coriolanus relies on no-one's feedback but his own, or it could be understood as his resistance to the early signs of the manipulation that is to follow from the political class: "*I had rather be their servant in my way,/Than sway with them in theirs.*"

It is not Coriolanus' contempt for the citizens that marks him out; all the patricians share the same view, but his refusal to 'go through the motions' of according them respect to achieve a political goal. Born with an impeccably martial lineage, Coriolanus has been raised to assume a rigid, arrogant and unquestioned soldierly identity and to follow a narrow set of precepts that prioritise action over thinking. Shakespeare has not here created one of his more intelligent protagonists; his ability to reflect on alternative pathways is strictly limited. His struggle for selfhood is worked out by conflict and opposition and by evoking hatred and fear. It is possible to construe the cry of "*There is a world elsewhere*" as containing a moment of triumphant apotheosis where he might escape his binds by leaving the field and facing the possibility of a period of aloneness, uncertainty and 'statelessness.'

In what could be seen as his first 'leaving home' experience, there is thus the heady but scary possibility of new adventures and, ironically, given the victory at Corioles, the promise of achievement: "*Farewell my wife, my mother; I'll do well yet. . . .* " The "*world elsewhere*" that is already prefigured by Coriolanus – *I wish I had cause to seek him there* – turns out to be a direct path to Aufidius' Antium and a re-entry into those very bonds he has briefly tried to escape.

Attachments, ambivalence and the "lure of the other"

The ambiguity of Coriolanus' seemingly desperate desire for autonomy is expressed in his relationships to the 'polis' and to his family ties as well as through his longing for another encounter with Aufidius. Aristotle, in depicting 'man' as a political animal, wrote that a man without a polis is "either a monster or a god"[7] and Coriolanus has a fair go at both of these identities. He rejects the Rome that defines him as a monster and is temporarily embraced by the Volscians as a god.

The contradiction sitting at the heart of a desire for autonomy is that it can only exist in relation to the very bonds that it attempts to reject or deny.

It is thus dependent on them. The moments of greatest dramatic tension in the play occur when the powerful emotional draw that these bonds exert is intensified in the very act of trying to shake them off. This reaches its apotheosis in Act 5, scene 3. Many commentators have remarked upon the impossibility of Coriolanus escaping from the mother who created him (or 'Mother Rome' since Rome and her own womb are quite explicitly linked by Volumnia and in trying to control her son she is serving the republic's interest). I have already described the creative repertoire Volumnia draws upon in this pursuit. What is so interesting in *Coriolanus* is the way that such beautifully choreographed interactions are performed at all stages of the play, when attachments are either threatened with their loss or challenged by their proximity.

In Act 4, scene 1, Coriolanus is faced – perhaps for the first time – by Volumnia's vulnerability at the very moment that he has made the bold move of escaping both her and the Senate's influence. He employs the same rhetorical strategy as in their earlier interaction; repeating back to her the exhortations she has always used on him, only this time it seems to emerge from a wish to help and hearten her:

> "*Nay, mother,*
>
> *Where is your ancient courage? You were used*
>
> *To say extremities was the trier of spirits....*" (4.i.3–4)

In a striking reversal of Act 3, scene 2, Coriolanus acts in a fatherly, reassuring way to Cominius – *"droop not"* – urging temperance on his mother and trying to calm her. For Coriolanus the cutting off of bonds with Rome, his native city and his close intimate relationships carries with it the expectation that he will be missed – *"I shall be loved when I am lacked"* – and that he will exist as a consistent image in the minds of those he has left behind: *"While I remain above the ground you shall/Hear from me still: and never yet of me aught/But what is like me formerly."* Beneath the rather messianic overtones of this message is, however, a plea for being kept in mind so that others will maintain those very attachments that he is rejecting.

In the final scene between Coriolanus and his family, the emotional dilemmas of both attachment and autonomy are pushed to their limits. Volumnia employs a remarkably similar range of rhetorical strategies to those she used in Act 3, scene 2, including appeals to her son's 'better nature,' to his vanity, reasoning about strategy, and outright guilt tripping: *"thou hast never in thy life / showed thy dear mother any courtesy."* The scene is structurally consistent with the earlier one, but with more intense emotional loading. A.D. Nuttall maintains that "the strongly formed soldier resists her reasoned plea for mercy but cannot hold out when hit by the word of terrifying conditioning power 'mother.' "[8] On the contrary, Coriolanus holds out against this very well.

At the beginning of the scene, Coriolanus reflects on his performance in dismissing Menenius and reassures Aufidius that *"Fresh embassies and suits/ Nor from the state nor private friends/ Will I lend ear to."* No sooner has he said this than the three women and young Martius appear. Coriolanus' injunction to himself to: *"Never/ Be such a gosling as to obey instinct, but stand/ As if man were author of himself/And knew no other kin"* is juxtaposed with his acknowledgment that he will be find this hard as *"Great nature cries 'Deny not'."* The dilemma is that disavowal of kin can only be performed in relation to the claims of kinship that are pressed by others. The fragility of this aspiration leads Coriolanus, after Virgilia lays claim to him, to meditate wearily: *"Like a dull actor now/ I have forgot my part."*

The crucial turning point occurs, however, when, instead of pressing kinship ties, Volumnia, having exhausted every other persuasive device, herself disavows kinship and begins to take her leave:

> "*Come, let us go.*" *(they rise)*
>
> "*This fellow had a Volscian to his mother.*
>
> *His wife is in Corioles, and his child*
>
> *Like him by chance.*" (5.iii.179–181)

It is then left to Coriolanus, faced with the terror of abandonment, to re-invoke and cling to the kin relationship *"Oh mother, mother!"* It is not the word 'mother' that unsettles him but that he is suddenly left with no kinship claims from her that he can reject. In what can be played as their mutual shock at what has unfolded and the awareness on each side of its fatal implications, mother and son could be seen as acting in silent synchrony enacting a powerful internal drama around the meaning of what has been sacrificed. Volumnia's role is left ambiguous after this point. On her return to Rome to the adulation of the patricians, she is given no words. She could already be mourning the son who is once again to be sacrificed for the good of the city, she could already be grooming young Martius to be her new surrogate warrior or, seduced by the rhetoric of *"patroness of Rome,"* she could be carried away by a sense of her own potency.

Behind Volumnia's harsh rhetoric there are hints of the great sacrifices she has made in unleashing her son upon the enemies of Rome "*when for a day of kings' entreaties a mother should not sell him an hour from her beholding . . . to a cruel war I sent him.*" What is striking is the contrast between her stance after Corioles, when it appears that her sacrifice has been triumphantly vindicated and her son about to fulfil all her dreams and her position after his banishment. Here, she wails as she were the most over-protective mother in the world: "*My first son/Whither wilt thou go? Take good Cominius/With thee awhile.*" The difference between sending a sixteen-year-old off to a '*cruel war*' and seeing the adult son leave the city alone is that she was in control of the former and could see within it a promise of success but she has no control over the latter which is also contaminated with failure.

If we think, as Bateson failed to, about the context within which his 'double-binding' mothers operated, Volumnia can be understood in more complex ways. The affective range that might have been available to her includes the language of blood and sacrifice, the imperative to serve and the self-censorship of all emotions that might be defined as weak, erotic or feminised. The constraints of her gender are obvious to all, as Sicinius sarcastically, reminds her: "*Are you mankind.*" Her robust reply "*Ay, fool. Is that a shame?*" still involves her positioning herself as her father's daughter: "*Was not a man my father?*"

The relationship between Coriolanus and Virgilia is often overlooked because her character is under-developed and because she is easily portrayed as passive and submissive, dominated by her mother-in-law and easily ignored by her husband. It would be hard for even the most enthusiastic revisionist to make much of her feeble bleats of "*Oh Heavens, oh heavens*" and "*Oh the Gods*" in Act 4, scene 1, and, when she does berate the tribunes, she follows Volumnia's lead. Overall she says very little and Coriolanus himself calls her "*My gracious silence.*" Frank Kermode comments that Shakespeare's interest in silence might mark "a general development away from rhetorical explicitness and towards a language that does not try to give everything away."[9] Thus, the way in which Virgilia's silence is portrayed on stage is crucial and there is scope for a more nuanced reading of both her speech and her silence. Her interactions with Coriolanus have a tenderness that is absent from any other part of the play, but which clearly struggles to find a 'voice.'

In the early scenes with Volumnia, Virgilia stands up for her own definition of the bond between husband and wife. This is presented as one of loyalty and protectiveness, in contrast to the instrumental language used by Volumnia. Indeed, tension between the two women emerges in relation to the sensual reverence for the body expressed by Virgilia, and Volumnia's belief that the body with its wounds is a marketable commodity to be exploited in the quest for political power. The two brief scenes where this dynamic is played out offer flashes of Virgilia's alternative reality, but even when the women's responses converge in their grief and anger at the banishment of Coriolanus and when they beg him to save Rome, Virgilia's voice has little salience. The emotional connection between her and Coriolanus is, however, expressed in tender, poetic, language quite unlike that of the rest of the play. "*My gracious silence, hail . . . ah my dear*" and "*O, a kiss/ Long as my exile, sweet as my revenge.*"

The tenderness, softness and sensuality of Virgilia's relationship to her husband, hinted at in Act 1, scene 3, is derided and ridiculed by Volumnia, perhaps because it excites envy, perhaps because it represents a threat to Coriolanus' need to be single-mindedly attached to his martial identity. We can also assume that they have different views about whether to encourage young Martius in his cruelty to animals. When Virgilia takes up a more ambivalent and sceptical stance towards her husband's military triumphs in Act 2, scene 1, she and Coriolanus could be seen as the dyad most in tune with each other. She does not rush to praise him but instead her silence opens up the momentary opportunity, soon crushed by Menenius, for Coriolanus to reflect on the human cost of this war: "*Ay, my dear/Such eyes the widows in Corioles wear/And mothers that lack sons.*" Menenius quickly steps in: "*Now the gods crown thee!*"

Coriolanus' relationship with Aufidius is often noted for its strong homoerotic overtones, or, in psychoanalytic terms, as a narcissistic object choice that, because it must contain strong elements of rivalry, is inherently unstable. These are compelling views; yet there is an additional way of exploring the relationship, which is in terms of its symmetrical and complementary patterns. These show how, at the same time as the relationship enacts the desire for the 'perfect rival': "*he is a lion that I am proud to hunt,*" its context is inevitably organised by patterns of domination and submission. These two elements intersect contrapuntally in the construction of the other as the ideal oppositional match – "*we hate alike*" – with its intimate, interdependent, collaborative nuances: "*. . . if I fly, Martius/Holloa me like a hare.*" The desire for an intimate encounter as physical equals – "*beard to beard*" – is, however offset by reminders of Coriolanus' military superiority: "*. . . Alone I fought in your Corioles' walls/And made what work I pleased.*" Aufidius faces up realistically to the prospect that he will never defeat Coriolanus in face-to-face combat and that he has to rely on guile: "*I'll potch at him some way/ Or wrath or craft may get him.*" At the moment of their passionate reunion in

Antium, power discourses are also embedded in each of their dialogues. After Coriolanus arrives at the Volscian camp, a competitive exchange occurs as he insists on being recognised by his former enemy and Aufidius refuses to grant him recognition. Coriolanus then persists in withholding his name. The name itself, as well as the person, is imbued with power, referring as it does to his earlier victory at Corioles.

> Aufidius "*Why speak'st not? Speak, man. What's thy name?*"
>
> Coriolanus (unmuffling) "*If, Tullus,*
>
> *Not yet thou know'st me, and seeing me, dost not*
>
> *Think me for the man I am, necessity*
>
> *Commands me name myself*"
>
> Aufidius "*What is thy name?*"
>
> Coriolanus "*A name unmusical to the Volscians' ears*
>
> *And harsh in sound to thine.*"
>
> Aufidius "*Say what's thy name?*"
>
> Coriolanus "*Prepare thy brow to frown./Know'st thou me yet?*"
>
> Aufidius "*I know thee not. Thy name?*"
>
> Coriolanus "*My name is Caius Martius.*" (4.v.54.66)

There is nothing more challenging to narcissism than not being recognised but, rather than allow this escalation go into a 'runaway' leading to his ejection from the city or worse, Coriolanus concedes and states his name. He follows this by taking the further complementary position of supplicant: "*And make my misery serve thy turn:*" but this position is clearly such a troubled one that he reverses the complementarity by daring Aufidius to kill him, offering advice and a provocative challenge: "*My throat to thee and to thy ancient malice/Which not to cut would show thee but a fool.*" By taking one complementary position (potential victim) and then reversing it (advice giving) he is thus able to maintain the competitive edge between himself and Aufidius.

These patterns are not just descriptive but also indicative of the constant and uneasy enactment of power dynamics between two men who are simultaneously antagonists and deeply attracted to one another. Behind the erotic hyperbole, however, Aufidius has obviously been doing some rapid calculations about military strategy. This is echoed later in Act 5, scene 3, when he witnesses the scene between Coriolanus and his family.

Here, as well as being *"moved withal"* he is already deciding how to *"work myself a former fortune."*

While the processes of their idealised 'twinning' and common military aims could work in favour of collaboration – perhaps what each of them longs for – the patterns of domination and subordination are too strong. Coriolanus has been raised to dominate and the adulation he receives from the Volscian soldiery, who treat him as *"their God"* is in stark contrast to his experience of the Romans. Even the cynical Aufidius is shocked by the reversal in their respective roles. It is as if the hierarchical patterns, inherent in warfare were waiting to assert themselves over their brief comradeship. Other observers, attuned to the workings of power, had already cut through the illusion of equality and taken note of Aufidius' dilemma in teaming up with Coriolanus.

> Third Serving Man "*Why, here's he that was wont to thwack our general, Caius Martius.... Our general himself makes a mistress of him ... But the bottom of the news is, our general is cut i'th'middle and but one half of what he was yesterday....*" (4-v.182–183,199–204)

While Martius distinguishes himself in the military field, it is Aufidius who retains the ability to think. Coriolanus, despite his awareness that in yielding to his mother's (and Rome's) entreaties, he has signed his own death warrant, proceeds to act as if this were not the case. He busies himself with diplomacy, ignoring Aufidius' likely response to being deprived of the pleasure of sacking Rome. In the final scene, however, while Coriolanus initially acts 'rationally' with negotiations and documents and Aufidius is bent on revenge, they both collaborate in brushing aside the intervention of the second lord:

> Second Lord ..."*Stand Aufidius,/And trouble not the peace*"
>
> Coriolanus (drawing his sword) "*O that I had him,/With six Aufidiuses..*"
>
> Aufidius "*Insolent villain.*"

At the end, it is the conspirators rather than Aufidius himself who cut Coriolanus down. His death produces an immediate sense of loss in Aufidius: *"My rage is gone/And I am struck with sorrow."*

Politics, power and positioning

Widening the lens again, all these interactions are played out and given significance in the context of a fierce and fateful political conflict within

Rome where the conservative metaphor of the 'body politic' is displaced by that of a struggle between the competing interests of citizens and senators, with the ambiguous role of the tribunes pivotal in the conflict that ensues.

In Act 3, as the political drama at the heart of the play unfolds; positions are taken up and then revisited strategically, public utterances are censored, relational dynamics are fluid and shifting and unlikely collaborations emerge. The relationship between the tribunes and the citizens is mirrored to some extent by that of the senators and Coriolanus. In each there is a part to be played that has to be scripted by others. Each develops in a way that reveals the many ambiguities of political representation.

The citizens are accorded the 'power' to approve Coriolanus as consul, a power to which they know there are strict limits. When Coriolanus grudgingly agrees to display his wounds, the citizens are not allowed to approach him as a group, but in twos and threes so that they cannot exercise a collective voice – *"He's to make his requests by particulars"* – and they are never actually shown the wounds that are the symbolic heart of the ritual. When they do give Coriolanus their assent, they are immediately challenged in this decision by the tribunes, who persuade them, using the power of their own office, that they have been cowed by the weight and status of Coriolanus' persona and lineage.

Claiming to provide the citizens with a convincing narrative to explain their change of heart, the tribunes are explicit in naming the ambiguity of their role as spokesmen: *"And this shall seem, as partly 'tis, their own/ Which we have goaded onwards."* They then pre-empt this carefully thought-out process by directly confronting Coriolanus themselves. This reduces the citizens and their influence to the status of, as Coriolanus names them, *"children's voices."* Menenius' earlier contemptuous comment to the tribunes – *"your abilities are too infant-like for doing much alone"* – has already revealed the assumption that, in the eyes of those with power, the tribunes are condemned by their very association with the despised citizens.

Throughout Act 3, the political imperative to appease the citizens and the tribunes for just long enough to get Coriolanus safely into power requires compliance on his part and a silence that he is unwilling to maintain. In scene 1, Coriolanus pronounced on the implications for the Senate if they allow the citizens influence: *"It will in time/Win upon power and throw forth greater themes/For insurrection's arguing,"* and in these scenes he again argues strongly for an authoritarian stance. This eloquence belies his description of himself as *"fleeing from words."* Ironically one of the senators upbraids him for speaking too much: *"No more words, we beseech you."* Coriolanus responds incredulously:

> *"How, no more?*
>
> *As for my country I have shed my blood,*
>
> *Not fearing outward force, so shall my lungs*
>
> *Coin words til their decay against these measles. . . ."* (3.i.78–81)

After his humiliating confrontation with Volumnia, Coriolanus resorts to invective and abuse. The tribunes had correctly calculated that it would be easy to provoke him to excess. Whether they predicted or not that Coriolanus would receive so little support from the patricians, the tribunes are certainly able to take advantage of it. They skilfully move the debate from that of competing political positions to the question of whether a single individual should be defined as a traitor. Since there is little justification for this accusation within Coriolanus' speech itself, it can be understood as emerging from the empty space opened up by the silence of the ruling class. Indeed, while Coriolanus' discourse is cruel, contemptuous and tyrannical, he initially puts forward a rational argument and it is the senators/patricians who attempt to silence both him and the tribunes:

> Coriolanus *"This was my speech and I will speak't again"*
>
> Menenius *"Not now, not now."*

In a telling interchange, the tribunes lambast Coriolanus for his arrogance and disrespect for the citizens:

> Brutus *"The people cry you mock'd them . . . call'd them*
>
> *Time-pleasers, flatterers, foes to nobleness."*
>
> Coriolanus *"Why, this was known before."* (3.i.44–47)

However, what was *"known before"* now has a different meaning. In a private exchange with the tribunes, Menenius made clear his own contempt for the *"beastly plebeians,"* a contempt he extends even more viciously towards those who represent them, their *"herdsmen," ". . . a brace of unmeriting, proud, violent, testy magistrates, alias fools, as any in Rome."* Indeed the very appointment – out of fear and expedience – of the tribunes has changed the context, so that public discourse too is required to change. Coriolanus has either not grasped this or is unwilling to comply with it.

It is important to note that at no stage do the patricians ever engage in any serious political debate. They do not wish to reveal their own authoritarian aims. If words are the currency of politics, they have to be exactly the right words and at the right time and this 'rightness' is of course contextualised by power. The combination of their own silence and their silencing of others could be said to emanate from a long history of entitlement. It opens up the space for a dual challenge to the status quo, both from the authoritarian posturing of Coriolanus and the pseudo-democratic arguments of the tribunes. In his later rantings against Rome, Coriolanus' rage against the tribunes is surpassed only by his fury with *"the dastard nobles."* In these two scenes, Alan Howard's Coriolanus confronts the senators with more emotional intensity than he does the tribunes and the people.[10]

When Coriolanus squares up to the tribunes, Menenius and Cominius try to intervene with rapidly diminishing success. Their interventions are solely aimed at damage limitation. Given his astonishment that the senators cannot see what he sees, Coriolanus vents his rage directly on the tribunes. One word is pivotal in summing up the changing power relationships. The word *"shall"* used by Sicinius serves more than anything to provoke Coriolanus:

> "*'Shall remain'?*
>
> *Hear you this Triton of the minnows? Mark you*
>
> *His absolute 'shall'? . . . They choose their magistrate,*
>
> *And such a one as he, who puts his 'shall,'*
>
> *His popular 'shall,' against a graver bench*
>
> *Than ever frowned in Greece.*" (3.i.106–109)

Despite, or perhaps because of this, the trio of Coriolanus, Brutus and Sicilius can be viewed, paradoxically, as being in collaboration in their different challenges to the senators. Each is prepared to go to the brink and beyond, so that eventually Menenius' and Cominius' interpolations become so much ineffectual noise. From their different positions, Coriolanus and the tribunes represent a radical challenge to the established order, a challenge that has the potential to destroy the republic. The tribunes have fundamentally misunderstood Coriolanus in assuming that he is strategising to gain political power and Coriolanus underestimates them by dismissing them as mere mouthpieces for the 'rabble' and not worth taking seriously. Nevertheless, as the play develops, they each recognise in the other a threat to their vital interests and, as such, an enemy to be defeated.

What Coriolanus and the tribunes have in common is their willingness to name the workings of power, expressed by Coriolanus in "*your people, I love them as they weigh*" and by Sicinius in "*Nature teaches beasts to know their friends*." In their different ways both Coriolanus and the tribunes are standing up a more 'localised' or 'particularised' approach to the acquisition of power. Coriolanus challenges the traditions and rituals that accompany the post of consul and questions the assumption that the language, culture and mores of politics is best served by circumspect talk. Sicinius and Brutus, challenging the idea that they are so much 'window dressing' to neutralise the plebeians, raise the proposition that public office needs to be acquired through suitability and political merit as well as by winning battles or being favoured by the Senate. We see this dynamic in action earlier when they carefully and politely raise this point, only to be slapped down by Menenius for whom their presence is purely cosmetic:

Sicinius "*We are convented*

Upon a pleasing treaty, and have hearts

Inclinable to honour and advance

The theme of our assembly"

Brutus "*Which the rather We shall be blessed to do if he remember*

A kinder value of the people than

He hath hereto prized them at."

Menenius "*That's off, thats off I would you rather had been silent.*

Please you To hear Cominius speak?"

Brutus "*Most willingly And yet my caution was more pertinent*

Than the rebuke you give it." (2.ii.52–62)

Coriolanus has already challenged procedure by refusing Cominius' offer of a tenth of the spoils from Corioles and then by declining to stay and hear himself praised in the Senate. Although Shakespeare strongly emphasises

Coriolanus' personal abhorrence of the ritual that requires showing his wounds to the citizens, he is only one of a number of participants who collectively act to close down certain options and make others seem more compelling. In this situation all is fluid; the energy and intensity of focus shifts from Coriolanus and the citizens, to the tribunes and the citizens, to Coriolanus and the senators and finally back to Coriolanus and the tribunes. The inertness of the senators can be seen to play a vital part in exacerbating the showdown between Coriolanus and the plebeians. We are not privy to any debates the senators might have had about strategy, but can assume that getting Coriolanus into a position of power as consul so that he can act as their repressive arm is the highest priority. They can then rely on him to neutralise the tribunes. The citizens need to be appeased as quickly as possible by visual symbols (being shown Coriolanus' wounds), but speech is to be avoided. Entering into political arguments about legitimacy and precedence is antithetical to achieving their aim. However, the effect is, and this emerges in the hiatus between the two 'public confrontation' scenes, that Coriolanus is singled out by all as 'the problem' in a way that obscures the underlying conflicts. These conflicts are, however, given added salience through the voices of other characters.

Voices off; citizens and serving men

As with all political dramas, on or off the stage, too intense a focus on the central protagonists has the effect of marginalising other participants, obscuring their contributions and thus limiting the richness of alternative perspectives. In *Coriolanus*, the voices of citizens, officers, soldiers and serving men provide a particularly acute and nuanced commentary on the personal and political dilemmas that coalesce around the practices of power and this in turn intensifies our understanding of the actions of the main protagonists.

In *Coriolanus*, Shakespeare gives the citizens a more compelling and sophisticated voice than those in *Julius Caesar*. They are by no means the rabble that Coriolanus portrays them as, and they are certainly not a mindless inarticulate, collective foil to the eloquence of the senators. In fact, they insist on their individuality:

> First Citizen " ... *he himself stuck not to call us the many-headed multitude*."
>
> Third Citizen "*We have been called so of many; not that our heads are some brown, some black, some abram, some bald, but that our wits are so diversely coloured*. ..." (2.iii.15–18)

The citizens debate strategy among themselves, question the virtues of complying with or resisting authority and tease away at the values and moral imperatives of Republican Rome. If the central dilemma for Coriolanus is that his striving for transcendence leads him to deny human bonds and refuse to acknowledge any kind of interdependence, this is encapsulated by the citizens, as it is by the tribunes and the officers in the single word, 'pride.' The accusation of pride towards Coriolanus is, however, considered in a nuanced way, from the perspective of childishness, moral flaw, nature or nurture and it is also posited as a protection against venality.

> First citizen "*He did it to please his mother and to be partly proud – which he is, even to the altitude of his nature*"
>
> Second citizen "*What he cannot help in his nature you account a vice in him. You must in no way say he is covetous.*" (I.i.35–40)

The citizens dissect the economics of privilege with a clarity that contrasts with the complacency and dishonesty of Menenius Agrippa's fable of the belly; his depiction of the 'body politic' as one organism is used solely as means of reinforcing hierarchy:

> First citizen "*I the great toe? Why the great toe?*"
>
> Menenius "*For that being one o'th' lowest, basest, poorest.*"

The citizens do not need to be told that political relationships are rooted in inequality; they readily grasp the idea of interdependence but reach radically different conclusions:

> First Citizen "*the leanness that afflicts us, the object of our misery, is as an inventory to particularise their abundance; our sufferance is a gain to them.*"

Pushed to breaking point by their hunger, the citizens are mocked by Coriolanus just as he pours scorn on the Senate's decision to appoint tribunes to represent them. His prescription is to wage war since it constitutes a win-win situation for those with power. War can both reduce the numbers of troublesome citizens – *"vent our musty superfluity"* – and divert demands for bread by exporting domestic need: *"The Volces have much corn. Take these rats thither/ To gnaw their garners."*

When Coriolanus has returned from Corioles, two officers charged with *"laying cushions"* debate the question, key to the play, of whether being overt about loathing the people – *"lets them plainly see't"* – is a more honest position and an easier one to deal with than pretending to love them: "*to seem to affect the malice and displeasure of the people is as bad as that which he dislikes, to flatter them for their love.*" This gets to the heart both of the performative element of the stand-off between Coriolanus and the tribunes as well as the different positions taken up by Coriolanus and Menenius and the dynamics and tensions it creates in their relationship. Menenius, as we have seen, makes a distinction between private and public utterances. Coriolanus does not.

The relative merits of states of war and peace, of warrior and civilian identities, another crucial framing for the play and for the fortunes of Coriolanus are debated by the serving men in Aufidius' court:

> First serving man "*Let me have war, say I. It exceeds peace as far as day does night, It's sprightly walking, audible and full of vent. Peace is a very apoplexy, lethargy; mulled, deaf, sleepy, insensible; a getter of more bastard children than war's a destroyer of men.*"
>
> Second serving man "*'Tis so. And as war in some sort may be said to be a ravisher, so it cannot be denied that peace is a great maker of cuckolds*"
>
> First serving man "*Ay, and it makes men hate one another*"
>
> Third serving man "*Reason: because they then less need one another. The wars for my money. I hope to see Romans as cheap as Volscians. They are rising, they are rising.*" (4.v.226–239)

In ironic juxtaposition, Shakespeare follows this scene with one in which the tribunes celebrate the outbreak of civic harmony following Coriolanus' exile. The audience is already aware of the attack that Coriolanus and Aufidius plan on the city. Sicinius waxes lyrical about: "*Our tradesmen singing in their shops and going/About their functions friendly,*" only to be thrown into confusion and disarray by news of the Volscian assault that is about to be unleashed on Rome, news that they initially dismiss as impossible: "*Tell not me/I know this cannot be.*"

The tendency to define reality expediently to buttress existing positions is an effect of power and highlights the complacency that so often results from unquestioned assumptions about power. That debates of the kind taking place between the "curs," " rats," "clusters" and "apron-men" touch upon such profound themes, serves to emphasise how, in *Coriolanus*, virtually no such debate takes place among those with power. The tribunes can only dismiss the news of the Volscian attack and whip the messenger. The senators, having mindlessly pursued the plan to make Coriolanus consul, have no other strategy other than to beg for mercy when he is poised to attack Rome. By investing Coriolanus with such transcendent power, they have divested themselves of their own capacity to think. However, although they demonstrate a simplistic understanding of power and its effects, the citizens have an acute awareness of its problems and the ritual character of their participation:

> First citizen "*Once, if he do require our voices, we ought not to deny him*"
>
> Second Citizen "*We may, sir, if we will*"
>
> Third Citizen "*We have power in ourselves to do it, but it is a power that we have no power to do. For if he show us his wounds and tell us his deeds, we are to put our tongues into these wounds and speak for them; so if he tells us his noble deeds, we must also tell him our noble acceptance of them.*" (2.iii.1–9)

The power/no power paradox "evokes a contradiction familiar to oppressed majorities: disunity prevents them from actualising their potential power, while the cause of that disunity is the very oppression which that power, if actualised, could overcome."[11]

When the citizens act in isolation, as for example when they are required to approach Coriolanus and his wounds in twos and threes, they are easily cowed. When they retract, albeit under pressure from the tribunes, it is collectively, and from a position of having reflected together and compared their different experiences. Knowledge of the ambiguous nature of whatever power they do have leads the citizens to have no qualms whatsoever in retracting their previous position when Coriolanus is about to attack Rome. This unabashedly self-interested flexibility is echoed by the serving men of Aufidius court when Coriolanus turns up:

> Third Serving Man "*What are you?*"
>
> Coriolanus "*A gentleman*"
>
> Third serving Man "*A marvellous poor one.*"

After Aufidius has made the guest so welcome, they rapidly change their tune: "*He's simply the rarest man in the world.*" These humorous and seemingly marginal contributions can be seen to reflect a deeper wisdom about the contextual nature of power and status than what is demonstrated by those who actually occupy positions of power. They are likely to take for granted that the person and their power are indivisible. Shakespeare had already highlighted in *Hamlet* precisely this tendency to respond to the acquisition of power by transforming contempt into flattery, as well as draw attention to inflationary processes of flattery:

> Hamlet "*for my uncle is King of Denmark, and those that would make mows at him while my father lived give twenty, forty, fifty, a hundred ducats apiece for his picture in little.*"[12]

In *Coriolanus*, only the plebeians and Volumnia, each, in their different ways, outside the circle of power but needing to observe its workings, show an awareness that political positions are unstable and that political rhetoric has to be managed with strategy and guile:

> Volumnia "*If it be honour in your wars to seem*
>
> *The same you are not, which for your best ends*
>
> *You adopt your policy, how is it less or worse*
>
> *That it shall hold companionship in peace*
>
> *With honour, as in war, since that to both*
>
> *It stands in like request?*" (3.ii.48–53)

Conclusion

To end with an exploration of the workings of power seems appropriate for one of Shakespeare's most sophisticated political plays. Political power so often involves the paradox, identified by Bateson, that belief in transcendent power, itself an illusion, leads to enacting processes that become increasingly unthinking and self-defeating.[13] This is because the attempt to exercise unilateral power involves blocking feedback, dismissing the circular and reciprocal nature of all interactions and thus drawing upon an increasingly narrow and rigid set of repressive practices.

Although Coriolanus is usually viewed as the personification of this restricted identity, I have argued instead that the rigidity of power positions is better illustrated by all the interactions between the senators and patricians, the tribunes, the citizens and Coriolanus himself. These struggles are not just about where power should be located, but crucially about whether and how power struggles should be named at all. At all levels of the play, relationships, both intimate and public, are infused with notions of power and hierarchy and are expressed in many of the details of speech and action, including such examples as the choreography of bodily positions, of kneeling and rising, sitting and standing.

We can learn much from cultural materialist perspectives about ideological positioning and from psychoanalytic perspectives about emotional underpinnings. What I have attempted here is to show how a focus on relational processes and positions can both highlight political dynamics and provide an understanding of the way that these dynamics bring forth such extreme emotions. Shakespeare created in Coriolanus a warrior-hero who is constrained by his rigid adherence to the masculine ideal of *virtus* and in Volumnia a formidably intelligent woman who promotes this ideal but has to subvert it if she is to be true to her political acumen and ambition. The emotional intensity of their interactions is set in the context of many other rich dialogues, by turns angry, dishonest, provocative, cynical, illuminating and ironic, all of which combine to expose the silence at the centre of power.

Notes

1 Kiernan Ryan, *Shakespeare* (Basingstoke: Palgrave Macmillan, Third Edition, 2003), 70.
2 Jonathan Dollimore, *Radical Tragedy* (Basingstoke: Palgrave Macmillan, Third Edition, 2004), 218.
3 Janet Adelman, 'Anger's My Meat: Feeding, Dependency and Aggression in Coriolanus', John Drakakis, ed., *Shakespearean Tragedy* (London: Longman, 1992).
4 Ibid., 353–373.
5 Gregory Bateson, 'Towards a Theory of Schizophrenia', *Steps to an Ecology of Mind* (St Albans: Paladin, 1973), 178.
6 Mikhail Bakhtin, *Problems of Dostoevsky's Poetics* (Minneapolis: University of Minnesota Press, 1984), 195–197.
7 Aristotle, 'Politics', in George Boys-Stones, Barbara Graziosi, eds., *The Oxford Handbook of Hellenic Studies* (Oxford: Oxford University Press, 2009).
8 Anthony Nuttall, *Shakespeare the Thinker* (New Haven and London: Yale University Press, 2007), 298.
9 Frank Kermode, *Shakespeare's Language* (London: Penguin, 2000), 10.
10 Alan Howard in *Coriolanus*, directed by Elijah Moshinsky (BBC Productions, 1984).
11 Jonathan Dollimore, *Radical Tragedy* (Basingstoke: Palgrave Macmillan, Third Edition, 2004), 223.
12 *Hamlet* (2.ii.259–362).
13 Gregory Bateson, *Steps to an Ecology of Mind* (St Albans: Paladin, 1973).

CHAPTER 8

"Let Rome in Tiber melt"

Subverting Roman identity in *Anthony and Cleopatra*

Anthony and Cleopatra begins and ends under the gaze of Rome. At the outset, it is a disapproving, if titillated gaze and, at the end, its tone reflects the reassuring re-establishment of Roman ascendancy and Roman ritual. The importance of gaze resonates throughout the play; Egypt in Rome's eyes is mysterious, exotic, fertile and treacherous and Rome in Egypt's eyes is powerful, rule-bound, sterile and charmless. Antony and Cleopatra, always conscious of the public gaze, put on a romantic performance for each other and for the world, concealing what is also for each of them a highly strategic relationship. The gaze of the other protagonists on this relationship fixes variably on dotage, decline, ensnarement, moral failing or aesthetics, depending on the point of view of the observer. As well as playing a crucial part in the changing construction of the lovers' relationship, these observers of Antony and Cleopatra also reveal their own ambitions and desires. Themes of intense loyalty, love and vulnerability co-exist alongside competitiveness, manipulation and dissembling, contributing to the rich, diverse and multi-levelled textures of this most complex and mercurial of Shakespeare's plays.

The series of oppositions in the opening scene sets up a motif for a play that has mutability, paradox and polarity embedded in its very structure. These oppositions recur throughout and are inscribed in the relationship between Antony and Cleopatra, where passion and power play are in constant tension. Hard, masculine, rational Roman values are set up in opposition to soft, yielding seductive feminine Egyptian sensuality, repeated in the metaphors of solid and reliable land versus the fluidity and treachery of river, slime and sea. Preoccupations with hierarchy and status are set against playfulness, irony and subversion. Others have drawn attention to the contrasts between the verbal and the physical: "the play assigns 'voice' alone to Rome, body alone to Egypt. Rome is a place of words, Egypt a place of actions. Rome is where love is talked of, Egypt is where love is made."[1]

However, although these oppositions work away at the level of the poetic imagination, it is important not to take them up in a reductionist way regarding the two protagonists and their relationship. An example of this tendency is A.D. Nuttall's description:

> the story of Antony in the play is the story of a political and military leader who fell in love, gloriously, disastrously with an Egyptian queen. The story of Cleopatra is the story of an erotic free spirit whose life became entangled, gloriously and disastrously with imperial Rome.[2]

I argue instead that the relationship between Antony and Cleopatra is set up so that these differences and contradictions are not located in either of the lovers but within each of them so that a 'political leader/free spirit' polarity is constantly undermined. It is also in constant motion, reflecting Antony's decline and the unstable power struggles surrounding his weakening grip on events. These political dramas concern the chaotic dying days of Republican Rome and the collapse of the triumvirate, soon to be supplanted by Imperial Rome.

Antony is often portrayed as a man divided against himself, wanting both to jettison and to preserve his heroic, martial reputation and identity. His contradictions are to some extent shown as manifestations of an inner struggle. Cleopatra, by contrast, is never presented in these terms but as possessing an inherently unstable and, contradictory persona, able to fashion herself into whatever she chooses to be, her "*infinite variety*." This can be seen as the 'role' of the colonised 'other'; to possess, rather than an intelligible inner world, a set of surfaces, which act as a screen upon which the desires and exigencies of the rulers can be projected. Antony is given inner dialogues: "*I must from this enchanting queen break off*," "*And though I make this marriage for my peace/ I' th' East my pleasure lies*." Cleopatra either *acts* inconsistently or impetuously or is *portrayed* in a contradictory manner; alternately a wonder, a whore or a vile treacherous Egyptian. Her own ruminations are expressed entirely through dialogues, mostly with her servants.

In the Roman view, Anthony has been seduced by Egypt and its queen; he has been devoured, not just in body but in his whole being. If he behaves like this in Cleopatra's company, he cannot truly be Antony, whose persona is fixed in the eyes of his Roman subordinates as a heroic and invincible warrior. He must be *"not Antony,"* falling short of *"that great property which still should go with Antony."* The explanation is as old as myth; a man's body and his reason have been subverted by an ensnaring female. His body – eyes which should *"glow like plated Mars"* and are now fixated on a *"tawny front,"* his heart which should *"burst the buckles on his breast"* but is now fanning a *"gypsy's lust"* – has been occupied. His power is now abused: *"The triple pillar of the world transformed/ Into a strumpet's fool."*

Against this grandiose rhetoric with its racist and misogynist overtones, the first encounter with Antony and Cleopatra invites the audience into a more ironic and multi-facetted mode of communication with power play at its heart. These four lines reveal the subtle way in which Shakespeare constructs the relationship.

Cleopatra *If this be love indeed, tell me how much*

Antony *There's beggary in the love that can be reckoned*

Cleopatra *I'll set a bourn how far to be beloved*

Antony *Then must thou needs find out new heaven, new earth.* (I.i.14–17)

Cleopatra opens with a rational, instrumental discourse on love – *"how much?"* – which Antony counters by dismissing the very idea of quantifying it. Cleopatra's rejoinder suggests that *she* will be in control of setting a boundary to their love and Antony responds by evoking a poetic view of the ineffability and immeasurability of love. In these lines, each disqualifies the discursive frame employed by the other and engages in competitive play about how their relationship is to be defined. The battle over whether love can be quantified and reduced to a bargaining tool or is of such a transcendent nature that it is immune from such self-serving considerations, sets the frame for the constant flow of contradictory and paradoxical messages exchanged between the lovers. The contingent and political nature of their relationship is never far beneath the surface of their most intense expressions of passion and desire and, crucially, these oppositions are never confined within one protagonist. Each is only too aware of the limitations to their commitment; Antony, because he must both appease and withstand Caesar, and Cleopatra, because Antony is only useful to her while he can act as her protector. The fact that each acts at times as if in denial of this reality and is shocked and enraged by its insertion into the relationship, maintains their interactions in a state of constant dramatic tension.

The wider contexts of politics, gender and power inevitably frame this couple relationship; however, their exquisitely co-ordinated yet contradictory interactive 'dances' undermine any fixed and stable reading. I will begin with a close exploration of the relationship itself, and then widen the frame to show how power politics and imperial interests penetrate into the intimacy of the relationship and define its limits.

Paradoxes, pretences and relational positioning

Looking systemically at Antony and Cleopatra's relationship, the concept of "distance regulation" is helpful.[3] In couple relationships where too much closeness might be experienced as claustrophobic or as a threat to other attachments, various strategies are employed to maintain a safe distance or equilibrium. For many couples, intimacy might be regulated by their work life, social activity or even by addiction to drugs or alcohol. A change in any of these activities requires a recalibration of the relationship. One of the ways that couples regulate their closeness and distance is through the involvement of a third party whose presence maintains this kind of equilibrium.

Antony is in a series of triadic relationships, including the triumvirate. His passion for Cleopatra is at its height when he is married to Fulvia. At her death he breaks off and returns to Rome, having acknowledged to himself that his rejection of Fulvia was based on the premise that she was reassuringly there in the background and that her importance to him only became evident through her absence: "*What our contempts doth often hurl from us/We wish it ours again. . . . She's good, being gone/The hand could pluck her back that shoved her on*" (1.ii.24–27). While Fulvia was alive Anthony had a ready excuse for not committing himself fully to Cleopatra.

As soon as he marries Octavia, Antony once again yearns for Egypt and Cleopatra. The waxing and waning of his love for her directly mirrors his conflicts over Rome and the desire to maintain his pride and reputation in the conflict with Caesar. When, having left Octavia and returned to Alexandria, publicly enthroning himself and Cleopatra and assigning territories to her and to their children, Antony is apparently fully committed to her, the war with Caesar creates catastrophic distance between them.

Cleopatra herself enacts distance regulation in a more immediate way by constant acts of pushing and pulling, inviting her servants into the fray and demonstrating greater intimacy with and trust of them:

> "*See where he is, who's with him, what he does:*
>
> *I did not send you. Iif you find him sad,*
>
> *Say I am dancing; if in mirth, report*
>
> *That I am sudden sick.*" (I.iii.2–5,)

While Antony rarely refers to Cleopatra when he is in Rome, Cleopatra's most high-flown expressions of love are reserved for the times when he is either absent or about to leave her. She then allows herself to speak as if her whole being is preoccupied with every detail of his existence:

> "*Oh Charmian,*
>
> *Where think'st thou he is now? Stands he or sits he?*
>
> *Or does he walk? Or is he on his horse?*
>
> *O happy horse, to bear the weight of Antony!*" (I.v.18–21)

A few lines later, however, she congratulates herself on her conquests of Caesar and Pompey, evoking images of her enduring sexual prowess:

> ". . . *I was*
>
> *A morsel for a monarch, and great Pompey*
>
> *Would stand and make his eyes grow in my brow.*" (I.v.30–32)

This allows Cleopatra to remind and reassure herself of her desirability but it also protects her from being too intensely focussed on one man and it opens up a space for Charmian to teasingly remind her queen (and the audience) that self-interest is never far from romantic rhetoric. Humour and teasing are also distance regulators that are used to great effect by Cleopatra.

Both lovers reassert the intensity of their love for each other as they face death, which could fairly be said to act as the greatest distance regulator. But even then, distancing processes enter into their discourse, revealing other, more prosaic, concerns. Antony is still obsessed with his competitive relationship with Caesar and with his reputation:

"... *the greatest prince o'the world,*

The noblest: and do now not basely die

Not cowardly put off my helmet

To my countryman."(4.xvi.56–59)

Cleopatra, even as she prepares to die and join her beloved Antony, still makes reference, after Iras' death, to his sexual peccadilloes:

"*If she first meet the curlèd Anthony,*

He'll make demand of her, and spend that kiss

Which is my heaven to have." (5.ii.300–302)

If Antony and Cleopatra were ever to devote themselves entirely to each other, the results for each would be catastrophic; for Antony because he would lose everything he depends on for his sense of self, i.e. his identity as a Roman hero, and Cleopatra would lose for exactly the same reason. If he becomes too much under her control, i.e. "*less than Antony*" he is no longer any good to her as a protector. What a systemic reading of *Antony and Cleopatra* suggests is that the lovers each hold in turn the positions of closeness and distance, of rapture and rationality, of a time-bound, contingent relationship and of a commitment for all eternity. When one takes one position, the other quite predictably occupies the opposite one. Each invokes the high-flown rhetoric of the relationship at key moments. As we have seen, Antony does this in Act 1, scene 1, but when he has decided to return to Rome the positions are reversed as Cleopatra takes up the poetic language of love:

"....*When you sued staying,*

Then was the time for words – no going then:

Eternity was in our lips and eyes,

Bliss in our brows...." (1.iii. 33–36)

Antony responds with a 'reasonable' plea for her to respect the "*strong necessity of time (which) commands/ Our services awhile.*" However, the reference to Antony as having once "*sued staying,*" calls up another period in which it was Cleopatra who held the more cautious and distant position.

The idea that the lovers' interactions are always collaborative in this way, even in the midst of conflict, is illustrated later in the play when Anthony vents his fury at Cleopatra for apparently cutting a deal with Caesar's emissary, Thidias. He lays bare in the starkest terms the brutal underlying power dynamics of their relationship:

> "*I found you as a morsel, cold upon*
>
> *Dead Caesar's trencher: nay you were a fragment*
>
> *Of Gneius Pompey's – besides what hotter hours*
>
> *Unregistered in vulgar fame you have*
>
> *Luxuriously picked out.*" (3.xii.117–121)

Cleopatra lets him rant, confining herself to terse and offhand comments until her "*What, not know me yet?*" produces Antony's "*Cold hearted towards me?*" leading Cleopatra to evoke a scenario of self-abasement, engaging in a florid disavowal of her own fertility and that of all her heirs. Antony then declares "*I am satisfied.*" As in many of their exchanges, this lends itself to different interpretations; Antony humiliating and humbling Cleopatra or Cleopatra skilfully handling Antony's temper tantrum and diverting attention away from her encounter with Thidias. It can also be seen as Cleopatra avoiding a symmetrical escalation, in which political realities might have to be faced, by taking a complementary 'one down' position. After this they return to safer ground; Anthony reasserts his sense of military and sexual potency and resumes his self-aggrandising rhetoric and Cleopatra reassures him that the world is theirs again.

Bertrand Evans' interpretation of Antony's attitude to Cleopatra is that, rather than being deeply in love with, let alone enslaved by her, he uses the public story of his 'dotage' to deflect attention from his fear of Caesar and to justify his inevitable defeat by the younger and more capable man, arguing that "to be known as the slave of passion is a lesser blemish on his character than to be known as one whose soul shrinks from Caesar."[4] Evans also argues that the lines "*I'the East my pleasure lies,*" rather than demonstrating Antony's yearning for Cleopatra, are a direct result of the soothsayer predicting his defeat by Caesar and advising him to put distance between them. Thus, he is not so much fleeing *to* Cleopatra as *from* Caesar. This interpretation certainly sharpens a focus on the central issue of Antony's decline, on his subtle shifts between public and private discourse and the fact that so many of his words to Cleopatra are disparaging rather than loving. However, Evans then goes on to argue that the one who 'truly' loves is Cleopatra and, while she certainly does everything she can to keep Antony and speaks lovingly of him when he is absent, it seems unnecessary to create too fixed a polarity between 'true love' and expediency. While to some modern Western audiences, the romantic ideal may dictate that a 'proper' relationship should not be dominated by materialist or political considerations, in practice these have always co-existed and continue to co-exist.

Whatever Shakespeare chose to portray as 'true love' in this case, he certainly presents Antony and Cleopatra as being in the throes of an intense and passionate sexual liaison in which each is the match of the other for narcissism and self-aggrandisement. They enthusiastically narrate theirs as the greatest love story the world has ever known. The hyperbole of this narrative is in inverse relationship to their human frailty, to their fears of ageing and loss of sexual prowess; they have to work exceptionally hard on the narrative, never more than when *in extremis*. The wider context that intensifies the attraction is the mutual encounter of power, status, fabulous wealth and lavish regal hospitality, a common enough narrative for colonisers' encounters with local elites.

Colonising, 'othering' and 'going native'

Egypt is represented as a feminised fertile 'body' projected in the Roman imagination as a source of both fascination and danger. In Edward Said's words, "The Orient is the stage on which the whole East is confined."[5] In this view, the erotic image of Egypt and its queen is an integral component of conquest and subjugation. However, in colonialist discourse, images shift, particularly at moments of resistance, 'bad faith' or duplicity. In these contexts, sensual language easily transmutes into derogatory terms such as 'whore' or 'harlot.' These terms then become detached from this context and are ascribed as qualities of the colonised, The need for colonisers to 'corrupt' their colonial vassals and then attribute this corruption to their innate defects, which then justify further domination, is an age-old process that continues to this day. It can be played out as much in intimate relationships as in the political domain. The other Romans always refer to Cleopatra in derogatory sexualised language but Anthony also takes up this discourse when he fears that Cleopatra has double-crossed or deceived him: "*triple-turned whore.*"

On the 'Oriental stage,' Cleopatra is a star performer, providing a mirror for a series of Roman conquerors on which their desires are reflected back to them. The famous account by Enobarbus of Cleopatra's journey up the Nile to meet Antony is a perfect example of this theatre. The description brings forth the erotic as well as the material capital of Cleopatra and highlights the aridity and emptiness of the invader:

> "*Anthony*
>
> *Enthroned i'th' market place, did sit alone*
>
> *Whistling to th'air, which but for vacancy*
>
> *Had gone to gaze on Cleopatra too*
>
> *And made a gap in nature*." (2.ii.221–224)

The power play between coloniser and colonised, which we see repeatedly enacted in Antony and Cleopatra's relationship, is illustrated by this first encounter when Cleopatra declines Antony's invitation to dine with him and insists that *he* join her. Although Cleopatra's 'local' power is dependent on the might of the military invader, she knows exactly how to employ what power she has. Her brilliance in gaining power through seducing Roman invaders represents a danger to 'Roman' values, at constant risk of being subverted and its leaders emasculated.

> "*She made great Caesar lay his sword to bed*
>
> *He ploughed her, and she cropped*." (2.ii.234–235)

In this rather unpleasant passage there is nevertheless a wonderfully complex interplay between women's power to subvert, disarm and emasculate men, and men's ability to 'plough' women, producing for the queen the valuable asset of half-Roman royal babies. The overt linkage between women and nature also highlights the elision of Cleopatra the queen and the land over which she reigns, 'ploughed' by its invaders.

In Rome, Antony is generally considered to have, as more recent parlance might have it, 'gone native,' succumbing to the excesses and carnal pleasures of Egypt. Caesar's disapproval is not just that Antony "*fishes, drinks and revels*" and "*tumbles on the bed of Ptolemy*" but also that he subverts social hierarchies; "*tippling with a slave*" and gender divisions. He "*is not more manlike/Than Cleopatra, nor the Queen of Ptolemy/More womanly than he.*"

Pompey, on the other hand, relishes the prospect of Cleopatra as an unwitting ally in his battle with the triumvirate:

> "*Let witchcraft join with beauty, lust with both,*
>
> *Tie up the libertine in a field of feasts,*
>
> *Keep his brain fuming!*" (2.i.22–24)

After Pompey has reluctantly accepted the peace treaty offered by the triumvirate, the feast that follows is framed by excited comparisons with the excesses of Egypt, by now a benchmark for all such jollities: "*This is not yet an Alexandrian feast*"/ "*It ripens towards it*"; "*Shall we dance now the Egyptian Bacchanals. . ..*" However, there is one small glimpse of something in Antony's 'gone native' discourse which presents Egypt in terms more challenging to Rome's sense of its own cultural and technological superiority:

> Antony *Thus, do they sir: they take the flow o'th Nile*
>
> *By certain scales i'th'pyramid; they know*
>
> *By th'height, the lowness, or the mean, if dearth*
>
> *Or foison follow. The higher Nilus swells,*
>
> *The more it promises.*" (2.vii.17–21)

Whoever this instructive, if sexualised, speech is directed at, it is Lepidus who answers, taking the conversation back to the more comfortable territory of Egypt as a source of the strange and exotic rather than of technical expertise, taking on the role, ignorant as he is, of educating the one person who actually knows the country: "*You've strange serpents there? . . . your serpent of Egypt is bred now of your mud by the operation of your sun: so is your crocodile.*" This small, drunken interchange, omitted in many productions, is nevertheless a beautiful example of the dynamics of centre/periphery relations. The preferred image of Egypt for Rome is that of a dangerous but fascinating place, full of moral decadence, excess and strangeness, but not a place from which anything can be learnt.

In this context an obsession with the corrupting and debilitating effects of Egyptian hedonism could be seen as constituting a 'moral panic' for Roman leaders, anxious to shore up their values and maintain their fighting spirit at a time when masculine, martial, republican values are under threat. This sets the frame for the anxiety shown by Antony's soldiers as they see these qualities diminish in him, an anxiety which, while it largely relates to age, confusion and alcohol intake, is primarily expressed in gendered terms.

Gender, power and sexuality

While Shakespeare sets up gendered oppositions and gendered anxieties: *"So our leader's led/ And we are women's men,"* he also creates contexts in which gender differences are subverted by playfulness and teasing:

> Cleopatra *"Ere the ninth hour I drunk him to his bed*
>
> *Then put my tires and mantles on him, whilst I wore his sword Philippan."*

The constraints of rigid gender identity and the instrumental uses to which they are put are plain to see in the play but so too are attempts to break free from them. Antony's 'dotage' in both its senses can be seen as a desperate desire to shore up his masculinity by frenetic sexual activity but also as a weariness with politics and power – *"Kingdoms are clay"* – and a desire to slip the constraints of his martial identity *"The nobleness of life is to do thus. (they embrace)"* At one point he even sends a messenger to Caesar in which he propositions for a different and freer life altogether: *"to thee sues/To let him breathe between the heavens and earth,/A private man in Athens."*

Cleopatra conveys no such need for alternative identities. She has seen many Roman invaders pass through her land, some of them through her bed, and her most pressing concern is to remain as monarch in her own territory. The fear of exile and the humiliation of being taken to Rome as a captive were the prompts for her suicide rather than Antony's death. The importance of being able to control her own physical space is illustrated by her retreat to the monument and her insistence that the dying Antony is brought up to her there, a subtle echo of the battle to control their first meeting place. Janis Krohn, in his psychoanalytic interpretation of *Antony and Cleopatra,* argues that the relationship is doomed because of the lovers' "inability to overcome the internal conflicts and fears posed in their relationship." Antony's dilemma is that the more he loves her, the less he is a man. For Cleopatra, "desiring Antony's masculinity and desperate for him to love her, the more he does so, the more his masculinity diminishes and he is no longer the man she loves."[6] While a paradoxical dynamic of this kind is certainly played out in the relationship, Krohn's analysis is replete with misogynist assumptions about emasculating women. He also fails to address either the dimension of power or the colonial context. In this context, Antony's dilemma might be seen to be that, just as the relationship with Cleopatra offers him a way out of the rigid constraints of his heroic Roman warrior identity – an identity which is of necessity diminishing with age – the relational dynamics constantly invite him back into it. This is because, however much she may disguise it, Cleopatra depends absolutely on his patronage and thus needs him to maintain his heroic status.

In Act 3, Scene 13, Antony's vicious diatribe against Cleopatra after her dalliance with Thidias takes us to the heart of the 'political' fault-lines of their relationship. He first denies her name, then refers to her age and promiscuous sexual past, disowns their own children by evoking the "*lawful race*" he could have begot with Octavia, by now transformed into a "*gem of woman*." In sum, he positions himself as the upholder of those very Roman virtues that he has supposedly rejected for the sake of this relationship. Cleopatra's apparently self-abasing lines also name the political realities behind her position; that her womb is the key to her survival and to that of Egypt, and that, without her Roman progeny, the whole population could be destroyed. This apocalyptic image appears to be enough to restore Antony's sense of potency, both sexual and military and, "*triple-sinewed, hearted, breathed*" he resumes his war-like, death-defying rhetoric, vowing to "*force/ The wine peep through their scars,*" promising Cleopatra "*There's sap in't yet*" and vowing to "*make death love me*." While Cleopatra enters into the fantasy, Enobarbus decides that "*a diminution in our captain's brain*" is the final proof that he must leave him.

Despite this utterly unconvincing charade on Antony's part, the discourse of the transcendent male subject who "*will appear in blood*" still has a compelling power, which both Antony and Cleopatra need to play up to. For Antony, the ageing hero, the relationship with Cleopatra may be an attempt to escape from realpolitik. For Cleopatra, as well as sexual gratification and pleasure, it *is* realpolitik, the means through which she has always survived by allying herself to invaders and bearing their children. Pompey, Caesar, Anthony and potentially Octavius Caesar all form part of a continuum. Antony thought he could split off politics and pleasure. Cleopatra knows she cannot.

As Antony becomes more obsessed with reasserting his heroic sense of himself, his need to feel powerful eventually centres on sexual anxiety: "an assertion of sexual prowess which has characterised his relationship with both Cleopatra and Caesar from the outset."[7] As we have seen, Antony's dying words are addressed more to Caesar and to Rome than to Cleopatra, reasserting the heroic narrative with which he sustains himself and without which he dissolves into nothingness, unable to "*hold this visible shape*."

Cleopatra, on the other hand, has no need to cling to such a one-dimensional identity; she seems at ease with a protean and performative version of self and is well aware of Antony's struggle to acknowledge this dimension, witheringly summarised in: "*I'll seem the fool I am not; Anthony will be himself*."

For a woman in Cleopatra's position, an autocratic queen, but a female colonial subject as well, the notion of guile, of subterfuge, of understanding what performances are required under the gaze of the coloniser as well as for her own people are all necessary parts of survival. She manages this paradoxical position with dexterity. Antony's obsession with Cleopatra destroys his capacity to think but it does not destroy hers. This could hardly be better illustrated than by the clumsy choreography of Antony's suicide and the carefully staged dignity of hers. Cleopatra's moments of greatest anxiety arise when she fears being separated from her land; Antony's are all about position *"I am Antony yet"* and the loss of it *"authority melts from me."*

When Antony chooses Cleopatra's option to fight by sea against the advice of all his soldiers, and then loses, his soldiers are quick to lay the blame on Cleopatra: *"yon ribanded nag of Egypt – Whom leprosy o'ertake,"* as a way of dealing with feelings of loss of manhood and unbearable shame.

Scarrus bemoans the fact that Antony:

"Claps on his sea – wing and, like a doting mallard,

Leaving the fight in height, flies after her

I never saw an action of such shame –

Experience, manhood, honour, ne'er before

Did so violate itself." (3.x.19–23)

Amid the rage and disappointment with Antony and his performance is the imputation that this ignominious flight marks a severance of the soldierly bond and reflects shame on those lieutenants whose professional advice was ignored so summarily by their leader, thus crucially undermining their loyalty.

Loyalty and 'speaking truth to power'

One of the distinctive features of *Antony and Cleopatra* is the number of short scenes within which a range of minor characters feature, often appearing briefly only to disappear from the action. While the focus remains on the main protagonists and their immediate circle, these voices provide a series of alternative observations about power, decline and the vanity of leaders.

As in many Shakespeare plays, key roles are allocated to the subordinate or servant whose loyalty and devotion is indisputable but who also acts as an intimate and challenging commentator on social realities and hidden truths or who warns against unwise actions. In *Antony and Cleopatra* Shakespeare has created several sophisticated and intelligent characters whose actions and commentary are integral to the plot. Indeed, their interventions are critical in exposing myopia, vanity, stubbornness and delusions. Pompey's Menas and Caesar's Agrippa also offer trenchant and unsentimental advice to their leaders, revealing the scope for political opportunism as well as its pitfalls. It also highlights the different ambience in Egypt and Rome. While Cleopatra's entourage speak to her freely and mainly encounter only light-hearted reprimands, the shift in context from Egypt to Rome signals a change in Antony's attitude to Enobarbus' humorous barbs. In matters pertaining to the triumvirate, he is firmly rebuked by his leader for overstepping his remit: "*No more light answers. Let our officers/Have notice what we purpose*" ... "*Thou art a soldier only: speak no more.*" The risk to subordinates if they over-reach themselves is beautifully expressed by Ventidius, Antony's officer, who, when urged to press on with his military conquests, reflects on the relationship between individual prowess and hierarchical position:

> Ventidius "*Oh Silius, Silius*
>
> *I have done enough. A lower place, mark well,*
>
> *May make too great an act. For learn this, Silius:*
>
> *Better to leave undone, than by our deed*
>
> *Acquire too great a fame when him we serve's away.*
>
> *Caesar and Antony have ever won*
>
> *More in their officer than person*
>
> *...Who does i'th wars more than his captain can,*
>
> *Becomes his captain's captain, and ambition –*
>
> *The soldier's virtue, rather makes a choice of loss,*
>
> *Than gain which darkens him.*" (3.i. 12–24)

This view of rulers in the eyes of their subordinates enriches our appreciation of how many adaptations are made to power and how language is tempered to fit the exigencies of the moment. Nowhere is this more elegantly and humorously expressed than by the messenger who brings the news to

Cleopatra of Antony's marriage to Octavia. After his initial terrifying encounter, he quickly learns to adapt his answers to gratify the Queen's vanity:

> Cleopatra "*What Majesty is in her gait? Remember,*
>
> *If e'er thou look'st on majesty*"
>
> Messenger "*She creeps:*
>
> *Her motion and her station are as one.*
>
> *She shows a body rather than a life,*
>
> *A statue than a breather.*" (3.iii.17–20)

As well as pay close attention to power, the various soldiers, servants, messengers and followers all take different positions in relation to love, loyalty, self-interest and survival. As Antony's authority collapses, these range from Canidius' calculated decision to desert to Caesar, to the public avowals of faithfulness from others: Antony "*Fly and make your peace with Caesar.*" All "*Fly? Not we.*" These differences are intensified in the way that Shakespeare juxtaposes in quick succession Eros sacrificing himself rather than obey Antony's command to kill his master, and Dercetus, arriving on the scene after Antony's suicide, removing the bloody sword with the aim of using it to gain favour with Caesar.

A range of emotional quandaries are expressed by Enobarbus in his struggle to reconcile his pride as a professional soldier with his love for Antony. Additionally, the role of Enobarbus – part cynical observer, part loyal lieutenant and part hedonist – is one which allows for a multi-facetted commentary on the mores of both Rome and Egypt since he plays a key part in representing each to the other. He also maintains the capacity to think that Antony himself has lost to fantasy, to macho posturing and to alcohol. Until this point Enobarbus has adopted a teasing way of describing Egypt to Romans, indicating how well he understands their hunger for tales of excess and indiscipline:

> Maecenas "*Eight wild boars roasted whole at a breakfast, and but twelve persons there – is this true?*"
>
> Enobarbus "*This was but a fly by an eagle. We had much more monstrous matter of feast, which worthily deserved noting.*" (2.ii.186–190)

Enobarbus' famous evocation of the meeting between Antony and Cleopatra draws upon quite another dimension; the majesty and charisma of Cleopatra, her ability to "*make defect perfection*" and, unlike Antony in Rome, her total control over her own domain. In her realm, no-one possesses the authority or the desire to restrain her: *"the holy priests/Bless her when she is riggish."* This contrasts perfectly with the dour disapproval of Antony emanating from Rome. Enobarbus, like his leader, is captivated by the excess but, unlike Antony, he remains consistent; eloquent, misogynistic, sardonic and yet professional, whether he is in Rome or Egypt. His political acumen is illustrated by his prediction of how Antony's marriage to Octavia and his relationship with Cleopatra are likely to play out in his dealings with Caesar.

Menas "*Then is Caesar and he forever knit together*"

Enobarbus "*If I were bound to divine of this unity, I would not prophesy so. . . . . . He will to his Egyptian dish again: then shall the sighs of Octavia blow the fire up in Caesar.*" (2.vi.114–126)

Crucially it is Enobarbus who reminds the audience, even when Antony is at his most pathetic and self-deluding, that his commander is a man who has inspired and can still inspire admiration and devotion. His loyalty until almost the end and then his agonies of guilt about defecting to Caesar, keep the complexity of the relationship in focus. If anything, it is Enobarbus, rather than Antony who most clearly exemplifies the theme of a struggle between love and duty, as, appalled and offended by his leader's catastrophic decision making, he still choses to *"follow/The wounded chance of Antony, though my reason/ Sits in the wind against me."*

Enobarbus' position is to some extent mirrored in Cleopatra's court by that of Charmian. She too is unafraid to speak her mind and firmly restrains her queen from physically assaulting the messenger who brings the news of Antony's marriage to Octavia *"Good madam, keep yourself within yourself/The man is innocent."*

Charmian gives Cleopatra advice – roundly rejected – about how to keep Antony, showing at least her understanding that he must, at all costs, be kept: *"In each thing give him way: cross him in nothing."* (1.iii.9). Later on, she reminds Cleopatra, as she is virtually cued in to do by her queen, that she has heard all the love and adulation heaped on Antony before:

Cleopatra "*Did I, Charmian,*

Ever love Caesar so?"

Charmian "*O, that brave Caesar!*"

Cleopatra "*Be choked with such another emphasis!*

Say 'the brave Anthony'."

Charmian "*The valiant Caesar.*"

Cleopatra "*By Isis, I will give thee bloody teeth*

If thou with Caesar paragon again

My man of men."

Charmian "*By your most gracious pardon*

I sing but after you." (1.v.66–74)

She and Cleopatra seem to be enjoyably collusive in their recall of Cleopatra's sexual history with Roman invaders and she and Cleopatra's other followers take a thoroughly disrespectful approach to their Roman overlords. At the end of the play, Cleopatra, Charmian and Iras reach the same conclusion that suicide is the only recourse, following the news that they will be taken as war booty to Rome. Charmian's understanding of the need for a royal performance even after death is poignantly evoked in her tending the body of her mistress:

"*Downy windows, close*

And golden Phoebus never be beheld

Of eyes again so royal. Your crown's awry,

I'll mend it, and then play." (5.ii.314–317)

Charmian, unlike Enobarbus, has no lines to share her inner dilemmas with the audience; nevertheless the dying moments of each of them can evoke more powerful emotional responses in the audience than those of either Antony or Cleopatra. They are each are given lines of unalloyed love, devotion and sorrow, uncontaminated by concerns about appearance or reputation.

The political context

Caesar exhorts the absent Antony to *"Leave thy lascivious wassails,"* and contrasts this self -indulgent hedonist with a past Antony, capable of enduring the most extreme hardships and privations:

"*and all this –*

It wounds thine honour that I speak it now –

Was borne so like a soldier, that thy cheek

So much as lanked not." (1.iv.68–71)

In the chaotic times leading up to the demise of Republican Rome, this may also be read as an expression of nostalgia for the courage, the asceticism and the self-discipline that is part of the Roman myth of *virtus*. It may also reflect anxiety and frustration on Caesar's part that he is dependent on Antony's bravery and leadership to defeat Pompey.

While Antony, the charismatic soldier/hero at one time personified the quality of *virtus*, Caesar represents a different kind of military leader, never a hero in physical terms but a brilliant strategist. "The clash between the glamour of the hand-to-hand armoured swordsman . . . and the personal prestige and comradeship which that confers, set against Caesar's logistical planning and efficiency, his ability to move troops and war materials rapidly to battle-fronts" provides the background to the competitiveness between the two men.[8] Rivalrous tensions and in their relationship were already signalled in *Julius Caesar* when the younger and more junior Octavius challenged Antony's battle plan on the plains of Philippi,[9] although Antony, reflecting back to this period, comments disparagingly that Octavius "*no practice had/In the brave squares of war.*"

Frequent references in *Antony and Cleopatra* to Octavius Caesar's youth: "*Scarce-bearded Caesar,*" "*the young man,*" "*the boy Caesar*" and Antony's age: "*this grizzled head,*" "*an old one dying,*" "*the old ruffian*" highlight one obvious aspect of their conflict. However, while clear differences in style and disposition are presented – nowhere more apparent than at Pompey's feast – the struggle between the two could be contained as long as Lepidus, the third in the triumvirate, was there to act as a foil and as long as there was a common enemy in Pompey. Indeed, before Pompey threatened Rome, it may have suited Caesar that Antony was out of the way in Egypt. When Caesar eliminates first Pompey and then Lepidus, the fight to the death between him and Antony commences. Enobarbus instantly grasps the significance of the triumvirate's collapse:

"*Then, world, thou hast a pair of chops, no more.*

And throw between them all the food thou hast.

They'll grind the one the other." (3.v.12–14)

Octavia, exploited by both men and possibly set up by her brother to provide justification for waging war on Antony, calculating that he would return to Cleopatra, has no influence whatsoever as a go-between. The symmetrical escalation between the two men involves provocation on both parts. Caesar initiates new wars against Pompey, depriving Antony of his share of the spoils. Antony crowns himself and Cleopatra, 'giving' her sovereignty over Egypt and allocating other 'Roman' territories to her and to their children. This last would have been of particular significance to Octavius Caesar, the adopted son of Julius Caesar, knowing that Cesarion – *"whom they call my father's son"* – might therefore inherit the land.

At this moment, Cleopatra, having previously been depicted by Caesar as an emasculating seductress, emerges as a military threat in her own right, supported by a whole bevvy of other monarchs, although this new status does not, of course, earn her any more respectful language:

> Caesar "*He hath given his empire/Up to a whore, who now are levying/The kings o' th'earth for war.*"
>
> Maecenus ..."*and gives his potent regiment to a trull/ That noises it against us.*"

The war that follows, which sets the scene for the disintegration of Antony and Cleopatra's relationship and leads to their deaths, is open to many different interpretations, especially over the disastrous decisions and actions taken by the pair. Extremes of emotion, from rage, fear, shame and self-abasement to pride, hubris and passion keep the tragedy on the edge of melodrama and farce. While Caesar is fixed in a cold determination to crush and humiliate the lovers, we are left guessing as to Antony's reasons, especially for the decision, against the advice of all his commanders to fight at sea. Bertrand's explanation is that he deliberately chooses this course, following Cleopatra's fleeing ships to propagate the public story of 'all for love.' This provides a coherent narrative of Antony's behaviour throughout, but coherent narratives are not a particular characteristic of this play. After learning the scale of Caesar's rapid and relentless advance, Antony's capacity to think is diminished and his explanation for fighting at sea: *"For that he dares us to't"* is as likely as any other motive and fits with his absurd offer to settle the war with Caesar by one-to-one combat.

In exploring the rivalry between the two men, however, commentators often ignore Cleopatra's own political stance and how her position might have changed, following her enthronement and the expansion of her realm. Certainly her rebuttal of Enobarbus' misogynist put-down about her involvement in battle suggests a Cleopatra determined to operate in the wider political and military sphere:

> Enobarbus "*Your presence needs must puzzle Antony,*
>
> *Take from his heart, take from his brain, from's time,*

What should not then be spared. He is already

Traduced for levity; and 'tis said in Rome

That Photinus an eunuch and your maids

Manage this war."

Cleopatra "*Sink, Rome, and their tongues rot*

That speak against us! A charge we bear i'th'war,

And, as the president of my kingdom will

Appear there for a man. Speak not against it,

I will not stay behind." (3.vii.10–19)

In battle, Cleopatra, as well as Antony, seems to prefer the impulsive grand gesture rather than the wise strategy. She seems excited by, rather than fearful of the danger they are in, although it could certainly be argued that having already decided to throw in her lot with Caesar, she wanted Antony to lose.

As much as playing out the oppositions of 'love and duty' the play also reveals the relationship between individual tyranny and autocracy and loyalty to the polis. Cleopatra, for all that her territory is colonised by Rome, represents an image of unilateral power. Her much vaunted charisma is as much contextualised by power and position as is Antony's *virtus*. The priests who "*bless her when she is riggish*" would have had little choice in the matter. We are not left in much doubt either that Cleopatra could have had the messenger from Rome put to death had she chosen. In the play's final scenes, when the macro-conflicts of warfare are over, political battles continue to be played out, this time in the intimate setting of Cleopatra's court. Although everyone present knows that suicide is Cleopatra's default weapon with which to evade humiliation by Rome, a series of negotiations are nonetheless played out which, leave the audience guessing as to whether she is still hoping for a deal with Caesar. In the scene with Cleopatra's treasurer, Seleucus, we do not know whether he has innocently or deliberately exposed her financial dishonesty or indeed whether it is all an elaborate performance to deceive Caesar. As well as this ambiguity, the interchange with the clown who brings Cleopatra the asp keeps an element of humour and farce playing out until the end.

Conclusion

Antony and Cleopatra is a play of such complexity and contradiction that every potentially coherent interpretation creates a response in this author's mind that echoes the play's first words: *"Nay, but . . . ."*

The *"infinite variety"* embodied in the person of Cleopatra applies also to the myriad characters who, while they appear in short scenes only to disappear again, nevertheless contribute greatly to the texture and richness of the play in their range of perspectives and commentaries on the central relationships. Attending to this 'infinite variety' of viewpoints as well as to the relationship between Anthony and Cleopatra seems particularly important if the lovers' actions are to be appreciated within their wider contexts. The importance of resisting what Keats called "an irritable reaching after fact and reason"[10] means that embracing uncertainty and lack of resolution can be an active position rather than 'failure' to find a coherent explanation.

Antony and Cleopatra contains in its structure a strategy which requires us to simultaneously believe and disbelieve in its high flown poetry and rhetoric; this creates what Janet Adelman terms a paradox of faith: "the imaginative vision of the play is based firmly on the two rhetorical figures that are themselves dependent on this strategy: paradox and hyperbole."[11] An appreciation of paradox is key to the enterprise of psychotherapy in all its forms as it means accommodating at some level to two domains simultaneously, that of belief and that of scepticism. It has a particular relevance for psychotherapists who engage with relational systems since they so frequently encounter these paradoxical processes, where rhetoric constantly contradicts reality and where relationships can at one and the same time involve sexual passion, love and desperate need for attachment, alongside distancing, self-interest, cruelty and duplicity.

Notes

1 Terence Hawkes, ' "King Lear" and "Anthony and Cleopatra": The Language of Love', in John Drakakis, ed., *Antony and Cleopatra* (Basingstoke: Palgrave Macmillan, 1994).

2 Anthony Nuttall, *Shakespeare the Thinker* (New Haven and London: Yale University Press, 2007), 321.

3 John Byng Hall and David Campbell, 'Resolving Conflicts in Distance Regulation: an Integrative Approach', *Journal of Marital and Family Therapy*, 7:3 (July 1981), 321–330.

4 Bertrand Evans, *Shakespeare's Tragic Practice* (Oxford: Clarendon Press, 1979), 242.

5 Edward Said, *Orientalism* (New York: Pantheon, 1978), 63.

6 Janis Krohn, 'The Dangers of Love in Antony and Cleopatra', *International Review of Psychoanalysis*, 13 (1986), 89–90.

7 Jonathan Dollimore, *Radical Tragedy* (Basingstoke: Palgrave Macmillan, Third Edition, 2004), 210.

8 Margot Heinemann, ' "Let Rome in Tiber Melt": Order and Disorder in "Antony and Cleopatra" ', in John Drakakis, ed., *Antony and Cleopatra* (Basingstoke: Palgrave Macmillan, 1994), 170.

9 *Julius Caesar*, 5.i.

10 John Barnard, ed., *John Keats, Selected Letters* (London: Penguin Classics, 2014), 79.

11 Janet Adelman, 'Nature's Piece against Fancy: Poetry and the Structure of Belief in Antony and Cleopatra', in John Drakakis, ed., *Antony and Cleopatra* (Basingstoke: Palgrave Macmillan, 1994), 63.

CHAPTER 9

"The noblest-hateful love"

Contradiction and irreverence in *Troilus and Cressida*

Unlike the other plays in this volume, *Troilus and Cressida* is not formally classified as a tragedy, since its eponymous hero and heroine are left alive at the end. It lends itself perfectly, however, to a systemic approach. As well as providing two scenes of compelling family interaction, Shakespeare displays his irreverence towards ideals of heroic individualism and emphasises the gulf between aspirations, rhetoric and actions. To sustain multiple perspectives and demonstrate connections, he makes use of debates, and processes of mirroring and reflection. His protagonists move between conveying a sense of time as frozen and suspended and an equally acute sense of the waxing and waning over time of fame, fortune and emotional bonds.

Above all the play's exploration of contextual and relational identity compels us to look at patterns and processes rather than the individual psyche. Indeed, the absurdity of which individuals are capable when they lose contact with whatever rationale originally guided their actions can only be understood through the idea of a system having acquired its own crazy logic. Within this context, protagonists frequently seem to act in mindlessly repetitive and quasi-ritualistic ways. This is, of course, a highly relevant theme for many protracted military conflicts across time and across cultures.

Helen, the supposed focus of the prolonged and static war between the Trojans and the Greeks, is virtually absent from the play and Janet Adelman argues that her 'vacuity' when she does briefly appear is "emblematic of the sense of absence or hollowness at the core . . . where there is no centre from which meaning can radiate, where high rhetoric, exalted statements, heroic battles, even the logic of the plot itself, perpetually seem on the point of collapsing into meaninglessness."[1] A sense of emptiness and indeterminacy certainly does pervade the text, so a reading that does not require meaning to radiate from an inner core but embraces contradictions and engages with diverse and unstable positions is essential.

This is partly because the play itself is so replete with paradox; it features several weighty philosophical debates that address questions of power, hierarchy, law and justice but at the same time demonstrates how these philosophical positions can be outweighed by pragmatics and abandoned, seemingly at whim. In the context of two opposing armies holding each other in mutual gaze, display counts more than substance. As time erodes the purpose of the war, metaphors of disease and decay prevail and the play can be seen as an attack on the idealisation of both love and war. Indeed, discourses from both sexual and military domains constantly overlap, creating an eroticisation of war and a militarisation of love, tropes that are reiterated as the play's action moves between the Greek and the Trojan sides. They form the background to the relationship between Troilus and Cressida and its collapse into betrayal and recrimination. The entanglement of love and warfare is intensified by a collapse of authority on both sides so that erotic performances tend to take precedence over military action and, indeed, whether to fight or not is often decided arbitrarily and capriciously.

Connection and attraction between the enemies

This is a play in which the importance of image and appearance looms large. Its protagonists strut, swagger and parade in front of each other, making it hard for the audience identify with them in any depth. René Girard regards *Troilus and Cressida* as the paradigmatic mimetic play.[2] In his conception of mimesis our desires, rather than arising from within the psyche and directed at forbidden or taboo objects, are provoked by the desire of another person for the same object. In other words, they are always relational. He challenges the illusion of autonomous desire and instead stresses the centrality of processes which are driven by envy and jealousy which, he argues, lead invariably to the threat or the enactment of violence. The object itself loses its importance and fades away, leaving behind a symmetrical escalation between the protagonists.

The iconic Helen has long since been transcended as an 'object' to be fought over by the Greeks and the Trojans, leaving them stuck in a sterile and ritualistic series of set-piece exhibitionistic battles in which they have lost all sense of purpose and question their aims in fighting at all. "The only reason the Greeks want her back is because the Trojans want to keep her. The only reason the Trojans want to keep her is because the Greeks want her back."[3] War does not, however, really polarise the enemies; in fact it increases their fascination with each other. The ritualised nature of much of the fighting suggests an inability or unwillingness to make any decisive move that would bring the war to an end.

Reluctance or squeamishness about making the 'killer move' is variously personified by the characters of Achilles and Hector. Raising the question of what the Greeks represent to the Trojans and vice versa reminds us that in wars fought between proximate ruling dynasties, there will invariably be family connections, heightening their preoccupation with each other. Ajax and Hector are cousins and, even at the height of the fighting, Achilles is negotiating for the hand of Polyxena, daughter of Priam and Hecuba and, of course, sister to Hector and cousin to Ajax. The dilemma of fighting a blood relative is summed up by Aeneas, reflecting on the impending combat between Hector and Ajax:

> "*This Ajax is half made of Hector's blood*
>
> *In love whereof half Hector stays at home;*
>
> *Half heart, half hand, half Hector comes to seek*
>
> *This blended knight, half Trojan and half Greek.*" (4.v.83–86)

When they prematurely stop fighting, Hector elaborates: "*The obligation of our blood forbids/A gory emulation twixt us twain.*" These obligations are even more complex in the case of Achilles. Hector is portrayed as holding stubbornly to a chivalric ideal that some, including his own brother Troilus, consider outmoded. Shakespeare casts Achilles in a highly unflattering light; on the one hand retreating to the private world of his tent where he and Patroclus mock and ridicule the Greek leadership, especially Agamemnon, and, on the other, showing a vain obsession with his image and reputation: "*What, am I poor of late?*" This is adroitly exploited by Ulysses, who reminds Achilles to "*marvel not/ That all the Greeks begin to worship Ajax.*"

Ulysses also reminds Achilles that *"All the commerce that you have had with Troy"* is well-known and warns him of the opprobrium that would ensue if he refuses to fight Hector because he is courting Polyxena. While Ulysses intends this as a threat, and Patroclus urges him to *"rouse yourself,"* Achilles, having already sworn an oath to Polyxena that he will not harm Hector, clearly prefers to meet her brother in a social rather than a military context:

> *"I have a woman's longing,*
>
> *An appetite that I am sick withal,*
>
> *To see great Hector in his weeds of peace."* (3.iii.236–238)

As well as actual and potential family bonds, connections take place at many other levels. In late twentieth-century Britain, meetings between old soldiers and their former enemies, German or Japanese, could still seem to contain a sense of wonder, so many years later, that the enemy 'other' is a human being 'just like us,' a person who can be identified with. In *Troilus and Cressida,* acceptance of the humanity of the 'other' is explicit within the present time frame of the war. The Trojan, Aeneas and the Greek, Diomedes, have no trouble in recognising this and agreeing on the ambiguity and interdependency of their relationship:

> Aeneas "*No man alive can love in such a sort*
>
> *The thing he means to kill more excellently*"
>
> Diomedes "*We sympathise. Jove, let Aeneas live,*
>
> *If to my sword his fate be not the glory*
>
> *A thousand complete courses of the sun!*
>
> *But, in mine emulous honour let him die*
>
> *With every joint a wound, and that tomorrow*"
>
> Aeneas "*We know each other well*"
>
> Diomedes "*We do; and long to know each other worse*"
>
> Paris "*This is the most despiteful-gentle greeting,*
>
> *The noblest-hateful love that e'er I heard of.*" (4.i.24–35)

This wonderfully expressed sense of what the 'other' represents is partly a product of the immediacy, physical intimacy and homo-eroticism of fighting and partly a reflection of the fact that the leaders in the opposing sides – princes, aristocrats and demi-gods among them – have more in common with each other than with their own soldiery; as Pandarus so charmingly calls them: *"Asses, fools, dolts! Chaff and bran, chaff and bran! Porridge after meat."*

In addition to mutual admiration, each side observes meticulously the injunction to protect emissaries when they enter the opposing camp, thus highlighting the shameful anomaly of Achilles having Hector murdered whilst he is unarmed. Ulysses and Aeneas, the two 'thinking' soldiers on either side, frequently meet up to compare notes across the battle lines. As well as these meetings and exchanges of information, there is much common language between the two sides. One connecting trope is that of Menelaus as cuckold, mercilessly evoked by all, including Cressida when she arrives at the Greek camp:

> Menelaus "*An odd man, lady? Every man is odd.*"
>
> Cressida "*No. Paris is not: for you know 'tis true*
>
> *That you are odd and he is even with you.*" (4.v.41–43)

Menelaus is indeed the universal butt, especially on his own side:

> Achilles "*What! Does the cuckold scorn me?*"
>
> Diomedes "*... he like a puling cuckold.*"

This repetition underlines the generally acknowledged absurdity of using Helen's abduction as a continuing motive for war. The remedy, however, is one about which the protagonists tend to take contradictory positions at different stages in the play, thus failing to act consistently or strategically. "Collectively," argues Jonathan Dollimore, "the inhabitants of the world of Troilus and Cressida are responsible for a war and the ideology which legitimates and thereby perpetuates it; individually they are more or less powerless to escape either the war or its ideology."[4]

The frequent crossing of the battle lines reaches its apogee in Hector's visit to the opposing camp in Act 4 when the Greeks compete with each other in paying homage to him and Achilles, who has been longing for this moment, struts before him – *"behold thy fill"* – challenges Hector's cursory glance – *"Thou art too brief"* – ignores his discomfort and proceeds to indulge his own fantasies of dismembering his enemy, fantasies which seem to require Hector's witness and acquiescence:

"Tell me you heavens, in which part of his body

Shall I destroy him?– whether there, or there, or there?"

Warfare and food metaphors converge as Achilles imagines Hector as a dish to be relished before it is disjointed:

"I'll heat his blood with Greekish wine tonight

Which with my scimitar I'll cool tomorrow.

Patroclus, let us feast him to the height." (5.i.1–3)

The mutual need among the adversaries for the judgement/approval of the other is also expressed by Paris, who acting as Achilles' narcissistic double in the Trojan camp, wastes no time, once he has Diomedes alone, in interrogating him:

Paris *"And tell me, noble Diomed, faith tell me true,*

Even in the soul of sound good-fellowship,

Who, in your thoughts, deserves fair Helen best,

Myself or Menelaus?."(4.i.52–54)

Above all there is the symmetry between Helen and Cressida in their experiences of being uprooted and seduced/ raped. Helen was snatched from Greece to live in Troy; Cressida, a Trojan, is forcibly removed to live with her father who has defected to the Greek camp. Each woman is loved by both a Greek and a Trojan. When Cressida is delivered to the Greek camp, her situation replays Helen's: "a beautiful woman is forced to leave one man (Menelaus/ Troilus) and is carried away by a foreigner (Paris/Diomedes)."[5] Moreover, both women are made to bear responsibility for the men's decision to trade them; in Helen's case, responsibility for the whole genesis and cost of this war:

Diomedes *"For every false drop in her bawdy veins*

A Grecian's life hath sunk: for every scruple

Of her contaminated carrion weight

A Trojan hath been slain." (4.i.70–74)

In Cressida's case, she is first held responsible by Troilus for diverting him from his proper military role – *"Why should I war without the walls of Troy/*

That find such cruel battle here within?" – and at the end for the fact that Troilus brutalises himself and determinates to fight:

> *"Farewell, revolted fair, and, Diomed,/ Stand fast and wear a castle on thy head."*

The symmetry is heightened in the final battle scene when Thersites, for whom 'lechery' and war are one and the same, shows an almost orgasmic excitement at witnessing the 'wronged' or cuckolded men finally fight their adversaries. As Troilus and Diomedes fight, he revels: *"I would fain see them meet. . . . Hold thy whore, Grecian! Now for thy whore, Trojan,"* and he is equally ecstatic when Paris and Menelaus fight: *"The cuckold and the cuckold-maker are at it. Now bull! Now dog! 'Loo Paris! Loo now, my double-horned Spartan!"*

In this sexualised military context, both Helen and Cressida bear the burden of being simultaneously idealised and oppressed and demeaned, each performing a diminished and compromised self. Cressida is at least able to articulate this whereas Helen is reduced to erotic pantomime. Both women are abused as whores by virtue of having been seized and imprisoned by men, regardless of whether they are 'consenting' or enjoying their relationship with their captors. While Helen is constantly described by others as a piece of merchandise, Cressida reflects on the gendered language of trade and exchange: *"Men prize the thing ungained more than it is."* As she predicts, this instrumental domain penetrates into her relationship with Troilus, destroying its intimacy, as political exigencies intervene. An indication that among Troilus' competing relationship priorities is the strong desire to advance his position among his brothers emerges in the family debate in Act 2, scene 2.

Family dynasties and family dynamics

Throughout the play, positions taken up by individuals are generally portrayed as strategic and self-serving rather than an expression of sincerely held opinions. However, Hector's 'volte face' in the Trojan royal family's debate about whether or not to return Helen has aroused much critical comment. It has variously been seen as a reflection of the cynicism of the play as a whole, as 'rough handiwork' on Shakespeare's part, occasioned by his "lack of love for his characters"[6] or as an undermining of universalising ideologies: "Hector invokes in some detail the apparatus of natural law only to advocate action which flatly contradicts it."[7] René Girard suggests that, despite his eloquent advocacy of peace, Hector simply becomes "a victim of the *infection* that he shrewdly denounced a few lines before."[8] While the whole play is riddled with inconsistencies, paying too much attention to Hector's individual position obscures the extent to which this change is influenced by the interplay of relationships. The debate takes place exclusively between siblings. Four brothers are involved with occasional interjections from their father and sister. Priam, Hecuba and their six children constitute one of the very few large intact families in all of Shakespeare's canon. This configuration alone, not to mention the sibling rivalry that is enacted in the two scenes, makes it well worth a family therapist's time to take a more detailed look.

Priam opens up the dialogue by conveying yet another request from the Greeks for Helen's return. It is not clear from the text whether this message was sent before or after Aeneas delivered Hector's challenge to the Greeks. Priam never directly states his own opinion, although during the debate he chastises Paris for his self-indulgence. One might hypothesise that Paris has his mother's protection so that Priam, if he is to thwart this son by deciding on Helen's return, needs the protective ballast of his other sons. Hector's reasoned and authoritative 'older brother' opening speech stating unequivocally *"Let Helen go"* is responded to by Troilus, the youngest, in a way that gives every sign that he will stop at nothing to win an argument. He accuses Hector of being disrespectful to their father by implying that all lives, royal and commoner, are equivalent:

> "*Fie, fie, my brother!*
>
> *Weigh you the worth and honour of a king*
>
> *So great as our dread father's in a scale*
>
> *Of common ounces?*" (2.ii.25–28)

This in turn evokes a put-down from Helenus and an exchange of brotherly insults ensues which is interrupted by Hector in magisterial tones that might suggest he thinks this should be the end of the matter: *"Brother she is not worth that what she doth cost/ The keeping."* When Troilus rejoins: *"What's aught but as' tis valued?,"* an argument between relativist and objectivist theories of value follows, in which Hector continues his lofty, moralising tone: *"Tis mad idolatry To make the service greater than the god."* Troilus, given remarkable leeway as the youngest to expound his arguments and perhaps realising that his previous interjections were vacuous, moves onto the ethics of responsibility for decisions. He reminds Hector that the abduction of Helen was one they all agreed on: *"You all cried 'Go, go' . . . , you all clapped your hands and cried 'Inestimable'."* This offers Paris, perhaps hiding behind his bold and passionate younger brother, the chance to follow this line of argument, but not before Cassandra, *"our mad sister"* intervenes, daring, under cover of madness, to disrupt male discourse. Only Hector takes her views seriously, accusing Troilus of being less rational than his 'mad' sister. Perhaps because he is the youngest male, Troilus is especially scathing about his sister's *"brainsick raptures"* and, perhaps offended by Hector's comments, is at pains to point out that *"I am no more touched than all Priam's sons."*

After Paris' salvo of self-serving and self-pitying hyperbole, earning a rebuke from Priam, suggesting that he has a low opinion of this son, Hector proceeds to bring matters to a close. He sums up his argument, pronounces on his brothers' eloquence, but lack of philosophical depth and states his final argument, in favour of natural law. This dictates that Helen is Menelaus 'property' and as such she must be returned to him. Having pronounced: *"Hector's opinion/Is this by way of truth,"* he then aligns himself with his brothers' preferred course of action which is to keep Helen. He can give in to his *"sprightly brethren"* precisely because he is sure they have lost the moral argument.

Taking sibling relationships as a context for Hector's 'volte face' could lead to several different interpretations. One is that Hector, having already issued the challenge to the Greeks, was hoping to be persuaded out of it, but needed his family's backing. He may have been taken by surprise at the ferocity of Troilus' argument. The tendency to back away from the 'killer argument' mirrors Hector's tendency, as seen with Ajax, Achilles and even Thersites, not to press home a victory if it does not accord with his own heroic self-image. It could be argued that pressing home his advantage over his brothers might have been too challenging to his father Priam, diminishing his '*valiant offspring*' in his presence. Priam, as the next family scene shows, is in decline and Hector's assumption of his powers is being challenged by Troilus. As in so much of the play, and here enacted between the brothers, strongly argued moral positions crumble in the face of relational imperatives.

The second family scene in Act 5, scene 3, again revolves around Hector and Troilus as key protagonists and can be read more explicitly as a power struggle between these two brothers as the ageing Priam's authority wanes. As in the previous scene with Cressida, it also marks the silencing of women as the men prepare for an orgy of killing. Andromache's and Cassandra's attempts to persuade their husband and brother not to fight are dismissed by Hector who evokes his own honour as well as his promise to the Gods. Not having access to a hot line to the deities, the two women seek out their father to back them up. In the intervening period, however, Troilus appears and Hector in turn urges *him* not to fight:

> "*No, faith, young Troilus: doff thy harness, youth.*
>
> *I am today i'th' vein of chivalry.*
>
> *Let grow thy sinews till their knots be strong,*
>
> *And tempt not yet the brushes of the war.*" (5.iii.31–34)

While this intervention seems strange, given that Ulysses earlier praised Troilus' bravery in battle, in the family context it could make sense. Hector of all the brothers is the one most likely to listen to his sister Cassandra and take her warnings seriously, so he manages his dilemma by diverting the injunction not to fight onto Troilus. He faces, however, a 'savage' Troilus, who not only brushes aside his older brother's attempt to protect him but criticises him for his "*fair play*" in battle, deriding it as "*fool's play*." Hector's eventual decision to defy his father is bolstered by Troilus declaring that *he* would not be deterred from fighting not by "*Priamus and Hecuba on knees,/Their eyes o'ergallèd with recourse of tears*" and certainly not by their sister, Cassandra, dismissed as "*this foolish dreaming, superstitious girl.*" Priam, however, supports the women's position, adding Hecuba's and his own premonitions of disaster to that of the other women:

> "*Come Hector, come, go back.*
>
> *Thy wife hath dreamed: thy mother hath had visions:*
>
> *Cassandra doth foresee: and I myself*
>
> *Am like a prophet suddenly enrapt to tell thee that this day is ominous:*
>
> *Therefore, come back.*" (5.iii.63–67)

Hector initially pleads with his father:

> "*You know me dutiful; therefore dear sir*
>
> *Let me not shame respect, but give me leave*
>
> *To take that course by your consent and voice*
>
> *Which you do here forbid me, royal Priam.*" (5.iii.72–75)

At this moment, Cassandra and Andromache intervene to support Priam, and perhaps because the scene is witnessed by the 'savage' Troilus, Hector rounds on his wife:

> *"Andromache I am offended with you*
>
> *Upon the love I bear you, get thee in." (Exit Andromache)*

From this moment on Hector's position hardens and he reproaches Priam for being influenced by Cassandra – *"you are amazed my liege, at her exclaims"* – and enjoins him to *"Go in and cheer the town."* As Cassandra has correctly divined, Priam's power is diminishing and Hector is now Priam's *'crutch.'* Her voice, however, remains the only one in the family to cut through the rhetoric and mock heroics of war to expose their bloody consequences.

Acts of deconstruction and irreverence

In *Troilus and Cressida,* Shakespeare certainly takes an iconoclastic and sceptical view of the glory and heroism of the Iliad. With its recurring images of disease and deformity, it is sometimes described as a 'sick play.' Thersites, source of the most repulsive imagery, also ensures that no pretensions go unchallenged, contributing to the process whereby all universalising ideas such as natural law or a divinely sanctioned order as well as aspirations to fidelity, chivalry or morality are shown to be violated in practice. In *Troilus and Cressida,* appeals either to divine order or natural law stand in inverse relation to actual experiences of disorder or injustice. The desire for order and adherence to the norms and rules of hierarchy voiced by Ulysses is matched by Hector's appeal to natural law; both men immediately cancel by their actions the very rules they have just upheld. Ulysses sets up an elaborate deception to entice Achilles to fight, which involves rigging the rules and Hector, as we have seen while arguing for the lawful necessity of returning Helen, dramatically changes his position. Equally, even when protagonists appear to be able to reflect on their positions, they themselves are likely to undermine that very process. Achilles does this in a beautiful example of double speech. Having expressed fears about his diminished status: *"What am I poor of late?"* he reflects on the relational effects of loss of power: *"What the declined is/He shall as soon read in the eyes of others."* He then rebounds from this realistic appraisal into a consoling message to himself: *"But tis not so with me."* Since Shakespeare immediately takes up the same theme in Ulysses' speech, the subject is replayed through dialogue; this time, since Ulysses is in control, it is entirely in the interests of strategy and power politics.

Margot Heinemann describes an interview with Nigel Lawson (Chancellor of the Exchequer under Prime Minister Margaret Thatcher) in which he says that Shakespeare "was a Tory, without any doubt." In support of this argument he quotes Ulysses: "*Take but decree away, untune that string/And hark what discord follows*."[9] If we took this speech out of context and assumed this was what Shakespeare himself actually thought, Mr Lawson might have had a point. However, he fails to see that Ulysses' argument to Agamemnon here is as much prescriptive as it is descriptive – a common failure in those who, like Lawson, are in positions of power. Since Ulysses, as Agamemnon's subordinate, is flouting decree through the very act of taking charge then we are not meant to attach too much literal truth to his words. What Ulysses presents to Achilles is a much more radical and typically Shakespearean perspective on how far rank and reputation are dependent on context and on the feedback of others, rather than having any essential or enduring status: "*No man is the lord of anything/Though in and of him there be much consisting,/ Til he communicate his parts to others*."

After a paean of praise about Ajax, Ulysses utters the deadly phrase to *Achilles*:

> "*Time hath, my lord, a wallet at his back*
>
> *Wherein he puts alms for oblivion*" adding "*Perseverance, dear my lord,*
>
> *Keeps honour bright: to have done is to hang*
>
> *Quite out of fashion, like a rusty mail*
>
> *In monumental mock'ry.*" (3.iii.145–153)

That Ulysses delivers this particular speech to Achilles and the quite different one to Agamemnon is an example of how context-bound are all ideological positions in the play. Agamemnon's leadership is barely holding; his authority is openly challenged by Achilles and he is dependent on the ever-resourceful Ulysses for survival. Agamemnon is trapped by his oath to fight on behalf of his brother, Menelaus, the much-derided cuckold, and, in the Trojan camp, while the authority of Priam is not openly challenged, he is still unable to persuade the cuckold-maker, his son Paris, to relinquish Helen and bring them peace. In a context of continuing failure on both sides, the resultant disrespect for hierarchy is evident, as Achilles, Patroclus and Thersites demonstrate in the Greek camp and Troilus, in his contempt for his older brother, Hector, in the Trojan. Ulysses' solemn speech about hierarchies and the risk of subverting them has playful and subversive echoes at various points in the play, including Cressida's sardonic comments to Pandarus as they witness the "march-past" in Act 1.

As Ulysses resorts to gimmicks to break the stalemate between the Greeks and Trojans and to entice Achilles to fight this, his strategy too is mercilessly mocked as Ajax is set up to fight Hector:

> Thersites "*Ajax goes up and down the field asking for himself*"
>
> Achilles "*How so?*"
>
> Thersites "*He must fight singly tomorrow with Hector, and is so prophetically proud of a heroical cudgelling that he raves in saying nothing.*" (3.iii.243–248)

The undermining of rules and the irreverence towards 'high ideals' is paralleled by the ways in which possibilities for intimacy or closeness are eroded. Shakespeare finds various ways of disrupting scenes of possible emotional intensity, one of which is through the insertion of a third person to create distance. This is most evident in the case of Pandarus, who acts as procurer/impresario in the first love scene between Troilus and Cressida. He hovers and gloats over their sexual consummation, urging them to "*press the bed to death*" and rushes in to learn the results: "*how now, how now! How go maidenheads?* He inserts himself into their parting scene, dismissing Cressida's grief as immoderate and then indulging in his own.

Thersites, set up as more of a licensed fool in the Greek camp, keeps any idea of idealism, moral grandeur, or noble intention at bay. His comic turns on the battlefield underline the fragmented, truncated and chaotic nature of the encounters where, it appears, any adversary will do as long as class distinctions are observed:

> Hector "*What art thou Greek? Art thou for Hector's match? Art thou of blood and honour?*"
>
> Thersites "*No, no I am a rascal; a scurvy, railing knave, a very filthy rogue*"
>
> Hector "*I do believe thee. Live ....*" (5.iv.24–260)

> Margarelon "*Turn, slave, and fight*"
>
> Thersites "*What art thou?*"

Margarelon "*A bastard son of Priam's*"

Thersites "*I am a bastard too. I love bastards...*" (5.vii.13–16)

He, like Pandarus, plays a distancing role, often being called upon as a 'third' in the interactions between Achilles and Patroclus. This disrupts the intensity of their relationship when, alone together after Ulysses' intervention, they face the consequences of their period of indulgent withdrawal from the rest of the Greek camp:

Patroclus "*I stand condemned for this:*

They think my little stomach for the war

And your great love to me restrains you thus.

Sweet, rouse yourself, and the weak wanton Cupid

Shall from your neck unloose his amorous fold...

And danger, like an ague, subtly taints

Even then when we sit idly in the sun."

Achilles "*Go call Thersites hither, sweet Patroclus.*" (3.iii.218–233)

Finally, in Act 5, scene 2, speaking mostly to the audience, Thersites disrupts identification with the plight of either Cressida, whom he gloatingly abuses as a whore, or Troilus, whose self-delusion he witheringly demolishes: "*Will'a swagger himself out on's own eyes*?" In this respect, much as Pandarus has done, he diminishes the possibilities for empathy, making it harder for audiences to become emotionally involved in the development and denouement of the love story. The message that this is not a story that can or should be taken too seriously is mirrored in the way the lovers themselves describe their relationship.

Troilus and Cressida: gender, sex and power

Critics seem to have struggled over Cressida's character and intentions in ways that go to the heart of those familiar processes through which women are either idealised or demonised, where a woman can only be seen as misunderstood or victimised if she can also be claimed to be 'innocent.' In Shakespeare, Desdemona fits this requirement; Cressida does not. Even some feminist critics seem to sigh as they reluctantly accept that she has a sexual relationship with Diomedes: "let's be plain in Cressida's case, faithlessness."[10] Apparently, she cannot both love Troilus, genuinely mourn his loss, and at the same time submit to the plainly coercive overtures of Diomedes. This scene alone provides a good argument for the importance of linguistically uncoupling 'innocent' from 'victim' in our discourse since 'innocent' in this context is so readily equated with goodness on the one hand and passivity on the other. Cressida, whose 'goodness' is not relevant and who is anything but passive, needs to be understood in a more nuanced way. Her lover, Troilus' behaviour is best understood in the context of his need to find a position among his siblings. Initially competing with Paris in the pursuit of love, he moves into challenging Hector in the 'bravery stakes.'

In the opening scenes Shakespeare presents Troilus and Cressida as equal protagonists, each narrating their separate versions of the relationship. Cressida's inner world as well as that of Troilus is revealed to the audience and her spirited reaction to the plan to send her to the Greek camp sets her up as a person of moral courage and steadfastness. At the end of the play, Cressida's voice has been stifled and she becomes, in the scene with Diomedes, the object of male gaze with no opportunity to present her point of view. If the play had fulfilled the 'tragic requirement' that its main characters die and if Cressida had remained at the heart of it, we might have anticipated her suicide after Diomedes cruelly sends her Troilus' horse as proof that he has "*chastised the amorous Trojan*." Instead, we hear no more from her after Act 5, scene 2, other than a letter that Troilus tears up. Troilus' agony over her supposed faithlessness, followed by his immersion in the world of the heroic and 'savage' male warrior emerges as the emotional heart of the play.

Both Troilus and Cressida present ambivalent accounts of their feelings as, from their different standpoints, they 'collaborate' in the assumption that love cannot last. Troilus, despite his declarations of passion, already anticipates disappointment as the time for consummation approaches:

"*I fear it much, and I do fear besides*

That I shall lose distinction in my joys,

As doth a battle, when they charge on heaps

The enemy flying." (3.ii.24–27)

These overt connections between sex and warfare have been foreshadowed in earlier speeches when Troilus speaks of his lack of commitment to fighting, attributing it to his alternative struggle to conquer

Cressida, a reluctance he associates with femininity: *"But I am weaker than a woman's tear."*

His scepticism about the war – *"Fools on both sides. . . . I cannot fight upon this argument:/ It is too starved a subject for my sword"* – reiterates the absurdity of love as a casus belli. However, it could also be read as a desire for his own heroic love story to compete with that of his brother, Paris. The 'Helen story' might act as a background for Troilus' fears about the precariousness of love within this erotically charged climate of warfare. Here, Helen has to perform endless desirability, Paris limitless desire and Menelaus is forever reminded of his cuckolded state. While we see little of Helen and Paris together, there is a suggestion of how much effort has to go into the performance of conjugal ecstasy and how vacuous it has become:

> Helen "*Let thy song be love. 'This love will undo us all.'*
>
> *O Cupid, Cupid, Cupid!*"
>
> Pandarus "*Love? Ay, that it shall, i'faith*"
>
> Paris "*Ay, good now, 'Love, love, nothing but love'.*" (3.i.102–104)

This is perhaps a necessary performance when so many lives are lost in protecting the relationship. Troilus, however, has little sympathy for his brother:

> *"Let Paris bleed: 'tis but a scar to scorn:*
>
> *Paris is gored with Menelaus' horn."*

Nevertheless, Paris is still the lover of the iconic Helen, whereas there is a hint of shame from Troilus as he confesses to his obsession with Cressida, shame that is perhaps connected to her father's treachery:

> *"At Priam's royal table do I sit,*
>
> *And when fair Cressid comes into my thoughts –*
>
> *So traitor! When she comes? When is she thence?"* (1.i.30–31)

Cressida's own ambivalence about the relationship stems from her acute reading of the power relations involved in sex and her knowledge of her own lack of social capital. As daughter of the 'traitor Calchas,' she would be acutely aware of her devalued status. Pandarus himself views her as something of a liability *"She's a fool to stay behind her father. Let her to the Greeks, and so I'll tell her the next time I see her"* and he makes it clear that she has to rely on her erotic resources. A match between her and Troilus, while it is never actually suggested, might have suited Pandarus perfectly. His distress at Cressida being sent to the Greek camp is expressed on Troilus' behalf rather than hers. The absence of Cressida's father (there is no mention of her mother) and her dependence on a prurient pimp for a guardian provides a marked contrast with the solidity of Troilus' family ties.

We first meet Cressida engaging in lewd banter with her uncle and, playfully subverting the hierarchy of human value that he is obsessed with, both his use of Helen as the coinage of all desirability and his judgements in the 'march-past' scene. She is presented as a young woman who knows she has to fend for herself: *"Upon my back, to defend my belly; upon my wit to defend my wiles, upon my secrecy, to defend mine honesty; my mask to defend my beauty."* The voice she draws upon in dialogue with Pandarus is transformed into one of thoughtful pragmatism in her soliloquy as she reflects on her reasons for deliberately diverting Pandarus and for 'holding off' the ardent Troilus:

"*Words, vows, gifts, tears, and love's full sacrifice,*

He offers in another's enterprise;

But more in Troilus thousandfold I see

Than in the glass of Pandar's praise may be.

Yet I hold off: women are angels wooing;

Things won are done – joy's soul lies in the doing.

That she beloved knows nought that knows not this:

Men prize the thing ungained more than it is.

That she was never yet that ever knew

Love got so sweet as when desire did sue.

Therefore this maxim out of love I teach:

'Achievement is command; ungained, beseech'

Then though my heart's content firm love doth bear,

Nothing of that shall from mine eyes appear." (I.ii.268–281)

This speech both echoes the play's cynicism but also undermines it by presenting the human cost of suppressing desire. Cressida's shrewd appraisal of gender and power involves dissecting the rules governing female sexuality. She simultaneously expresses her own desire, knowledge of the risks she runs in fulfilling it and awareness that Pandarus is acting in Troilus' interests and not in hers. What sets Cressida apart from the other protagonists is that she interrogates principles rather than simply state them and then proceed to violate them in practice.

In the Act 3 scene with Troilus, Cressida's ambivalence is central. She struggles to find a new voice through which she can directly express feeling. Rather than attempt to show consistency, she confounds Troilus and frustrates Pandarus by changing her position from moment to moment. Cressida's dialogues encompass multiple aspects of her identity: the wary, cautious self of the devalued outsider, the sceptical self of the intelligent observer of social mores, the teasing irreverent self that she uses with Pandarus and the passionate self she struggles to communicate to Troilus.

Initially in this scene each of the lovers agrees on the paradox that love is at one and the same time exquisite, monstrous and bound to disappoint: "*the will is infinite and the execution confined: that the desire is boundless and the act a slave to limit*" and that "*all lovers swear more performance than they are able.*" However, Troilus, not the most emotionally intelligent of Shakespeare's heroes, struggles to understand Cressida's gnomic and ambivalent communication. Expressing uncertainty and vulnerability about her compromised position, she moves between sincere declarations of love and anxious retreat from anything that might be perceived as sexual manipulation:

> *(He kisses her)*
>
> Cressida "*My lord I do beseech you, pardon me*
>
> *Twas not my purpose thus to beg a kiss*
>
> *I am ashamed.*"

Cressida's self-censorship is overt – "*perchance my lord I show more craft than love*" – as she takes up one position only to withdraw from it: "*The gods grant – O, my lord!,*" justifying her "*pretty abruption*" by referring to her pessimism and fear. In these interchanges, Cressida not only responds directly to Troilus and to her own fear of rejection but also to the internalised view of her promulgated by her uncle. His construction of her as a commodity is reinforced at every stage by the way he crudely urges the lovers to go to bed. His intrusive presence in what might otherwise be an intimate scene – "*What blushing still? Have you not done talking yet?"* – invites Cressida back into her ironic and teasing voice: *"Well uncle, what folly I commit, I dedicate to you."* Pandarus devotes all his efforts towards procuring his niece for Troilus rather than acting on her behalf. She is an object, a vessel; if she becomes pregnant, the child will be his: *"If my lord get a boy of you, you'll give him to me."* When Cressida is sent to the Greek camp, all of Pandarus' sorrow is on behalf of Troilus: *"Would thou hadst ne'er been born! I knew thou wouldst be his death."*

Ironically it is when Pandarus reassures Troilus that the women in his family are faithful: *"Our kindred though they be long ere they are wooed, they are constant being won. They are burrs I can tell you: they'll stick where they are thrown,"* that Cressida is emboldened to directly declare her love, suggesting what a burden her father's notoriety might have been to her. Even then she corrects and contradicts herself:

"I love you now: but not, til now, so much

But I might master it. In faith I lie!

My thoughts were like unbridled children, grown

Too headstrong for their mother." (3.ii.113–116)

Troilus' speech is more straightforward, having no doubts about his entitlement to woo Cressida. This a gendered truism that she is all too aware of:

"But though I loved you well I wooed you not;

And yet, good faith, I wished myself a man,

Or that we women had men's privilege

Of speaking first." (3.ii.119–122)

After a long struggle, she finally takes up the required performance, to the obvious relief and satisfaction of the males: *"Go to, a bargain made . . . Amen."* While Pandarus dismisses all the complexity she had been struggling to articulate as that of *"tongue-tied maidens,"* Troilus at least attempts to understand her – *"Why was my Cressid then so hard to win? . . . What offends you lady?"* – Cressida acknowledges her inner splits and tensions:

"I have a kind of self resides with you

But an unkind self that itself will leave

To be another's fool." (3.ii.137–140)

The self-division that emerges from a struggle between desire and social sanction is only expressed in Cressida's part of the dialogue. Troilus never displays this degree of reflexivity, projecting on to Cressida all his anxieties about the fragility and impermanence of love, so that she has to prove herself faithful no matter what he does nor in what circumstances she finds herself. Moreover, the tropes of falsehood and treachery epitomised by Calchas emerge and contaminate the joy of a first sexual encounter. The yardstick for relationships, provided earlier by Troilus in relation to Helen – *"What's aught but as 'tis valued?"* – inserts itself, as Cressida predicted, into the relationship. She is only too aware that by 'submitting' to Troilus, her 'value' has sunk. This 'commodifying' of Cressida is reinforced by her father's offer to the Greeks to barter her for Antennor –*"in right great exchange."*

The morning after their love-making, Troilus is eager to be off. Here, the Greeks come to his rescue, enabling him to extricate himself from Cressida under compulsion – *"no remedy"* – and still consider himself honourable. In the exchange with Antenor, he has the perfect opportunity to be rid of his lover. Only Cressida challenges this decision, dismissing her father's right to make any claim on her behalf, but also conveying her loneliness and emotional dependence on Troilus.

> *"I will not, uncle. I have forgot my father;*
>
> *I know no touch of consanguinity;*
>
> *No kin, no love, no blood, no soul so near me*
>
> *As the sweet Troilus."* (4.ii.94–97)

The contrast between the prolonged debate about whether or not to keep Helen and the casual handing over of Cressida, presented as a foregone conclusion could not be starker:

> Troilus *"Is it so concluded?"*
>
> Aeneas *"By Priam and the general state of Troy*
>
> *They are at hand and ready to effect it."* (4.ii.65–67)

Troilus after a brief eruption of self-pity – *"how my achievements mock me"* – is eager to re-enter the male soldierly world and to erase evidence of his night with Cressida:

> *"I will go meet them; and, my Lord Aeneas/ We met by chance: you did not find me here."*

With his desire to distance himself from his lover now fulfilled, Troilus can afford to indulge in some sentimental regrets: *"Cressid I love thee in so strained a purity/That the blest gods, as angry with my fancy . . . take thee from me."*

Incredulously, Cressida challenges him: *"Have the gods envy?"* Ignoring Pandarus' interventions, she insists on clarity and makes a final plea for her lover to take her side: *"What, and from Troilus too?"* On his: *"From Troy and Troilus,"* her rejoinder: *"Is't possible"* could be played with fury or with a weary and cynical resignation, since this betrayal could be said to lie within the realm of the 'already known.'

René Girard suggests that, in using the phrase *"a woeful Cressid 'mongst the merry Greeks,"* thus reminding Troilus of the Greeks' erotic reputation, Cressida stimulates a resurgence of Troilus' desire for her because of the mimetic envy it unleashes. "With seven words she has caused a second revolution in her relationship with Troilus."[11] While this interpretation reflects Cressida's ability to think on her feet and employ her wit, it underplays the preposterousness of Troilus delivering Cressida to what amounts to sexual slavery and expecting her to protect her own virtue. Despite her grasp of the power politics of this situation – *"what wicked deam is this?"* – Cressida, having challenged Troilus' demand for her to be faithful – *"Oh heavens! Be true again!"* – finally submits to his construction of her as potentially false: *"But I'll be true."* Troilus' earlier words to Paris suggest that he knows full well that Cressida is to be delivered, not to her father but to Diomedes personally:

"*I'll bring her to the Grecian presently:*

And to his hand when I deliver her,

Think it an altar, and thy brother Troilus

A priest, there off'ring his own heart." (4.iii.6–9)

If there were any doubt about what the deal is, Diomedes quickly dispels it:

"*When I am hence,/ I'll answer to my lust.*"

From this moment on, Cressida's position as victim to the whims of sexually predatory males makes discussion of her fidelity or falseness irrelevant. The scene when she arrives in the Greek camp represents further trauma – "the verbal and osculatory equivalent of gang rape"[12] – and begins the process of her silencing. "This normally vocally assertive woman (is silent) for a full 20 to 30 lines" while the Greeks take turns to eye, comment on and kiss her. [13] When she recovers her wit and repartee and assumes some control, this is seized upon by Ulysses, who has been at the receiving end of it, as a sign of her promiscuity:

> *Ulysses "Fie, fie upon her!*
>
> *There's language in her eye, her cheek, her lip*
>
> *Nay her foot speaks; her wanton spirits look out*
>
> *At every joint and motive of her body*
>
> *O these encounterers, so glib of tongue*
>
> *That give accosting welcome ere it comes,*
>
> *And wide unclasp the tables of their thoughts*
>
> *To every tickling reader! Set them down*
>
> *For sluttish spoils of opportunity*
>
> *And daughters of the game."* (4.v.54–63)

Ulysses' attempt to transform Cressida's mind and voice into a pornographic image emphasises the way that calling women who stand up for themselves 'whores' or 'sluts' acts as a means of control and silencing. It is small wonder that, in this context, Cressida seeks protection from Diomedes who does not join in his fellow Greeks' attempts to kiss her and who removes her just as Ulysses becomes menacing. As her 'guardian' to whom her father is only too ready to hand her over, he may seem to be her only hope.

In Cressida's final scene where she 'betrays' Troilus, Ulysses' portrayal of Cressida as whore is eagerly taken up by Thersites: "*And any man may sing her, if he can take her clef; she's noted.*" In this scene Cressida again takes up a series of contradictory positions, alternating between cowed acquiescence, flirtatiousness and defiance. Rather than duplicity, this could be seen as attempting to take some control in a situation where, as Diomedes' property, she has virtually no power. Alone and unprotected she resolves her dilemma by submitting to Diomedes' bullying but continuing to assert her love for Troilus. As in all her interactions, Cressida persists in naming her inner conflict even though at the end she appears to have internalised the myth of women's 'frailty.' However, while one level of the drama features Cressida's simultaneous resistance to and placation of Diomedes, this is interwoven contrapuntally by the voices of the three observers. Here, Troilus' anguished and judgemental interjections are met by Ulysses' attempts to restrain and calm him and joined by Thersites' scurrilous commentary. As if *she* has overheard *them*, and it could easily be played in this way, Cressida ends up performing an abject version of herself:

> "*Ah, poor our sex! The fault in us I find,*
>
> *The error of our eye directs our mind;*
>
> *What error leads must err.*" (5.ii.107–109)

She could then turn to the three males at the final lines;

> "*O, then conclude*
>
> *Minds swayed by eyes are full of turpitude.*"

If a drama that so strongly features processes of mirroring were played in this way, Cressida could be reflecting the gaze back to her audience of three and, beyond them, to the wider theatre audience who are witnessing this unpalatable spectacle. Since Shakespeare created a woman with such an ability to expose hypocrisy, betrayal and abuse of power and then proceeded to deprive of an active voice it is tempting to try to restore some agency to her at the end.

Conclusion

Troilus and Cressida is a play where protagonists act as if they are trapped in a continuous present, while at the same time being acutely aware that "*injurious time*" which has "*a wallet at his back*" creates the imperative to act differently. In this context of simultaneous stasis and chaos, no ideological or moral position seems to survive the exigencies of the moment nor the blandishments of others. The one action that could bring the war to an end – the handing back of Helen – has been ruled out to preserve family unity. Agamemnon cannot give up the attempt to win her back for the same reason. In the light of this, rhetoric and display take the place of action. When action in the form of an orgy of killing finally erupts in the final scenes, it is depicted as confused and anarchic, not arising from any strategy but from diverse personal motives; Troilus' desire to avenge the loss of Cressida, Achilles' to avenge the death of his lover, Patroclus and Hector in response to his younger brother's provocations.

There is no heroic denouement. The much-heralded set-piece duel between Hector and Achilles – "*Where is this Hector? Know what it is to meet Achilles angry*" – is replaced by a squalid assassination of the unarmed Hector, not even by Achilles himself but by his Myrmidon henchmen. Troilus' grandiloquent speech with its suitably heroic final line: "*Hope of revenge shall hide our inward woe,*" instead of ending the play, is immediately followed by the re-entry of Pandarus who, roundly rejected by Troilus, ends the play instead with a self-pitying account of his venereal disease and a warning to the audience about their own likely contamination.

These connections in the play between sex, war and disease can hardly be missed and they find expression in the contamination of the relationship between Troilus and Cressida by the brutal realities of power. Their one-sided love story does, however, capture other levels; in particular, the paradoxes of desire and its fulfilment, the inequality between the sexes and the struggle to find a way to express a divided self. Cressida speaks throughout of the split within herself. Troilus is puzzled by this discourse but, unable to reflect on his own contribution, can only project his confusion onto her: "*This is and is not Cressida.*" In doing so he frees himself from ambivalence or uncertainty and takes up the unitary identity of the successful warrior son of Priam that he has all along been striving for.

Cressida stands out in this play of narcissistic males as the one person whom Shakespeare allows to be self-reflexive and who interrogates practices of power. This is particularly striking in a play that is full of people who contradict themselves but show little awareness that this is what they are doing. Cressida's relationship with Troilus succumbs to the same combination of cynical manipulation, undermining of ideals and trivialisation of intimacy as suffuses the drama as a whole. Although *Troilus and Cressida* is not a play that invites us into a profound emotional engagement with any of the protagonists, the fact that it is a play mainly of 'surfaces' has its advantages. It opens up a way to appreciate the processes that evolve within 'stuck systems' where everyone has given up on the idea that anything can change. In this context, unexpected connections and alliances emerge, hierarchy is subverted, performance and display assume greater significance and despised "*scurvy knaves*" like Thersites are able to flourish and can wield unexpected influence. When protagonists have few occasions in which to experience pride in their actions, we see them employ whatever ingenious means they can to maintain some agency, dignity, humour and pleasure within the crazy system engendered by a prolonged war whose pointlessness everyone at least agrees upon.

Notes

1 Janet Adelman, *Suffocating Mothers: Fantasies of Maternal Origin in Shakespeare's Plays, 'Hamlet' to 'The Tempest'* (New York: Routledge, 1992), 44.
2 René Girard, *A Theatre of Envy* (New York: Oxford University Press, 1991).
3 Ibid., 123.
4 Jonathan Dollimore, *Radical Tragedy* (Basingstoke and New York: Palgrave Macmillan, Third Edition, 2004), 47.
5 Laurie Maguire, *Helen of Troy* (Chichester: Wiley-Blackwell, 2009), 94.
6 Anthony Nuttall, *Shakespeare the Thinker* (Newhaven: Yale University Press, 2007), 217.
7 Jonathan Dollimore, *Radical Tragedy* (Basingstoke and New York: Palgrave Macmillan, Third Edition, 2004), 43.
8 René Girard, *A Theatre of Envy* (New York: Oxford University Press, 1991), 151.
9 Margot Heinemann, 'How Brecht Read Shakespeare', in Jonathan Dollimore and Alan Sinfield, eds., *Political Shakespeare* (Manchester: Manchester University Press, 1994), 227.
10 Barbara Hodgdon, 'He Do Cressida in Different Voices', in Kate Chedgzoy, ed., *Shakespeare, Feminism and Gender* (Basingstoke: Palgrave Macmillan, 2001), 186.
11 René Girard, *A Theatre of Envy* (New York: Oxford University Press, 1991), 131.
12 Laurie Maguire, *Helen of Troy* (Chichester: Wiley-Blackwell, 2009), 94.
13 Ibid.

CHAPTER 10

"Tis but thy name that is my enemy"

Freedom and constraint in *Romeo and Juliet*

Appropriated by Shakespeare from earlier texts, the story of Romeo and Juliet has subsequently been told and retold in myriad formats from musical to film and replicated in any number of different social, political and cultural contexts. The effect of this diversity has been, paradoxically, to narrow the focus onto the lovers themselves. As they confront whatever ethnic, religious or political divide they are shown to be trying to overcome, the complexity of the play's representations of love and sex can be obscured. Over the centuries the play has become, as Joseph Porter points out, "far more canonical a story of heterosexual love than it was when it came to Shakespeare's hand, when gender, sexuality and eroticism would have assumed more fluid and contested forms."[1] Julia Kristeva's somewhat a-historical view, that "Young people throughout the entire world, whatever their race, religion or social status, identify with the adolescents of Verona," has been a more prevalent one.[2] This takes material form in the locus of Juliet's supposed house in Verona which, complete with its inevitable balcony, has been appropriated as a site on which to inscribe the graffiti of lovers from all over the world.

While Romeo and Juliet's story of romantic love has thrived because of its constant repetition over the centuries, many writers have also located it within the changing ideologies of family and state, of power and patriarchy, looking at how these contexts impact upon the construction and enactment of desire.[3] The moments of greatest relational tension occur as a result of the two lovers failing to act according to prescribed codes of social behaviour, even while the relationship itself remains a secret. Romeo fails to act as his friends believe he should and Juliet likewise disappoints her family. As well as choosing a sexual partner proscribed by their social milieu, each can be seen to be pushing at the limits of how young men and women are expected to enact their gendered roles. In doing so, they lay bare the rules of patriarchal society and, "as individuals who try to advance beyond their ideology but cannot undo its constitutive influence, there is no feasible way to live."[4] How these contexts, societal and familial, influence the course of the relationship will form the core of this chapter.

Violence and patriarchy

The feud between the two Veronese families – Montague and Capulet – provides the critical background to the play and within the constricted ambience of the city's urban space, all the characters, from the prince through members of the warring families and their friends, down to their serving men, enact their relationships according to its exigencies. The Prologue forewarns the audience that this unspecified 'ancient grudge' will end only when the two "star-crossed lovers" have given their lives for it. The play duly ends with the feuding parents apparently extending the hand of friendship and according the lovers proximity and memorialisation in death. Since Romeo and Juliet enact an overtly predetermined plot, their language is correspondingly suffused with references to death and to the grave. The audience is never allowed to escape the interweaving of the language of love and death which emerges at all stages of the relationship once the lovers have learnt of each other's identity. These linguistic couplings are echoed in ritual practice where funeral observances are overtaken by marriage preparations, which are, in turn, transformed into funerals

The feud, much as Shakespeare depicts the siege of Troy in *Troilus and Cressida*, has taken on a life of its own, which the participants and even the prince and his officers seem unable or unwilling to control. We are introduced to this dynamic in the opening scene via a brawl that erupts between the serving men of each house, assuming the form of street theatre and allowing for comedy, sexual banter and misogyny. Their repartee also alludes to the way that policing sexual contact across the divide is a crucial, if unstated, aspect of the feud in which violence and sexuality are inextricably linked:

> Samson "*I will push Montague's men from the wall and thrust his maids to the wall..I will be civil with the maids, I will cut off their heads ... or their maidenheads.*"

The rapid escalation through appearances as if on cue of the younger kinsmen, Benvolio and Tybalt, followed by old Capulet and Montague and finally Prince Escalus provides a vivid introduction to the symmetrical and predictable nature of this feud and the participation in it of so many members of the community as Benvolio describes:

> "*While we were exchanging thrusts and blows*
>
> *Came more and more, and fought on part and part,*
>
> *Till the prince came, who parted either part.*" (I.i.109.111)

The prince, however, only has the temporary solution of 'banging heads,' which is no solution at all but allows things to continue as before. The feud's immersion in codes of male behaviour is illustrated by the determined but ineffectual attempts of both wives to restrain their husbands:

> Capulet "*What noise is this? Give me my long sword, ho!*"
>
> Capulet's Wife "*A crutch, a crutch – why call you for a sword?*"
>
> Capulet "*My sword I say. Old Montague is come*
>
> *And flourishes his blade in spite of me.*"
>
> Montague "*Thou villain Capulet! (To his wife) Hold me not, let me go*"
>
> Montague's wife "*Thou shall not stir one foot to seek a foe.*" (I.i.71–76)

Clearly a feud that continues despite the head of state issuing such threats as "*If ever you disturb our streets again/Your lives shall pay the forfeit of the peace*" operates at more complex levels. Despite his threats to all, Escalus has one language for the general citizenry – "*Rebellious subjects, enemies to peace. . . . You men, you beasts*" – and another for the families themselves. "*You Capulet, shall go along with me:/And Montague, come you this afternoon/ To know our further pleasure in this case.*" For the scions of these powerful and wealthy families, negotiations are best held in private where Escalus can be more conciliatory. Terminating the feud means directly challenging the power of the Montague and Capulet families. Escalus acknowledges his half-heartedness when, at the end of the play, he blames himself for *"winking at your discords."*

Uncontrolled street violence can signify social systems in states of change, instability or dysfunction. The Montague and Capulet families are 'alike in dignity' and the feud is ancient. Disorder spreading outwards from conflict at the heart of competing families would not have been unusual in either Elizabethan England or Renaissance Italy and the state, personified by Prince Escalus, would have been determined to keep it under control without sacrificing his own advantageous links with either of the families. After all, one nephew, Paris, is suing for the hand of Juliet and the other, Mercutio, is a close friend of Romeo. We are given no explanation of what this particular feud is actually about, which heightens the impression of its arbitrariness. "The members of the rival houses belong to the same culture and use the same verbal and behavioural language. When the Montagues intrude on the Capulet festivities, only their faces have to be covered: nothing else in their bearing or manners marks them as outsiders."[5] Susan Snyder argues that the feud "most closely represents the workings of ideology; its origins are obscure and it operates by the production of beliefs, assumptions and especially practices which reduce everything to sameness."[6] However, the workings of the feud also represent profound shifts in social organisation, the effects of which are experienced at many levels:

> The move from the family allegiance based on feudalism to those identified with centralisation of the state constitutes the overarching narrative of *Romeo and Juliet*. That is the shifting configurations of patriarchal law and the changing formations of desire which attend it comprise the structure and substance of Shakespeare's text.[7]

In *Romeo and Juliet* these shifts are enacted through Romeo and Juliet's marriage, which can be seen to represent the beginning of the modern family of capitalist development, presented as a more significant site of sexual and emotional satisfaction than its early modern precursor. The lovers, in pursuing their desire in this way, take up new and more challenging positions than simply attempting to escape together from the feud and its violence.

Violence is indeed pervasive and weapons appear at the slightest provocation. According to Coppelia Kahn, the feud is the "deadly *rite de passage* that promotes masculinity at the price of life."[8] Violent conflict tends to lead participants, especially males, into mindless repetitive actions and this is what is enacted in the opening scene as more and more bodies pile into the fight. Fighting language is invariably sexualised: *"My naked weapon is out,"* thus enacting patriarchal norms at many levels. But while we could see the young as having internalised the imperatives of the feud in the process of becoming adults, there are also – as with all ideologies – many sites of resistance. The relationship between Romeo and Juliet is clearly the principal site of resistance, as they reject both the feud and the demeaning sexual language of patriarchy, but it is not the only one. None of the actors need be seen as mindless enactors of hatred or violence. There are times when the young attempt to avoid it, as Benvolio does in Act 1 and Romeo in Act 3, and times when it can be suspended for the sake of other imperatives, such as Capulet's insistence on the rules of hospitality in Act 1, scene 4. Capulet even compares his own kinsman, Tybalt, unfavourably to Romeo, the son of his enemy. The positions taken up in relation to violence and revenge are much more complex and multi-faceted than at first appears. The only person who seems to take the feud utterly seriously is Tybalt and he is presented as an isolated, humourless and presumptuous figure – a *saucy boy* according to his uncle – apparently lacking the peer group that surrounds Romeo. This would have allowed him other means of enacting a young male identity such as jokes, puns and homo-erotic performances. Certainly Tybalt's excessive sensitivity to insult and his enthusiasm for fighting are what Shakespeare highlights as finally tipping the feud into murder.

Until then, the feud itself seems well regulated if intractable. Everyone is inured to it and at some level it can seem harmless or even comic. At the outset of the play, while blood has been shed, we do not know for sure that anyone has died from it. It is a system in some kind of equilibrium, partly because, since they could always rely on the prince to intervene at points of excessive violence, neither Capulet nor Montague has needed to take any responsibility for ending it. The death of Mercutio at the hands of Tybalt, killed by Romeo shortly afterwards, changes everything and destroys this equilibrium. Mercutio treats it as a joke almost until the moment before his death when he erupts with rage – *"A plague o' both houses"* – as if he has only just realised that this is no mere play. As the prince's own kinsman, Mercutio's death does not fit with the 'rules of the game' and, subsequently, the Capulets are denied what they consider to be their rightful redress; the death of Romeo in exchange for that of Tybalt. This change in social context has repercussions for relationships throughout the entire system and most of all within the Capulet family. It culminates in the shocking violence and misogyny of Capulet's assault on his daughter Juliet.

The families

Shakespeare provides a richer and more detailed account of family relationships among the Capulets than the Montagues, reflecting perhaps the different ways in which each family is involved in their children's lives. The first introduction to Romeo's family is Montague's rather endearing expression of bewilderment about the mental state of his son. Romeo is displaying what to a modern audience appears quintessentially adolescent behaviour:

> *"Away from light steals home my heavy son,*
>
> *And private in his chamber pens himself,*
>
> *Shuts his windows, locks fair daylight out.*
>
> *And makes himself an artificial night...*
>
> *... But he his own affection's counsellor*
>
> *Is to himself – I will not say how true –*
>
> *But to himself so secret and so close."* (I.i.133–146)

Once Benvolio has offered to *"know his grievance,"* and invites Montague – *"So please you step aside"* – the father, in what could be a lesson for many anxious and overly intrusive parents of today's adolescents, complies: *"I would thou wert so happy by thy stay./ To hear true shrift. Come madam, lets away."*

We never actually see Romeo and his parents together, although we learn that he and his friends dine at their house and that, even in his extreme distress at the reported death of Juliet, Romeo still finds time to write to them. As the scene between Montague and Benvolio suggests, Romeo is more intimate with his peer group than with his parents, although Benvolio, as an extended family member, provides a link to them. Before his banishment, Romeo, unlike Juliet, has a group of friends to confide in and to help him reflect on alternative courses of action. Given this fact, it is even more striking that Shakespeare depicts Juliet as the more mature, thoughtful and decisive of the pair.

Unusually for Shakespeare's plays, we are given a vivid account of Juliet's upbringing and her intimate relationship, not just with the nurse (her wet nurse), but also with the nurse's late husband. Juliet's 'special qualities' are encoded in the narrative that the nurse repeats to Lady Capulet and her daughter, to the obvious irritation of both:

> "*For even the day before she broke her brow,*
>
> *And then my husband – God be with his soul,*
>
> *A was a merry man – took up the child.*
>
> *Yea, quoth he, "dost thou fall upon thy face?*
>
> *Thou wilt fall backward when thou hast more wit,*
>
> *Wilt thou not, Jule?" And by my holidam,*
>
> *The pretty wretch left crying and said 'Ay'*" (I.iii.40–46)

This anecdote serves several functions; it prefigures Juliet's courage and resilience, it emphasises the greater intimacy she has with the nurse's family than with her own and it illustrates the sexualised ambience Juliet has grown up in. The nurse and her husband remind her from an early age that sex and procreation are to be her destiny in life.

Before we meet Juliet, she is already the subject of marriage negotiations. When Paris, kinsman to the prince, approaches old Capulet for the hand of his daughter, Capulet is at first cautious, still preoccupied with the prince's earlier pronouncement and concerned about maintaining parity of favour between him and Montague. He cites Juliet's young age and the need for her to give consent, implying that his decision will be conditional on hers:

> "*My will to her consent is but a part;*
>
> *And she agreed, within her scope of choice*
>
> *Lies my consent and fair according voice.*" (I.ii.17–19)

Lady Capulet also uses the language of consent when she asks her daughter *"What say you, can you love the gentleman?"*

In these scenes, the Capulet family, as representatives of the feudal social order, can be seen to be negotiating a complex pathway between paying lip service to autonomy and individuality on the one hand and insisting on obedience to family rules on the other. When young women voluntarily agree to their parents' marriage choice, these family rules are not put to the test. Initially, the Capulet parents take a relaxed stance; there is plenty of time and no reason to think that Juliet will oppose their choice. As far as Capulet is concerned, the situation between him and Montague is contained by the authority of the prince and still in balance: *"But Montague is bound as well as I/ In penalty alike."* His relationship to the prince does not especially trouble him and he has therefore no particular imperative to please Paris, his kinsman.

Families and other relationships can continue, however uncomfortably, in some kind of equilibrium without the need to change until episodes occur, either within the development of the family itself (Juliet reaching marriageable age) or in the wider system. The challenges then posed can make overt and call into question the hidden assumptions that have previously organised them. The deaths of Mercutio and Tybalt mark such a turning point. Initially the families are slow to understand the implications of this shift in context from their finely balanced feud to the murder of the prince's own relative:

> Capulet's wife "*I beg for justice, which thou, Prince must give:*
>
> *Romeo slew Tybalt; Romeo must not live*"
>
> Prince "*Romeo slew him, he slew Mercutio.*
>
> *Who now the price of his dear blood doth owe?*" (3.1.180–183)

Montague is quick to seize advantage: *"Not Romeo, Prince, he was Mercutio's friend."* At the end of this scene, the prince, in banishing Romeo, makes it clear the game has changed:

> "*I have an interest in your hearts proceeding:*
>
> *My blood for your rude brawls doth lie a bleeding.*"

He cuts off further protests from the Capulets:

> "*I will be deaf to pleading and excuses;*
>
> *Nor tears nor prayers shall purchase out abuses.*"

Capulet suddenly feels at a disadvantage vis-a-vis the Montagues and Lady Capulet, for her part, feels deprived of justice. This leads Capulet urgently to seek to seal an alliance between his family and the prince's and Lady Capulet to swear that she will avenge Tybalt by having Romeo killed herself. At the age of only twenty-eight and married to 'old Capulet' with his imminent need of crutches, her feelings for Tybalt might plausibly be stronger than those of kinship, as Franco Zeffirelli's film suggests.[9] Tybalt's waywardness has already been highlighted in Act 1, scene 4, and Capulet, smarting under its catastrophic consequences, is ready to displace his rage elsewhere. The change in the context of the feud is thus echoed in Capulet family dynamics where the parents' sense of loss, disadvantage and disappointment erupt when their daughter refuses to fit in with their plans.

The significance of this turning point in the feud is reinforced by the form of the play in its shift from comedy to tragedy. This shift, Snyder argues, introduces a different time frame; a tragic one in which "a sense that time is limited and precious grows with our perception of an inevitable outcome."[10] This is perfectly illustrated by the contrast between Capulet's first and second encounters with Paris. After the murders of Mercutio and Tybalt, Capulet is desperate to assure Paris that he can deliver Juliet as a bride whether she likes it or not:

> "*Sir Paris, I will make a desperate tender*
>
> *Of my child's love. I think she will be ruled*
>
> *In all respects by me. Nay more, I doubt it not"*
>
> *...A Thursday let it be-a Thursday, tell her*
>
> *She shall be married to this noble earl*
>
> *Will you be ready? Do you like this haste?"* (3.iv.12–22)

The collapsed time frame also has Lady Capulet, at her husband's insistence, coming to Juliet at dawn apparently just after Romeo has left her bed as he commences his banishment. The lovers are not the only ones to elide day and night *"Who is't that calls? It is my lady mother/. Is she not down so late or up so early?"*

In the first scene between Juliet and her mother, Lady Capulet is tentative with her daughter, needing the presence of the nurse to support her when she broaches the subject of marriage and raising the possibility of Juliet having a choice. The second time she is in a highly aroused state after the death of Tybalt and full of rage at being deprived of revenge. She has also been charged in no uncertain terms by her husband to ensure that Juliet will accede to the marriage with Paris. Mothers forced into unhappy marriages themselves at a young age are no less likely to expect their daughters to submit to a similar fate as they are to wish to protect them from it, especially if the relationship has never been close. Juliet appears to be highly adept at confusing and neutralising her mother and does so with word games, which play upon desire and death:

> *"Indeed I never shall be satisfied*
>
> *With Romeo till I behold him – dead –*
>
> *Is my poor heart so for a kinsman vexed."* (3.v.93–95)

What follows after Capulet enters is a vivid portrayal of a family drama in which all members for secret, or at least unstated reasons, are under extreme emotional duress. In an echo of the external violence, they convey the impression of fighting for their lives. Lady Capulet might be doubly disempowered by Juliet's ability to confound and bemuse her with verbal games and by her refusal to agree to the marriage, probably having had no such opportunity herself at fourteen to refuse a husband many years older than her. After all she is presenting Juliet with *"a gallant, young and noble gentleman."* She also knows her failure will enrage her husband. When Capulet enters, he deals peremptorily with his daughter's attempts at evasion: *"How, how, how, how, chopped-logic?"* and sweeps aside Juliet's objections by threatening to impose his will by force:

> *"But fettle your fine joints 'gainst Thursday next*
>
> *To go with Paris to Saint Peter's Church*
>
> *Or I will drag thee on a hurdle thither."* (3.v.152–154)

At this point the whole tone and timbre of the speech changes, the metre becomes disjointed and Capulet erupts into a violent invective that seems quite detached from the rest of the speech:

> *"Out, you green-sickness carrion! Out, you baggage,*
>
> *You tallow face!"*

What provokes this sudden volley of abuse could be, depending on the production, a defiant or a pleading gesture from Juliet or a silent intervention by Lady Capulet or the nurse. However, if the actor pauses before *"Out,"* it could be performed as the intrusion of an inner voice – an invisible interlocutor in Bakhtin's sense – representing the ideology of patriarchal power.[11] A father who has never before been disobeyed and whose self-image is that of a tolerant, reasonable and benign man, might be horrified at the thought that he *has* to threaten his daughter with force when she should help maintain this self-image by obeying him. The eruption could thus signify something like "You have forced me to display a side of me that I prefer not to recognise and which affronts my dignity. I cannot forgive you for that." That his speech has moved into a totally different register is witnessed by Lady Capulet's intervention: *"Fie, fie, what, are you mad?"* Undeterred, or perhaps further enraged, Capulet continues to abuse his daughter and threaten her with physical violence: *"my fingers itch"* and finally banishment:

> "*Graze where you will, you shall not house with me...*
>
> *An you be mine, I'll give you to my friend;*
>
> *An you be not, hang, beg, starve, die in the streets!*" (3.v.188–192)

This scene lays bare the workings of power in the patriarchal family as its inherent violence becomes visible in the face of disobedience or resistance. Juliet's whole identity as daughter is suddenly contingent on accession to her father's will. Capulet implausibly presents his entire purpose as a father as having been to secure a good marriage for his daughter:

> "*Day, night, hour, tide, time, work, play,*
>
> *Alone, in company, still my care hath been*
>
> *To have her matched.*" (3.v.176–178)

It is of course not marrying Juliet off in itself that preoccupies him but allying his family as quickly as possible with the prince's. Each woman who intervenes is abruptly silenced: *"Speak not, reply not," "Peace you mumbling fool."* For all that she tries to restrain her husband from his excesses, Lady Capulet too, in the face of *"O sweet my mother, cast me not away,"* refuses to engage further with her daughter:

> "*Talk not to me for I'll not speak a word.*
>
> *Do as thou wilt, for I have done with thee.*"

It is as if the violence, alienation and distancing of the feud have now found their way into the interior of one of its participant families.

The dilemmas raised by exposing the brutal power dynamics underlying intimate family relationships are further illustrated in Act 4 scene 2.

Here, we see Capulet determinedly continuing with the wedding preparations while continuing to complain about and abuse his daughter: "*A peevish, self-willed harlotry it is.*" However, when Juliet returns from Friar Lawrence and announces her change of heart, his relief and joy are palpable: "*My heart is wondrous light.*" He has been much more dependent on her acquiescence than he could admit. She has restored to her father the experience of his power being once more in equilibrium with his self esteem and his emotions. When Juliet reassures her father that: "*Henceforward I am ever ruled by you,*" the contradiction this creates for a woman supposedly about to acquire another male overlord is overlooked by all. Now that his family authority is restored and he no longer fears humiliation in front of Paris and the prince, Capulet can confidently return to the wider political considerations that underlay the marriage in the first place: "*Let me see the County . . . fetch him hither.*"

In the previous family scene, Shakespeare further dramatises Juliet's despair and isolation by having the nurse too withdraw her support, when she advises Juliet to forget Romeo and marry Paris:

> "*Oh he's a lovely gentleman!*
>
> *Romeo's a dish clout to him.*"

Juliet is quick, in this over-heated atmosphere of relationship rupture, to disavow the nurse in turn:

> "*Ancient damnation! O most wicked fiend! . . .*
>
> *Go counsellor;*
>
> *Thou and my bosom henceforth shall be twain.*" (3.v.235–240)

The bond between Juliet and the nurse has an ambivalent side, contextualised as it is by an uneasily competitive relationship between Juliet's 'two mothers.' Juliet is the same age as the nurse's deceased daughter, Susan, and her appropriation of Juliet's affections thus leaves both her and Lady Capulet in a similar position; being separated from a daughter. The relationship between Juliet and the nurse has all the ambiguity of child and mother-substitute on the one hand and mistress and servant on the other, incongruities that are accentuated when Juliet reaches marriageable age. The imperative to maintain the relationship with all its advantages, both emotional and material would be enough to propel the nurse into advocating on behalf of Paris who is prestigious and close at hand rather than

Romeo who is now far away in Mantua: "*Your first is dead, or 'twere as good he were,/As living here and you no use of him.*" Conveniently obliterating the fact that Juliet would be committing bigamy by marrying Paris, the nurse is doing no more than Capulet in thinking of marriage from a purely strategic point of view.

The nurse is generally played as a comic role but, as the shift from comedy to tragedy intensifies, so she reveals a darker side. This has already manifested itself when she brings the news of Tybalt's death and prolongs Juliet's agony by leading her to believe that it is Romeo who is dead. Later, in her need to accommodate to patriarchal power by backing Paris over Romeo, she fails to recognise Juliet's sense of abandonment. Interestingly, she takes this seemingly callous stance just after Lady Capulet has rejected her daughter so emphatically, as if perhaps she no longer needs to compete with her. In a world in which family life is quite overtly an extension of politics, the nurse's instrumentalism and realism is understandable but it also reveals the fragility of Juliet's emotional bonds and the loneliness that follows her act of dissidence and transgression in falling in love with Romeo.

The teenage lovers

I have deliberately, if somewhat unromantically, left my exploration of the relationship between the famous "star-crossed lovers" for the last sections of this chapter. Romeo and Juliet's relationship is touching and appealing to audiences, partly because of their attempt to transcend those rigid strictures and structures of their families and their society, which have been explored above. For this reason, while their relationship dilemmas are clearly historically and contextually located, they have been, and will continue to be, endlessly reinvented and re-appropriated for contemporary audiences. The vision Romeo and Juliet enact of facing death for the sake of an ideal of boundless, unconfined love is a romantic trope that is at once located in and transcends its historical context. "In the estranged idiom of the lovers can be read the tragedy's estrangement from its era, the imprint of its commerce with futurity."[12]

Dympna Callaghan, exploring the ways that desire is reconfigured under a transfer of patriarchal law, is careful to point out that, despite the fact that the mode of desire disapproved of in the old order becomes valorised in the new one, it does not mean that the play "circulates around only one discourse of desire. Rather, multiple and contradictory discourses of desire are negotiated in the isolation and idealisation of romantic heterosexual love."[13] Shakespeare has also created in Mercutio a young man who expresses his desire for Romeo intensely and passionately, if obliquely.

While Romeo and Juliet's exquisite language of love and desire in their secret trysts is what touches audiences, they have only four scenes together, two of them very brief. Most of the action takes place in wider contexts and our first encounter with them is in the dialogue of others, mainly that of their parents. This emphasises their youth, their identities as son and daughter and their dependency on family decisions and family bonds, inevitably requiring immersion in their families' conflict. Each has, however, found in Friar Lawrence a surrogate father who provides a close confiding relationship detached from the family feud and this is an important context for alternative ways of thinking.

Romeo is first introduced to us as a troubled and suffering human being; Juliet, by contrast, only as marriageable commodity, invited by her mother to be the decorative cover that should beautify the "*precious book of love*" that is Paris' life. Romeo's unsuccessful pursuit of Rosaline and Juliet's invitation by her mother to consider marrying Paris form an important background to their first encounter. While, usually played as a '*coup de foudre*,' Romeo and Juliet's passionate response to each other is perfectly set up by the previous scenes. Romeo is advised by Benvolio to cast his eyes around the Capulet ballroom to weigh: "*Your lady's love against some other maid/That I will show you shining at this feast.*" Juliet, approached by her mother to consider marriage, despite her elegantly phrased and diplomatic reply – "*It is an honour that I dream not of*" – agrees to keep her eyes open for Paris at the feast and to "*look to like, if looking liking move.*" Lady Capulet, by her intervention, has inadvertently given her daughter permission to be on the lookout for eye-catching men.

Both Romeo and Juliet are thus, for different reasons, primed to be on the alert for sexually attractive partners. The play is one of Shakespeare's most sexually explicit and its raunchy language creates a highly charged background for their encounter. Romeo is encouraged by his friends and Juliet by the nurse, who is easily Mercutio's equal in sexual badinage, bawdiness and innuendo. This serves to emphasise the very different language of their actual encounter and it enables Shakespeare to show us two young people who will develop their own quite independent style of relating. Their dialogue, with its innocent and unworldly metaphors of Saints and Pilgrims, has also however also been prefigured by Romeo's deliberations on Rosaline:

> "*She will not stay the siege of loving terms*
>
> *Nor bide th'encounter of assailing eyes,*
>
> *Nor ope her lap to saint-seducing gold*." (I.i.208–210)

Assailing with eyes and seducing saints is the very stuff of this encounter. The fact that Romeo is masked and that each is unaware of the other's name, contributes to the creation of a temporary unregulated space within which social codes can be suspended, mutual gaze can be met and kisses exchanged. Their dialogue also highlights their different styles and different language use. The artifice of the Petrarchian sonnet form that Romeo employs to declare his love for Rosaline continues to be his mode of expression when he first encounters Juliet. Both have often been described as using constrained formal speech before their encounter and freer and more spontaneous speech afterwards. "Words are the chains that bind the lovers to the sexual norms and social imperatives of Verona; their struggle for fulfilment expresses itself as a struggle to escape the way Verona has taught them to speak."[14] What is more striking, however, is that the extent to which Shakespeare accords Juliet the privilege of breaking free from convention and modelling for Romeo a new way to speak. Before meeting her, and in the early stages of their encounter, Romeo's speech is formal and full of ossified romantic clichés. Juliet bursts through these conventions by breaking up Romeo's sonnet form and teasing his formality: "*You kiss by the book.*"

In their second scene, with Romeo still in the position of supplicant, Juliet unquestionably takes charge of the dialogue; she initiates the metaphors that suffuse their speech; she suggests the practical steps for their marriage; she leaves and returns while Romeo waits for her. Shocked that Romeo has risked his life to climb into the Capulet orchard, for twenty lines she cuts short all of his romantic excesses with pragmatic concerns: "*How camest thou hither?,*" "*If they do see thee, they will murder thee.*" Her speech unfolds in a way that is fresh, spontaneous and daring. Shakespeare created in Juliet a young woman of courage and passion as well as fierce intelligence. The more tentative Romeo struggles at times to keep up with her.

It is initially through Juliet's speech that the lovers create the impression of embodying a love that reaches beyond their own place and time.

Juliet's speech *"Thou knowst the mask of light is on my face"* is an extraordinary mixture of reflexive awareness of what convention demands, grasp of the way that passionate women may be viewed by their suitors: *"If thou thinkest I am too quickly won,"* and an impatient desire to cut through all the requisite speech and behaviour and go straight to the heart of the matter: *"Dost thou love me?"* She even answers this question herself: *"I know thou wilt say ay"* and then goes on to propose marriage and suggest how it might be implemented. Juliet is, of course, on her own territory; acting confidently and probably used to getting her own way, having in the nurse a mother-figure whom she can bend to her will. Leading a more secluded life, Juliet has only indirectly been involved in the feud that is inevitably enacted in public space. She is therefore perhaps better able to question its premises and the limitations these place on relationships: *"'Tis but thy name that is my enemy."*

Romeo, emerging from the shadows of the Capulet orchard and from his sterile and unreciprocated pursuit of Rosaline, seems overwhelmed to discover that his love can be reciprocated so immediately and passionately. His life so far has embodied a favourite Shakespearean theme – the dilemmas for young men as they negotiate the apparent transition from the intensity and intimacy of same sex bonds to the socially sanctioned world of heterosexual love and marriage.[15] Romeo's non-existent love affair with Rosaline has an air of such unreality about it (he does not seem troubled that *she* is a Capulet) that its purpose may be to give him an excuse for both titillating and distancing himself from his demanding male friends, especially the attention-hungry and intense Mercutio. He indeed quite literally escapes them to seek out Juliet. Benvolio seems concerned with his friend's welfare, Mercutio to be threatened by Romeo's defection, attempting to provide a misogynous counter narrative to his friend's changing priorities, hoping to attract him back into the old pattern of relationships and reassured when Romeo is coaxed back into out-punning him: *"Why is this not better now than groaning for love? Now art thou sociable, now art thou Romeo. . . ."* It is unclear whether it is Romeo or Mercutio himself who is *"groaning for love."* We could see a symmetry in Romeo's unrequited love for Rosaline and Mercutio's for Romeo. Rosaline offers the opportunity for Mercutio to express sexual excitement vicariously: *"I conjure thee by Rosaline's bright eyes. . . . By her fine foot, straight leg and quivering thigh. . . ."*

Romeo, faced with these potentially painful relationship dilemmas, opts for concealment. While he shared his supposed feelings about Rosaline with his friends, he says nothing whatsoever about Juliet. The performance of hopelessly unrequited love for Rosaline could be accommodated within a discourse of male friendship since it provides opportunities for bawdy quibbles, male solidarity and inventive strategies. Romeo's requited passion for Juliet makes for an uneasy fit in this world where the young men have not yet developed a language for the experience of mutual love between men and women: *"Now Romeo is belov'd and loves again."*

Juliet, on the other hand, is sequestered in a secluded and largely female world where her only opportunity for an unaccompanied excursion is to head to Friar Lawrence's cell for confession. That this is a somewhat ambiguous and potentially subversive space is expressed by her father:

> Capulet "*What is my daughter gone to Friar Lawrence?*"
>
> *(Enter Juliet)*
>
> Nurse "*See where she comes from shrift with merry look.*"
>
> Capulet "*How now, my headstrong, where have you been gadding?*"

It seems, that within her sequestered world, she has absorbed, as well as the nurse's sexually charged talk, many stories about romantic love. One of the few hackneyed phrases employed by Juliet suggests that she, who has presumably never left Verona, has been waiting for an opportunity to express it:

> *"And all my fortunes at thy feet I'll lay,*
>
> *And follow thee, my lord, throughout the world."*

In the first two scenes between Romeo and Juliet, there are many examples of teasing and playfulness, including metaphors of mastery and control: *"O for a falc'ners voice/ To lure this tassel gentle back again."* However, the kind of games-playing that results either from mutual mistrust, power imbalance or excessive worry about social codes is absent. The play does not deal with power struggles between the couple but between them and the outside world. Some of the same language, such as contrasting measurable and ineffable love and switching between pragmatism and idealism, is employed by those older, worldly wise and cynical lovers, Antony and Cleopatra, but the contrast is obvious. Whereas Antony and Cleopatra's relationship is embedded in complementarity, i.e. coloniser/ colonised, Romeo and Juliet's relationship emerges out of symmetry. They are immersed in a conflict between two families which are "*alike in dignity.*" Romeo is a young man whom even Juliet's father acknowledges is a "*virtuous and well governed youth.*" The lovers thus have the frisson and excitement that comes with forbidden love without too many other complications. The audience too has the pleasure of revelling in their love without having to witness any falling off from what Cleopatra recalls of her and Antony's beginnings: "*Eternity was in our lips and eyes,/Bliss in our brows. . . .*"[16]

There are many differences between Romeo and Juliet's modes of speech, some of which challenge gender stereotypes, reflecting as they do his impulsivity and her more pragmatic bent. Conventionally, it is the male lover who expresses impatience for sexual consummation; here it is given to Juliet:

> "*Come civil night*
>
> *Thou sober-suited matron all in black,*
>
> *And learn me how to lose a winning match,*
>
> *Play'd for a pair of stainless maidenhoods.*
>
> *Hood my un-mann'd blood, bating in my cheeks. . . .*
>
> *. . O I have bought the mansion of a love*
>
> *But not possessed it; and though I am sold*
>
> *Not yet enjoyed.*" (3.ii.10–17)

Although Shakespeare clearly intended her to be bold, passionate and keen to experience sex, this speech also heightens an appreciation of Juliet's innocence, not least because of the contrast between her ideas about sex and the crude language used by the nurse:

> "*Now comes the wanton blood up in your cheeks*
>
> *. . . I am the drudge and toil in your delight*
>
> *But you shall bear the burden soon at night.*" (2.iv.69–75)

In Romeo, Shakespeare also presents a different kind of masculinity from the swaggering macho of the feud or the misogyny of Mercutio. He speaks respectfully to Tybalt and, at the end of the play, expresses his empathy for Paris whom he has just killed. He is unafraid to express strong emotions, he is tentative and diffident in his initial approaches to Juliet and he does his best to avoid fighting. However, this is a complicated stance for a young man. Although he blames himself for Mercutio's fatal injury, Romeo soon lapses into drawing upon a familiar trope of men's emasculation by women.

> "*My very friend hath got this mortal hurt*
>
> *In my behalf... O sweet Juliet*
>
> *Thy beauty hath made me effeminate,*
>
> *And in my temper softened valour's steel.*" (3.i.110–115)

At a time of such stress and sorrow he is easily called back into gendered discourses that define how men should behave. The contradictions Romeo faces in trying to adopt a different way of living re-emerge when he takes refuge in Friar Lawrence's cell. His state of emotional collapse on learning of his banishment has the priest upbraiding him by evoking the usual gendered norms "*Art thou a man? . . ./ . . . thy tears are womanish . . . /unseemly woman in a seeming man.*"

Relationship priorities

Romeo and Juliet may relish the experience of overcoming social restrictions and, in Kieran Ryan's somewhat overblown terms, of "laying siege to the legitimacy of a world that deprives men and women of boundless love."[17] As we have seen, however, the greatest challenge to their brief relationship arises in the aftermath of the deaths of Tybalt and Mercutio. Friar Lawrence has agreed to marry the pair in the hope that their alliance will transform relationships between their warring families:

> "*For this alliance may so happy prove,*
>
> *To turn your households rancour to pure love.*"

This optimistic ideal remains with Romeo as he is confronted by Tybalt. He can barely contain himself from sharing his news:

> "*I do protest I never injured thee,*
>
> *But love thee better than thou canst devise*
>
> *Til thou shalt know the reason of my love*

And so good Capulet, which name I tender

As dearly as mine own, be satisfied." (3.i.67–71)

Keen to inaugurate a new inter-familial accord, he takes a position above the fray by allying himself with Escalus' strictures – "*Tybalt, Mercutio, the Prince expressly hath/ Forbid this bandying in Verona's streets.*" However, he totally misunderstands the context. In his eagerness and idealism, Romeo fails to recognise the extent to which his friend Mercutio is immersed in a different context; preparing to fight, chastising him for his moderation – "*O calm, dishonourable, vile submission!*" – goading Tybalt and diverting him from attacking Romeo. In this scene Romeo's changing priorities are exposed, to the utter bemusement of his friend for whom they ultimately prove fatal: "*Why the devil came you between us? I was hurt under your arm.*" The shocking experience of his friend's death and guilt about his part in it leave Romeo particularly vulnerable when Tybalt returns. At this point, Shakespeare writes Romeo back into the constrained and clichéd language of the feud and of revenge:

"*Away to heaven, respective lenity*

And fire-eyed fury be my conduct now."

The illusion that Romeo could, through his own agency, bring about a change in the toxic Montague/Capulet relationship dies along with Mercutio and Tybalt. After killing his adversary, Romeo is left rooted to the ground, bemoaning his impotence: "*O, I am fortune's fool!*" In the whole of the scene in Friar Lawrence's cell, while Romeo expresses various extremes of despair, he never once refers to Mercutio's death. It is as if the world of his friends is erased both from the play (Benvolio does not re-appear and nor is he referred to again) and seemingly from Romeo's mind, which is now full of the unbearable loss of Juliet.

Juliet for her part is also drawn back into the language of the feud with its assigned forms of subjectivity as she absorbs the news that her lover has killed her cousin. Her speech now takes the form of an outraged Capulet, suddenly constrained into "hackneyed images and formally balanced end-stopped lines."[18]

"*Oh serpent heart hid with a flow'ing face*

Did ever dragon keep so fair a cave?

> *Beautiful tyrant, fiend angelical!*
>
> *Dove-feathered raven, wolfish-ravening lamb!*" (3.ii.73–76)

What is remarkable, however, is that, unlike Romeo who has to be coaxed out of despair by the friar and the nurse, Juliet quickly talks herself out of her stance as a feuding Capulet. Here, she is unwittingly aided by the position taken by the nurse who, when she echoes the opprobrium of Romeo, enables Juliet to rebound into another position

> Nurse "*Shame come to Romeo.*"
>
> Juliet "*Blistered be thy tongue for such a wish! . . . O, what a beast was I to chide at him!*" (3.ii.89–91)

Tybalt's death and Romeo's banishment challenge Juliet to re-assess her relationship priorities in a way she has not previously needed to. Here, the fact that she is actually married to Romeo enables her to name her conflict as being between two different types of social bond rather than as a conflict solely between desire and family duty:

> Nurse "*Will you speak well of him that killed your cousin?*"
>
> Juliet "*Shall I speak ill of him that is my husband?*"

These lines signify the wider shift from primary loyalty to family to primary loyalty to husband, as women's sexual desire is seen as 'properly' located within the confines of marriage.[19] While Romeo expresses his anguish only at being separated from Juliet, she additionally locates her distress in ideological and moral terms. By giving in to the demand that she marry Paris, she would be not only be betraying Romeo but committing bigamy:

> "*O God! O Nurse, how shall this be prevented?*
>
> *My husband is on earth, my faith in heaven*
>
> *How shall that faith return again to earth,*
>
> *Unless that husband send it me from heaven*
>
> *By leaving earth?*" (3.v.204–208)

She will thus drink Friar Lawrence's potion as much for the sake of her moral status as to be reunited with Romeo: "*without fear or doubt/To live an unstained wife to my sweet love.*"

Disconnection and isolation

Many of Shakespeare's later tragic protagonists – Lear, Coriolanus, Hamlet – face the loss of their family ties through banishment or self-imposed exile. The experience of isolation and of being disconnected from others is usually accorded to males. Here, however, both Romeo and Juliet experience the agonies of actual or potential isolation. Both face banishment. Romeo is banished as a direct result of the feud and Juliet indirectly as a result of disobeying her father, whose disavowal of her also stems from the workings of the feud. Romeo, in solitary exile in Mantua, lives in a dream-like state alone with his imaginings and with no companion to sustain him or provide reality checks. Juliet, abandoned by her parents and the nurse, turns to the only person who will understand her plight, Friar Lawrence. Imploring him for help, she, as Romeo does in Act 3, scene 3, threatens suicide. This could be seen as teenage histrionics. Romeo, overwhelmed by remorse and guilt towards his lover whom he can now only imagine despising him, loses his capacity to think and has to be physically restrained from stabbing himself. Juliet, despite her florid language, appears to use it as a rhetorical device to urge Friar Lawrence to find a solution to her dilemma:

> "*Give me some present counsel; or behold*
>
> *'Twixt my extremes and me this bloody knife*
>
> *Shall play the umpire....*" (4.i.61–63)

In the scene that follows when Juliet, as instructed, retires to bed with her vial of distilling liquor, she faces for the first time the loss of all her family ties as well as the home she has known for her entire life. Because of the ensuing drama in the Capulet tomb, it is easy to forget that, had Friar Lawrence's plan succeeded, Juliet would be leaving home and family behind, possibly for ever: "*Farewell, – God knows when we shall meet again.*" The soliloquy that follows thus involves a moment of profound uncertainty and the desire to return to the security of her childhood before she rallies herself to her cause:

> *"I'll call them back again to comfort me.*
>
> *Nurse! – What should she do here?*
>
> *My dismal scene I needs must act alone."* (4.iii.17–19)

This decision is followed by a series of horrific visions – hallucinatory in nature – in which the thought of betraying generations of buried ancestors – let alone the recently murdered and still vengeful Tybalt – torments and terrifies her. She raises the possibility that Friar Lawrence might have actually given her poison so that his wrongdoing in marrying her and Romeo would not come to light. She imagines the foetid and stifling air of the tomb and the terror that would beset her if she wakes before time. She thinks ahead to the madness this might induce: "*shall I not be distraught?*" Marx's famous phrase: "The dead generations weighing like a nightmare on the brains of the living"[20] comes to mind as in her imagined madness, Juliet conjures up this scenario:

> *"And in this rage with some great kinsman's bone,*
>
> *As with a club, dash out my desp'rate brains?"*

However, what propels Juliet to drink the potion is the fantasy of rescuing Romeo from the clutches of the ghostly Tybalt. She thus positions herself, as she has throughout, as the active one who takes charge and thinks things through. Despite the fears and gruesome fantasies that precede her drinking the potion, Juliet wakes up apparently totally in control. She conveys a sense of relief at still being firmly ensconced within her family as she awakes in the tomb, with a calm and realistic sense of herself and her priorities. The fears and suspicions have melted away and her expectation and trust that the world will fall into place reasserts itself:

> *"I do remember well where I should be*
>
> *And there I am. Where is my Romeo?"*

At this point not only is her lover dead but the "comfortable Friar," having failed to persuade her to enter a nunnery, escapes, leaving her alone and to suicide. This is expressed in almost erotic terms "*O happy dagger, This is thy sheath.*"

With the deaths of Romeo and Juliet representing the ultimate pinnacle of their desire to be together, the play reverts, as it began, to the warring parents. At this point, the prince takes charge, both of investigating the deaths and, more importantly, of controlling the narrative. The Montague and Capulet families are duly reprimanded by Escalus; this time, however, he includes himself in the frame:

"*Capulet, Montague,*

See what a scourge is laid upon your hate

That heaven finds means to kill your joys with love;

And I for winking at your discords, too

Have lost a brace of kinsmen. All are punished." (5.iii.291–295)

His reference to all these losses, however, also signals a consolidation of his power over the errant families, a power that had been undermined by their refusal to give up the feud. Friar Lawrence too is firmly sidelined. Montague and Capulet's response is to make a belated public solemnisation of the marriage contract:

Capulet "*O brother Montague, give me thy hand*

This is my daughter's jointure, for no more

Can I demand." (5.iii.296–298)

Montague's response – "*But I can give thee more/For I will raise a statue in pure gold*" – can either be understood as the families burying their enmity or indeed as the opening up of a renewed form of competition, this time through commercial means.[21] Romeo and Juliet's relationship can, however, be safely celebrated in death in a way that would never been allowed in life.

Conclusion

The struggle for the young lovers as they seek a way to enact their relationship outside the control of their families is given dramatic form by the settings in which their intimate scenes together take place; at a masked ball, in darkness and in the liminal zone between day and night. Indeed, in their one night together, their desire to reinvent the world and to control nature is expressed in the poetic language through which they play with the oppositions of light and darkness, night and day, lark and nightingale. This desire to live 'out of context' is juxtaposed by all the signifiers of the constraints surrounding them. These constraints take the form not only of family and societal rules but also the internalised norms they draw upon and the extent to which, despite their rejection of it, they are at times 'captured' by the ideology of the feud. Juliet is also troubled by fears of divine retribution for bigamy and the weight of generations of Capulets oppressing her with such suffocating force.

Finding a 'feasible way to live' is beyond Romeo and Juliet's capacity. Their attempt begins with their mutual desire to escape the linguistic shackles imposed by their names and the restraints and commitments inscribed in them. They highlight in touching detail those profoundly ambiguous processes that arise in trying to reinvent themselves within a world that exerts such a profound control. The play charts the consequences of trying to advance 'beyond their ideology' as they live life at a cusp of social change.

Many couples trying to develop an intimate relationship in the face of social disapproval face similar dilemmas, inevitably finding that the constraints of their surrounding contexts enter into their own interactions. They therefore need to find creative ways of managing the ambiguous processes that develop between them. This often assumes the form of taking alternating positions at different moments in their interactions. These different positions might be expressed in relation to independence and obedience, pragmatism and impulsiveness, loyalty, love and sacrifice. These are some of the processes we witness in Romeo and Juliet's relationship. They are playfully enacted as they wake up from their one night together and take turns in describing the singing bird as a nightingale or a lark. This enables them to both accept and refuse reality simultaneously. "A way of life which had seemed unquestionable is exposed as a prison-house, whose walls are built of words. For Romeo and Juliet those walls prove in the end too strong, but their struggle to demolish them affords the prospect of a release, by confirming that what Verona enforces as normal is neither pervasive nor impregnable."[22]

Notes

1 Joseph Porter quoted in Dymphna Callaghan, 'The Ideology of Romantic Love: The Case of Romeo and Juliet', Dymphna Callaghan, Lorraine Helms and Jyotsna Singh, eds., *The Weyward Sisters* (Oxford: Wiley-Blackwell, 1994), 61.

2 Ibid.

3 Kiernan Ryan, *Shakespeare* (Basingstoke: Palgrave Macmillan, Third Edition, 2003).

4 Susan Snyder, *Shakespeare: A Wayward Journey* (Newark: University of Delaware Press, 2002), 191.
5 Ibid., 183.
6 Ibid., 185–186.
7 Dymphna Callaghan, 'The Ideology of Romantic Love: The Case of Romeo and Juliet', in Dymphna Callaghan, Lorraine Helms and Jyotsna Singh, eds., *The Weyward Sisters* (Oxford: Wiley-Blackwell, 1994), 72.
8 Coppelia Kahn, 'Coming of Age in Verona', in Carolyn Ruth Swift Lenz, Gayle Greene, and Carol Thomas Neely, eds., *The Woman's Part: Feminist Criticism of Shakespeare* (Urbana: University of Illinois Press, 1980), 171–193.
9 *Romeo and Juliet*, directed by Franco Zeffirelli (Paramount Pictures, 1968).
10 Susan Snyder, 'Romeo and Juliet: Comedy into Tragedy', in Susan Snyder, ed., *Shakespeare: A Wayward Journey* (Newark: University of Delaware Press, 2002), 20.
11 Mikhail Bakhtin, *Problems of Dostoevsky's Poetics* (Minneapolis: University of Minneapolis Press, 1984), 197.
12 Kiernan Ryan, *Shakespeare* (Basingstoke: Palgrave Macmillan, Third Edition, 2003), 83.
13 Dymphna Callaghan 'The Ideology of Romantic Love: The Case of Romeo and Juliet', in Dymphna Callaghan, Lorraine Helms and Jyotsna Singh, eds., *The Weyward Sisters* (Oxford: Wiley-Blackwell, 1994), 72.
14 Kiernan Ryan, *Shakespeare* (Basingstoke: Palgrave Macmillan, Third Edition, 2003), 80.
15 This theme is explored in many of the subsequent comedies such as *Much Ado About Nothing, Two Gentlemen of Verona* and *The Merchant of Venice.*
16 *Antony and Cleopatra,* 1.iii. 35–36.
17 Kiernan Ryan, *Shakespeare* (Basingstoke: Palgrave Macmillan, Third Edition, 2003), 83.
18 Susan Snyder, *Shakespeare: A Wayward Journey* (Newark: University of Delaware Press, 2002), 191.
19 Dymphna Callaghan, 'The Ideology of Romantic Love: The Case of Romeo and Juliet', in Dymphna Callaghan, Lorraine Helms and Jyotsna Singh, eds., *The Weyward Sisters* (Oxford: Wiley-Blackwell, 1994).
20 Karl Marx, *Eighteenth Brumaire of Louis Napoleon* (New York: Die Revolution, 1852).
21 Susan Snyder, *Shakespeare: A Wayward Journey* (Newark: University of Delaware Press, 2002), 193.
22 Kiernan Ryan, *Shakespeare* (Basingstoke: Palgrave Macmillan, Third Edition, 2003), 83.

CHAPTER 11

Endings

Arriving at the end of this book involves reconnecting to the pleasures and passions that led me to embark upon it and to the early joys of immersion in the treasure trove of Shakespearean drama and Shakespeare studies, a field that is as contradictory, multi-facetted and diverse as the tragedies themselves.

Completing the book has also freed me up to revel in the fact that, no matter how many times I read the tragedies, I know that the next time I read any of them, I will spot something that I never noticed before, upon which, most likely, someone else will have written a scholarly publication. This experience can now be restored to its rightful place as a pleasure and an advantage rather than a source of anxiety.

Renée Girard asserted that anyone adding to the vast number of volumes on Shakespeare should first of all issue a profuse apology, but I have been disinclined to follow his advice. First, the intellectual playground that is Shakespeare studies is enticing precisely because of its huge number of inhabitants and, in writing about the tragedies, I am engaging with them as much as with the Bard himself. Second, and more important, I do consider that systemic thinking has something new to contribute.

As I have argued throughout, the value of a systemic approach lies in its ability to link the level of close and intimate human interactions with their particular emotional dilemmas, their patterning, their language and dialogue, to the level of the wider world that shapes them. This inevitably means engaging with complexity and uncertainty.

Thus, one useful contribution from a systemic approach towards the study of tragedy lies in its ability to capture the ambiguous, unstable and paradoxical qualities of relationships. I have found the approach to be a particularly good fit with the multi-levelled interactions we encounter in Shakespeare's plays. A focus on individuals creates the temptation to uncover their inner reality, to fix them in some kind of essence, which does not do justice to the complexity of their interactions. A focus on relationships creates a more dynamic means through which identity can be revealed as fluid, contested and expressed in diverse ways, depending on the contexts, which confer meaning.

My focus in this chapter, which is entitled "Endings," is not on attempting the impossible task of drawing all the different strands together but on offering some reflections on the denouements in the plays themselves. I consider that a framework that emphasises multiplicity can actually heighten the sense of tragedy rather than diminish the intensity of the tragic hero/s emotional plight. Tragedy might reside in protagonists lumbering towards their demise, propelled by an inner 'tragic flaw,' a characteristic that becomes more overt and dominant as the play progresses. But it is perhaps more tragic if we highlight all the ways that Shakespeare shows his protagonists as able to act and think differently in different relational contexts. It is more of a tragedy if they then seem to act *as if* their identities are unitary, progressively stripping away alternative aspects of self or even alternative sources of information. Shakespeare clearly had a preference for exploring multiple ways of viewing the world, rarely going for closure and always holding onto ambiguity and complexity. This only heightens the anomaly of protagonists who are seemingly set on living and dying the narrative of the Aristotelean tragic hero, drawing upon only one rigid identity when all around them are nuances, alternative narratives and invitations to disrupt this (not) inexorable process.

Macbeth, Coriolanus, Othello and Mark Antony are all examples of this tendency to act as if they can only do what they do. As I have argued, this is most likely to be seen in conditions where dialogue has broken down, where other voices are absent, complicit or simply dismissed. There is a telling moment in *Othello* when, having interrogated Emilia about Desdemona's movements, Othello is perturbed and unsettled by her strong counter-narrative supporting Desdemona's innocence. "*That's strange,*" he says. Then he quickly talks himself out of his uncertainty: "*She says enough; yet she's a simple bawd/That cannot say as much.*" (4.ii.11–21) The significance of these lines lies in the levels of context they reveal. Othello initially constructs Emilia as a potentially reliable witness – *she says enough* – but immediately afterwards categorises her as a lower being – a servant and a woman, dismissed and abused as a bawd and whose words can therefore be discounted. It means that the contexts of hierarchy and male privilege prevent her speech act from having any influence. Her robust response might otherwise have led Othello to challenge his certainty about Desdemona, since by questioning Emilia he is actually inviting such a challenge.

Potential sources of feedback in relationships can thus be curtailed by hierarchy, as when Anthony, who is at times inclined to confide in Enobarbus, asserts rank and abruptly forecloses further conversation: "*Thou art a soldier only; speak no more.*" He thus blocks the contribution of a loyal soldier who is able to think. This process is also present in a gentler form in the relationship between Hamlet and Horatio. In systemic therapy, as well as aiming to enhance and expand dialogic possibilities, we are aware of how much power influences who speaks and who is listened to. There are examples – already discussed in Macbeth and Hamlet – where the absence or poverty of dialogue cramps the protagonists' ability to think outside their usual frame. In Shakespeare's tragedies, we are presented with many instances of the 'almost said' – with brief glimpses of the alternative narratives that can emerge from significant dialogue. I have discussed Emilia and Desdemona's potentially transformative conversation at the end of Othello, and Hamlet and Horatio almost discussing Hamlet's fear and vulnerability. Another 'almost dialogue' briefly takes place between Coriolanus and Virgilia about the human cost of war and this creates resonances for the very end of the play when Coriolanus sets about suing for peace between Romans and Volscians. At the denouement, Coriolanus' continuing habit of acting unilaterally and failing to take into account the possible reactions of others reasserts itself and seals his fate. While they have little else in common, I argue in *King Lear* that it is Cordelia's failure to take account of the context she is in that likewise contributes to her doom.

As in the process of drama's tragic denouements, therapists are often faced with families who act as if there is only one possible narrative; our task is to help people expand their sense of possibility when they may be restricting themselves to unitary identities and thus only see one future pathway. Part of the ethics of therapy is to support the expansion of choices, not in the glib sense of 'lifestyle choice' but as a process in which individuals and families can feel freer and more confident to enact relationships that bring them more pleasure, more dignity, or more of a sense of empowerment. The most helpful ways of supporting this process are through identifying those very constraints that limit them, which may include gender stereotypes, rigid beliefs about material success and achievement, or precepts about how parents and children should properly relate to each other. Identifying exceptions and counter-narratives is an intrinsic part of this process, a process that orientates us towards other possible futures. In Shakespeare's tragedies, even in their very last scenes, there are examples of alternative potentialities – flashes of reflectiveness, regret, humour or kindness – which continue to speak to other, more life-enhancing contexts or to further possibilities for dialogue. As I have argued, what we are most likely to see at the end of the tragedies is the breakdown or foreclosing of dialogue. At these moments, the effects of power, especially gendered power, will be most clearly in evidence. Hector heads to his death having disregarded or dismissed his sister Cassandra and his wife Andromache, Othello is deaf to Desdemona's pleading and the voices of Lady Macbeth and Ophelia are silenced in their 'madness' as potentially too dangerous or subversive to be heard. Of course, because this *is* tragedy, this is what happens, but focussing on what is being foreclosed creates a different perspective from which to challenge the idea of inevitability and which means engaging at some level with other possible futures.

As Mikhail Bakhtin observed, "there are no limits to the dialogic context . . . it extends into the boundless past and the boundless future. . . . At any moment in the development of the dialogue there are immense boundless masses of forgotten contextual meanings. . . . Nothing is absolutely dead: every meaning will have its homecoming festival."[1]

Note

1 Mikhail Bakhtin, *Speech Genres and Other Late Essays* (Austin: University of Texas Press, 1986).

APPENDIX

Plot summaries

Hamlet (1600–1601)

Hamlet's father, King of Denmark, has died and his Uncle Claudius has rapidly married his mother and become King. Hamlet is angry, grief-stricken and distraught. His friend, Horatio comes with the news that a ghost, resembling Hamlet's father, has appeared to the guards on the watch. When Hamlet goes with them, he speaks to the ghost of his father and learns that Claudius has murdered him. The ghost tells Hamlet he must avenge him.

After this, Hamlet pretends to be mad and enters into a series of agonised soliloquies about how he should proceed. He rejects Ophelia, the daughter of the King's Counsellor, Polonius, whom he had been courting. Claudius meanwhile, afraid of Hamlet's state of knowledge invites two of Hamlet's friends, Rosencrantz and Guildenstern, to the court to spy on him. When a group of travelling players arrive at the court, Hamlet takes the opportunity to have his father's murder enacted on stage so that he can observe Claudius' reaction. Claudius reacts violently, storming out of the room. He decides to send Hamlet to England with Rosencrantz and Guildenstern and have him put to death there. Meanwhile Hamlet visits his mother Gertrude in her room and fulminates against her for her betrayal of his father and for her sexual relationship with Claudius. Polonius has hidden behind the arras to overhear their encounter and Hamlet kills him, thinking it is Claudius.

Hamlet then departs for England. Meanwhile Ophelia goes mad with grief for her father's death and her rejection by Hamlet. Her brother, Laertes, returns from France, initially accuses Claudius over his father's death and then joins forces with him against Hamlet who has just set foot back on Denmark's shores. Hamlet has intercepted Claudius' letter with instructions to kill him and replaced it with instructions to have Rosencrantz and Guildenstern put to death instead. Meanwhile Ophelia has drowned, presumably by suicide. At her funeral Hamlet appears and is challenged by Laertes to a duel. Claudius, to make sure of killing his stepson, has poisoned the tip of Laertes' sword and arranged for Hamlet to drink from a poisoned goblet. Hamlet and Laertes fight; Hamlet kills Laertes but not before suffering a deadly wound from the poisoned rapier. Gertrude drinks the poison meant for Hamlet and dies. Before dying himself, Hamlet finally kills his stepfather. Horatio is left attempting to narrate the story of Hamlet. Fortinbras, son of the old King of Norway, arrives and prepares to take over the Kingdom.

King Lear (1605–1606)

The main protagonists are King Lear and his three daughters – Gonoril, who is married to the Duke of Albany; Regan, married to the Duke of Cornwall; and Cordelia, later married to the King of France – Lear's loyal follower, the Earl of Kent and Lear's fool. The sub plot characters consist of the Duke of Gloucester, his legitimate son Edgar, who is also Lear's godson, and later disguised as mad Tom and his illegitimate son, Edmund.

Lear has decided to divide up his kingdom between his three daughters as he grows old and approaches death. His daughters are asked to tell him how much they love him to get their share. Gonoril and Regan comply but Cordelia, his favourite, refuses and is disinherited and banished. The Earl of Kent who tries to intervene on Cordelia's behalf is also banished. Lear's relationship with Gonoril and Regan quickly deteriorates and he is cast out/casts himself out into the storm, with only the fool for company, Meanwhile Edmund, the bastard son of the Earl of Gloucester, has tricked his father into believing that Edgar is plotting against him and Edgar too is cast out and disguises himself as "Poor Tom," a bedlam beggar. Lear wandering in the storm is joined by the disguised Earl of Kent and takes shelter in a hovel that contains Tom. Meanwhile on the political front there are rumours of an imminent invasion from France and Kent has written to Cordelia, now Queen of France, to warn her of her father's plight. The Duke of Gloucester has also been in contact with France and, betrayed by his son Edmund, is apprehended by the Duke of Cornwall and Regan, who put out his eyes. He meets up with Edgar still in disguise as Tom and is led at his request to Dover where he intends to throw himself over the cliffs but, with Edgar's connivance, he fails.

Lear is also taken to Dover where he is reunited first with Gloucester and then with Cordelia. In the battle between Albany, Edmund and the forces of France, France is defeated and Lear and Cordelia are imprisoned. Edmund's betrayal of his brother and father is revealed and he fights a duel with Edgar, who kills him. Meanwhile Cornwall has earlier died from a wound sustained from a servant who tried to stop him blinding Gloucester. Gonoril has poisoned Regan because of their rivalry over Edmund and has proceeded to kill herself. Lear appears carrying the dead body of Cordelia, who has been put to death on Edmund's orders, and shortly afterwards he himself dies. Gloucester has meanwhile also died. Kent suggests that he is going to kill himself to follow Lear and only Edgar and Albany remain as the play ends.

Othello (1604–1605)

Othello, distinguished military commander in the Venetian army but considered an outsider because of his race and religion, has secretly married Desdemona, daughter of a Venetian senator. Her father Brabantio is alerted to this by Iago, Othello's ensign, who is full of resentment because Othello has made another man, Cassio, his lieutenant. Brabantio appeals to the Duke of Venice to have Othello apprehended but the Duke requires Othello to set sail to fight the Turks in Cyprus. Desdemona is granted leave by the Duke to accompany Othello. She has Iago's wife Emilia with her as lady-in-waiting. In Cyprus, Iago, using a Venetian gentleman Rodrigo, also in love with Desdemona, as a foil, sets about plotting against Othello. He first has Othello dismiss Cassio for drunkenness and then has Desdemona plead Cassio's case to her husband. He succeeds in arousing Othello's anxiety and suspicions of Desdemona by many insinuations and by a series of subterfuges, which include planting Desdemona's handkerchief, a gift from Othello, in Cassio's room. He then has Othello eavesdrop on a conversation with Cassio in which Cassio boasts about his sexual conquest of another woman, Bianca, leading Othello to think it is Desdemona he refers to. Meanwhile Desdemona innocently continues to plead for Cassio, further fuelling her husband's rage. Lodovico and Gratiano emissaries from Venice arrive with the news that Othello is to leave Cyprus with Cassio deputing for him. Iago, afraid that his machinations are about to be found out, incites Rodrigo to kill Cassio. This backfires; Cassio survives and Iago then kills Rodrigo. Meanwhile Othello has decided he must kill Desdemona and he strangles her in their marriage bed. Desdemona's maid and Iago's wife, Emilia, confronts him and tells the truth both to him and to the Venetian nobles before being stabbed to death by her husband. Othello kills himself and Iago is taken away to be tortured. Cassio is given Othello's command in Cyprus.

Macbeth (1605–1606)

Duncan, King of Scotland, has been waging war against Norwegian invaders aided by some Scottish thanes. They are defeated largely due to the heroic actions of Macbeth, Thane of Glamis. As Macbeth and his colleague in arms Banquo return from battle they encounter the "weird sisters" who predict that Macbeth will be firstly Thane of Cawdor and then King of Scotland. They also, however, predict that Banquo's heirs will be kings. When they meet up with Duncan, they learn that the Thane of Cawdor has been executed as a traitor and Duncan has conferred his title on Macbeth. Duncan also announces that his eldest son, Malcolm, will inherit the throne. Macbeth and Lady Macbeth play host to Duncan at their castle of Dunsinane and, after many misgivings on Macbeth's part and much urging by Lady Macbeth, they decide to kill Duncan and Macbeth carries out the deed. When the murder is discovered there are many suspicions about the part Macbeth played, especially from Banquo and from Macduff, Thane of Fife. However, Macbeth is duly crowned king. Malcolm and his brother Donalbain, fearing for their lives, have meanwhile escaped. Macbeth, who has no heirs, fears that Banquo and his son Fleance will pose a threat to his security on the throne. He gives orders for them to be killed. Banquo dies but Fleance escapes. At the ceremonial feast in honour of his kingship, Macbeth is haunted by the appearance of Banquo's ghost. He visits the witches again and this time they predict that he cannot be defeated until Birnam Wood comes to Dunsinane and that he cannot be killed by one of woman born. More worryingly for Macbeth they show him a whole line of Scottish kings emanating from Banquo's heirs. Macbeth embarks upon an orgy of killing, including Macduff's wife and young children. Macduff himself has fled to England and joins forces with Malcolm and English knights to attack Macbeth. Back at Macbeth's castle, Lady Macbeth has been sleepwalking and speaking of the murders. She is tended to by a fearful doctor but dies, presumably by her own hand. Meanwhile Macbeth prepares for battle and is confronted by the sight of a forest of trees, each branch held by one of Malcolm's soldiers advancing towards Dunsinane. Malcolm's forces invade the castle and Macduff (who was born by Cesearian section and thus strictly not of woman born) kills Macbeth. Malcolm is crowned King of Scotland.

Coriolanus (1607–1608)

In Republican Rome the hungry citizens are restless and angry, demanding bread and challenging the senators. They are placated by being offered tribunes to represent them, a move bitterly opposed by Caius Martius (later Coriolanus) who favours taking a hard line. Rome is being threatened by the Volscians under their leader Tullus Aufidius and Caius Martius goes off to attack their city, Corioles. He scores an outstanding victory, his individual heroism offset against the feebleness of the Roman generals and the cowardice of the Roman soldiers. He is ceremonially named Coriolanus. His return is eagerly awaited by his mother Volumnia and his wife Virgilia as well as his friend and mentor Menenius Agrippa. Volumnia is delighted that Coriolanus has sustained wounds as this will greatly enhance his reputation if he shows them to the people. Her ambition is that Coriolanus will become a consul.

At the Senate, Coriolanus absents himself from the speeches praising him, initially refuses to show his wounds and only reluctantly agrees to present himself to the people to gain their agreement for him to become consul. The two tribunes, who are deeply opposed to Coriolanus becoming a consul, raise objections. Questioning his fitness and encouraging the citizens to rescind their earlier assent to Coriolanus, they confront him and a bitter row erupts. Menenius removes Coriolanus from the fray. His mother, Volumnia, afraid that her son is over-reaching himself and ruining his political chances, persuades him finally to return to the tribunes and act more moderately. He sulkily agrees but quickly loses his temper again and abuses the tribunes and people. The tribunes demand his death, which they commute to banishment, and Coriolanus storms off, preparing to leave the city. After an emotional parting with Volumnia, Virgilia and Menenius, Coriolanus departs. Bitter and angry, especially with the senators, Coriolanus heads for Antium where Aufidius resides. The two of them agree to make common cause in attacking Rome. News of their advance causes consternation in Rome and Menenius is sent as an ambassador to Coriolanus, only to be dismissed by him. Then Volumnia, Virgilia and Coriolanus' son arrive to plead with him and finally Volumnia prevails upon him to save the city. Coriolanus sets about trying to make peace between Volscians and Rome. Aufidius, however, has other ideas and he has Coriolanus put to death.

Anthony and Cleopatra (1606–1607)

Anthony, ageing hero of the Roman republic and one of the triumvirate (with Octavius Caesar and Lepidus) is having a passionate love affair with Cleopatra Queen of Egypt, much to the disgust of some of his Roman soldiers. Cleopatra has a son by Julius Caesar, who was Octavius' adoptive father and she is rumoured to have slept with Pompey senior. Anthony receives news of his wife Fulvia's death and of conflict with Pompey junior and decides he must break with Cleopatra and return to Rome. There he makes peace with Octavius by marrying his sister Octavia. Cleopatra does not receive this news well. The triumvirate fight Pompey and then agree a peace accord followed by a riotous dinner on board Pompey's ship. Tension mounts between Anthony and Caesar; Caesar has waged new wars on Pompey and deposed Lepidus. Anthony accuses Caesar of plotting against him; he leaves Octavia and returns to Egypt where he and Cleopatra are enthroned, their illegitimate children declared kings. Caesar declares war on Anthony. Anthony is defeated in a sea battle off Actium, a defeat for which he and most of his soldiers blame Cleopatra because her ships fled the battle. Many of Antony's generals desert him at this point, including, after much agonising, Enobarbus, his most trusted follower. Cleopatra has also appeared to do a deal with Caesar to secure her throne. They row, make up and Anthony fights again, achieving a brief victory before being roundly beaten in another sea battle. This time he is so enraged with Cleopatra that he threatens to kill her, following which she takes refuge in the monument and sends a messenger to say she is dead. Anthony having failed to persuade his attendant to kill him, falls on his sword but bungles the attempt. He is taken to the monument where he dies in Cleopatra's arms. She is held prisoner by Caesar and, after learning that he plans to take her captive to Rome, kills herself by applying asps to her breast.

Troilus and Cressida (1601–1602)

The play opens when the Trojan War has been going on for several years. The Greeks, led by Agamemnon, are laying siege to Troy to recover Helen, the wife of Agamemnon's brother Menelaus, who has been abducted by Paris, son of King Priam of Troy. Things are not going well in the Greek camp since their premier warrior, Achilles is refusing to fight, not so much sulking in his tent it as disporting himself with Patroclus, his male lover and mocking the Greek leaders. Priam's youngest son, Troilus is in love with Cressida and is seeking, through her uncle, Pandarus, to arrange an assignation with her. Cressida too, although she disparages Troilus to Pandarus, declares her love for him. Priam's oldest son Hector, a famed warrior has issued a challenge to the Greeks that they should put forward one of their warriors (he assumes it will be Achilles) to fight him in single combat. Ulysses, the most strategic of the Greek soldiers suggests that they plot to put forward Ajax, a lesser warrior to arouse Achilles envy and provoke him into fighting. Achilles is troubled but does not rise to the bait. Meanwhile in the Trojan camp, Priam and his sons debate whether they should return Helen to the Greeks. Hector argues in favour but changes his mind in the face of vehement opposition from Troilus and Paris. Pandarus has finally arranged an assignation between Troilus and Cressida and they go to bed together. Meanwhile the Greeks send a deputation to the Trojans at the instigation of Cressida's father who has earlier deserted to the Greek camp. They demand that Cressida be delivered to the Greeks in exchange for Antenor, a Trojan prisoner. Just after their night of passion, Troilus agrees to this and sends Cressida off with Diomedes, a Greek soldier who has made it clear that his intentions are anything but honourable. Hector visits the Greek camp, fights a desultory battle with Ajax (who is actually his cousin) and then meets Achilles and is feted by the Greeks. Ulysses escorts Troilus to her father's house where they, together with Thersites, a scurrilous observer, witness Cressida and Diomedes together when it becomes clear that she is, however reluctantly, Diomedes' lover. Devastated, Troilus returns home and vows to fight and kill Diomedes. Meanwhile Hector has come under pressure from his wife, Andromache, and sister, Cassandra, who predicts his death, not to go and fight. But goaded by Troilus he does so and, after a bloody battle in which Hector slays Patroclus, Achilles has him killed while he is unarmed. The play ends with Troilus vowing revenge and roundly rejecting Pandarus, whose closing words to the audience involve sharing the news of his own imminent death from syphilis

Romeo and Juliet (1594–1595)

In Verona, the longstanding feud between the Montague and Capulet families erupts, at the opening of the play, in a street brawl, which is broken up by Prince Escalus, who issues a stern warning to the older members of each family. His nephew, Paris has asked Capulet for permission to marry his fourteen-year-old daughter, Juliet. Romeo, a young Montague, is obsessed with his unrequited love for Rosaline, a Capulet. However, he and Juliet meet and fall in love at the Capulet feast, where Romeo and his friends Benvolio and Mercutio have gone wearing masks. Later, Romeo climbs into the Capulet garden and he and Juliet exchange vows of love. The following day, with the assistance of Juliet's nurse, they are secretly married by the priest, Friar Lawrence. Soon afterwards, another fight breaks out between Juliet's cousin Tybalt, still enraged by Romeo's appearance at the Capulet feast, and Romeo's friend Mercutio, who provokes Tybalt to draw his attention away from Romeo. Tybalt kills Mercutio and, shortly afterwards, Romeo kills Tybalt. The prince, who is Mercutio's uncle, refuses to accede to the Capulet's demand for Romeo to be put to death as punishment for Tybalt's murder and orders his banishment instead. Distraught, Romeo goes to Friar Lawrence who, with the help of the nurse, arranges for the young husband and wife to spend one night together. Meanwhile Juliet's father has agreed to expedite her marriage to Paris. He threatens Juliet with expulsion from the family if she does not consent and Juliet's mother likewise disowns her. Desperate to escape this forced marriage and remain faithful to Romeo, Juliet begs Friar Lawrence for help. He gives her a potion that will make her appear dead for a period of forty-two hours. Laurence assures her that when she awakes in the Capulet tomb, he will have brought Romeo to her side and they can flee together to Mantua. Juliet's nurse duly finds her 'dead' in the morning and the family mourns. However, the messenger the friar sends to advise Romeo of this plan is overtaken by Romeo's servant Balthasar, who tells him that Juliet is actually dead. In despair, Romeo purchases poison and goes to Juliet's tomb where he meets Paris, who challenges him. Romeo kills Paris and then drinks the poison. The friar has arrived too late to tell him Juliet is not dead. Awakening shortly afterwards, Juliet discovers her dead lover and stabs herself to death. The two families and the prince mourn their losses and Montague and Capulet agree to end their feud.

BIBLIOGRAPHY

Adelman, J. (1992). *Suffocating Mothers: Fantasies of Maternal Origin in Shakespeare's Plays, 'Hamlet' to 'The Tempest'*. New York: Routledge.

Adelman, J. (1997). Iago's Alter Ego: Race as Projection in Othello. *Shakespeare Quarterly*, 48(2).

Bakhtin, M. M. (1981). *The Dialogic Imagination*. Austin: University of Texas Press.

Bakhtin, M. M. (1984). *Problems of Dostoevsky's Poetics*. Minneapolis: University of Minnesota Press.

Bakhtin, M. M. (1986). *Speech Genres and Other Late Essays*. Austin: University of Texas Press.

Barnard, J. (ed.), (2014). *John Keats: Selected Essays*. London: Penguin.

Bate, J. (2013). *The Genius of Shakespeare*. Oxford: Oxford University Press.

Bateson, G. (1958). *Naven*. Stanford: Stanford University Press.

Bateson, G. (1973). *Steps to an Ecology of Mind*. St Albans: Paladin.

Bateson, G. (1979). *Mind and Nature*. London: Fontana.

Belsey, C. (2007). *Why Shakespeare?* Basingstoke: Palgrave Macmillan.

Berger, H. (1996). Impertinent Trifling: Desdemona's Handkerchief. *Shakespeare Quarterly*, 47(3): 235–250.

Bradley, A. C. (1992). *Shakespearean Tragedy*. Basingstoke: Palgrave Macmillan. Third Edition.

Burck, C., & Daniel, G. (1995). *Gender and Family Therapy*. London: Karnac.

Burck, C., & Speed, B. (Eds.), (1995). *Gender, Power and Relationships*. London: Routledge.

Butler, J. (1990). *Gender Trouble*. New York: Routledge.

Byng Hall, J., & Campbell, D. (1981). Resolving Conflicts in Family Distance Regulation: An Integrative Approach. *Journal of Marital and Family Therapy*, 7(3): 321–330.

Callaghan, D., Helms, L., & Singh, J. (1994). *The Weyward Sisters*. Cambridge, MA: Wiley-Blackwell.

Chedgzoy, K. (ed.) (2001). *Shakespeare, Feminism and Gender*. Basingstoke: Palgrave Macmillan.

Cowen Orlin, C. (ed.) (2004). *Othello*. Basingstoke: Palgrave Macmillan.

Coyle, M. (ed.) (1992). *Hamlet*. Basingstoke: Palgrave Macmillan.

Cummings, B. (2013). *Mortal Thoughts: Religion, Secularity and Identity in Shakespeare and Early Modern Culture*. Oxford: Oxford University Press.

Dollimore, J. (1994). Antony and Cleopatra: *Virtus* under Erasure. In Drakakis, J. (ed.), *Antony and Cleopatra*. Basingstoke: Palgrave Macmillan.

Dollimore, J. (2004). *Radical Tragedy*. Basingstoke: Palgrave Macmillan. Third Edition.

Dollimore, J., & Sinfield, A. (eds.), (1994). *Political Shakespeare*. Manchester: Manchester University Press.

Drakakis, J. (ed.) (1992). *Shakespearean Tragedy* London: Longman.

Drakakis, J. (ed.) (1994). *Antony and Cleopatra*. Basingstoke: Palgrave Macmillan.

Drakakis, J. (ed.) (1996). *Alternative Shakespeares*. London: Routledge.

Eagleton, T. (1970). *Shakespeare and Society*. London: Chatto and Windus.

Eagleton, T. (1986). *William Shakespeare*. Oxford: Basil Blackwell.

Eagleton, T. (1996). *Literary Theory*. Oxford: Wiley-Blackwell. Second Edition.

Evans, B. (1979). *Shakespeare's Tragic Practice*. Oxford: Oxford University Press.

Foucault, M. (1972). *The Archaeology of Knowledge and the Discourse of Language*. New York: Pantheon.

Freud, S. (1899). *The Interpretation of Dreams*. Harmondsworth: Penguin.

Freud, S. (1927). *Autobiographical Study*. New York: W.W. Norton.

Girard, R. (1991). *A Theatre of Envy*. New York: Oxford University Press.

Greenblatt, S. (1980). *Renaissance Self-Fashioning*. Chicago: University of Chicago Press.

Greenblatt, S. (1988). *Shakespearean Negotiations*. New York: Oxford University Press.

Greenblatt, S. (1990). *Learning to Curse*. New York: Routledge.

Greenblatt, S. (2001). *Hamlet in Purgatory*. Princeton: Princeton University Press.

Greenblatt, S. (2010). *Shakespeare's Freedom*. Chicago: University of Chicago Press.

Greenblatt, S., & Platt, P. G. (eds.) (2014). *Shakespeare's Montaigne*. New York: New York Review of Books Classics.

Harré, R., & Van Langenhove, L. (1999). *Positioning Theory: Moral Contexts of Intentional Action*. Oxford: Wiley-Blackwell.

Jacobs, M. (2008). *Shakespeare on the Couch*. London: Karnac.

Jardine, L. (1996). *Reading Shakespeare Historically*. London: Routledge.

Kahn, C. (1993). The Absent Mother in *King Lear*. In Ryan, K. (ed.), *King Lear*. Basingstoke: Palgrave Macmillan.

Kermode, F. (2000). *Shakespeare's Language*. London: Penguin.

Knapp, J. V., & Womack, K. (Eds.), (2003). *Reading the Family Dance*. Newark: University of Delaware Press.

Loomba, A. (1994). Theatre and the Space of the Other. In Drakakis, J. (ed.), *Antony and Cleopatra*. Basingstoke: Palgrave Macmillan.

Maguire, L. (2009). *Helen of Troy: From Homer to Hollywood*. Chichester: Wiley-Blackwell.

Maguire, L. (2014). *Othello, Language and Writing*. London: Bloomsbury.

Nuttall, A. D. (1983). *A New Mimesis: Shakespeare and the Representation of Reality*. New Haven: Yale University Press.

Nuttall, A. D. (2007). *Shakespeare the Thinker*. New Haven: Yale University Press.

Orgel, S. (2003). *Othello* and the End of Comedy. *Shakespeare Survey*, 21: 105–116.

Pigman, G. R. (1985). *Grief and English Renaissance Elegy*. Cambridge: Cambridge University Press.

Rosslyn, F. (2000). *Tragic Plots: A New Reading from Aeschylus to Lorca*. Aldershot: Ashgate.

Rustin, M., & Rustin, M. (2002). *Mirror to Nature*. London: Karnac.

Ryan, K. (ed.), (1993). *King Lear*. Basingstoke: Palgrave Macmillan.

Ryan, K. (2002). *Shakespeare*. Basingstoke: Palgrave Macmillan. Third Edition.

Said, E. (1978). *Orientalism*. London: Vintage.

Seikkula, J. (2003). Dialogue Is the Change: Understanding Psychotherapy as a Semiotic Process of Bakhtin, Voloshinov and Vygotsky. *Human Systems*, 14(2): 83–94.

Shapiro, J. (2015). *1606: William Shakespeare and the Year of Lear*. London: Faber and Faber.

Singh, J. (1994). Othello's Identity, Postcolonial Theory and Contemporary African Rewritings of *Othello*. In Hendricks, M., & Parker. P. (eds.), *Women, Race and Writing in the Early Modern Period*. London: Routledge.

Snyder, S. (2002). *Shakespeare: A Wayward Journey*. Newark: University of Delaware Press.

Stallybrass, P. (1986). Patriarchal Territories: The Body Enclosed. In Ferguson, M. W., Quilligan, M., & Wilson, N. J. (eds.), *Rewriting the Renaissance*. Chicago: University of Chicago Press.

Swift Lenz, C. R., Greene, G., & Thomas Neely, C. (eds.) (1980). *The Woman's Part: Feminist Criticism of Shakespeare*. Urbana: University of Illinois Press.

Watzlawick, P., Beavin, J., & Jackson, D. (1967). *Pragmatics of Human Communication*. New York: W.W. Norton.

Welldon, E. (1992). *Mother, Madonna, Whore: The Idealization and Denigration of Motherhood*. London: Karnac.

Wells, S. (2010). *Shakespeare, Love and Sex*. Oxford: Oxford University Press.

Williams, R. (2006). *Modern Tragedy*. Toronto: Broadview.

Wise, I., & Mills, M. (eds.) (2006). *Psychoanalytic Ideas and Shakespeare*. London: Karnac.

Films

Antony and Cleopatra (2004). Directed by Trevor Nunn. Starring Janet Suzman and Richard Johnson. Royal Shakespeare Company.

Coriolanus (1984). Directed by Elijah Moshinsky. Starring Alan Howard. BBC Productions.

Hamlet (1964). Directed by Grigori Koznintsev. Starring Innokenti Smoktinovsky. Mr Bongo.

Hamlet (2009). Directed by Gregory Doran. Starring David Tennant. Royal Shakespeare Company.

Iago on the Couch (2009). British Psychoanalytical Society. Freud Museum.

King Lear (1971). Directed by Peter Brook. Starring Paul Scofield. Columbia Pictures.

King Lear (2008). Directed by Trevor Nunn. Starring Ian McKellen. Royal Shakespeare Company.

Macbeth (1978). Directed by Trevor Nunn. Starring Ian McKellen and Judi Dench. Royal Shakespeare Company.

Othello (2003). Directed by Trevor Nunn. Starring Willard White, Ian McKellen and Imogen Stubbs. Royal Shakespeare Company.

Ran (1985). Directed by Akira Kurasawa, Starring Tatsuya Nakadai. Nippon Herald Films.

Romeo and Juliet (1968). Directed by Franco Zeffirelli. Starring Leonard Whiting and Olivia Hussey. Paramount Pictures.

Throne of Blood (1957). Directed by Akira Kurasawa. Starring Toshiro Mifune and Isuzu Yamada. Toho Studios.

INDEX